The Ideological Origins of the Dirty War

The Ideological Origins of the Dirty War

Fascism, Populism,
and Dictatorship in
Twentieth Century Argentina

FEDERICO FINCHELSTEIN

OXFORD
UNIVERSITY PRESS

OXFORD
UNIVERSITY PRESS

Oxford University Press is a department of the University of Oxford.
It furthers the University's objective of excellence in research, scholarship,
and education by publishing worldwide.

Oxford   New York
Auckland   Cape Town   Dar es Salaam   Hong Kong   Karachi
Kuala Lumpur   Madrid   Melbourne   Mexico City   Nairobi
New Delhi   Shanghai   Taipei   Toronto

With offices in
Argentina   Austria   Brazil   Chile   Czech Republic   France   Greece
Guatemala   Hungary   Italy   Japan   Poland   Portugal   Singapore
South Korea   Switzerland   Thailand   Turkey   Ukraine   Vietnam

Oxford is a registered trademark of Oxford University Press
in the UK and certain other countries.

Published in the United States of America by
Oxford University Press
198 Madison Avenue, New York, NY 10016

Library of Congress Cataloging-in-Publication Data
Finchelstein, Federico, 1975-
The ideological origins of the dirty war : fascism, populism, and dictatorship in twentieth
century Argentina / Federico Finchelstein.
    pages cm
Includes index.
ISBN 978-0-19-993024-1 (hardback); 978-0-19-061176-7 (paperback)
1. Fascism—Argentina—History—20th century.   2. Political culture—
Argentina—History—20th century.   3. Political violence—Argentina—History—
20th century.   4. State-sponsored terrorism—Argentina—History—20th
century.   5. Antisemitism—Argentina—History—20th century.   6.   Church
and state—Argentina—History—20th century.   7. Peronism.   8. Argentina—
History—Dirty War, 1976–1983—Philosophy.   9. Argentina—History—Dirty War,
1976–1983—Atrocities.   I. Title.
F2849.F483 2014
982.06—dc23
2013040029

A Lauri, Gabi, y Luli

Contents

Acknowledgments

THIS TEXT OWES a great deal to many friends and colleagues.

I would like to thank Ben Brower, Pablo Piccato, and Enzo Traverso for their comments and suggestions. As always, I am greatly indebted to Dominick LaCapra for his encouragement and suggestions over the years.

In New York City, I would also like to thank Amy Chazkel, Seth Fein, Nara Milanich, and Caterina Pizzigoni. I would like to thank Jose Moya and Louise Walker and Brenda Elsey, Javier Fernández Galeano, Paul Gootenberg, Luis Herrán Ávila, Sinclair Thompson, Barbara Weinstein, and Eric Zolov. I am also grateful to Tulio Halperín Donghi.

I started working on this book in 2006. In many ways it continues the work of my two previous books on Argentine fascism, especially in thinking and researching the twisted path of fascism from interwar nacionalismo to the Cold War era and the military dictatorship of the *Proceso*. Different chapters of this book were presented in New York at The New School and at Columbia University, and also at the University of Macerata, Italy; The Hamburg Institute for Social Research; Arizona State University; the University of Notre Dame; New York University; the University of Texas at Austin; the University of Minnesota; Brown University; and Cornell University. I have also presented parts of the chapters in Mexico City, Montevideo, Munich, Montreal, Rome, Toronto, Washington DC, and Buenos Aires. I thank all the participants of the different workshops and lectures where these chapters and related topics were discussed.

In the United States, I would also like to thank Michael Steinberg, Vicki Caron, and Mary Roldán, as well as Jeremy Adelman, Alejandro Baer, Ed Baptist, Chris Bilodeau, Alicia Borinsky, Bruno Bosteels, Geoff Eley, Ray Craib, Ben Kiernan, Tracie Matysik, Sandra McGee Deutsch, Jeffrey Mehlman, and Camille Robcis.

Around the world, many colleagues and friends helped me with suggestions, comments, criticism, and encouragement. In France, I would like to thank Roger Chartier; in Israel, Amos Goldberg, David Bankier, Raanan Rein, Haim Avni, and Alberto Spektorowski; in Mexico, Victoria Crespo, Arturo Grunstein, and Christian Sperling; in Canada, Jorge Nallim, David Sheinin, and Ben Bryce; in Italy, Angelo Ventrone, Paul Corner, Martin Baumeister, Valeria Galimi, Lutz Klinkhammer, Claudio Pavone, Wolfgang Schieder, and Loris Zanatta; in Germany, Norbert Frei, and Tim Muller; in Spain, Xosé Manoel Núñez Seixas; in Portugal António Costa Pinto; in Uruguay, Roberto García Ferreira; in England, Tanya Harmer, Andrea Mammone, and Dan Stone.

In Argentina, *muchas gracias a* Andrés Bisso, Fabián Bosoer, Lila Caimari, Ale Cattaruzza, Mariano Plotkin, Daniel Lvovich, Elías Palti, Guillermo Saidon, Hugo Vezzetti, and Eduardo Zimmerman. Jorge Gelman invited me to write an earlier, much shorter instantiation of this book for his excellent history series at *Editorial Sudamericana* in Buenos Aires. I will be always grateful to him for his invitation and his subsequent commentaries to the text. I would like to thank the readers from *Sudamericana*. After that book was published I spent four more years researching and writing to produce this book. Once more, I am deeply indebted to my Argentine mentors, José Emilio Burucúa, Luis Alberto Romero, and José Sazbón.

I would like to thank Lucina Schell for her translation of earlier drafts of chapters 1, 2, 3, and 4. Also my thanks to Jane Brodie for her translations of very initial drafts from chapters 5 and 6. I thank librarians and archivists from many places, including The New School library, the NYU library, and the university libraries of Brown and Cornell. I also thank the archivists of the Bibliothèque de Documentation Internationale Contemporaine (BDIC) in Nanterre, France, and the Archivio Centrale dello Stato in Rome. I am grateful to the Argentine archivists and librarians at the Archivo General de la Nación (AGN), Biblioteca Nacional Argentina, Biblioteca del Congreso de la Nación, Archivo del Ministerio de Relaciones Exteriores y Culto (Argentine Foreign Ministry Archives), Instituto Judío de Investigaciones (IWO), Centro de Documentación e Investigación de la Cultura de Izquierdas en la Argentina (Cedinci), the Archivo y Biblioteca de Raúl Scalabrini Ortiz located at the Asociación del Personal de Dirección de Ferrocarriles Argentinos, Comisión por la Memoria de la provincia de Buenos Aires and its Archivo de la ex-Dirección de Inteligencia de la Policía de Buenos Aires (DIPBA) in La Plata, the archives of the Acción Coordinada de Organizaciones

Argentinas de Derechos Humanos (Memoria Abierta), Instituto de Historia Argentina y Americana "Dr. Emilio Ravignani," the Latin American Rabbinic Seminary in Buenos Aires, and also the New York Public Library and the Library of Congress in the United States. In Buenos Aires, I want to thank Carmen Lugones for allowing me to read the documents from the Lugones family archive.

At The New School I would like to thank my colleagues in the history department, especially Oz Frankel, David Plotke, Natalia Mehlman Petrzela, Ann Laura Stoler, Jeremy Varon, and Eli Zaretsky. Also at The New School, I would like to thank Andrew Arato, Andreas Kalyvas, Richard Bernstein, Juan De Castro, and Carlos Forment. My research assistants, Diego Cagueñas, Monica Fagioli, and Luis Herrán Ávila provided invaluable help.

I would like to thank Susan Ferber, the executive editor of Oxford University Press, for her meaningful support. I am very thankful to the two anonymous reviewers for OUP for their insightful suggestions.

I wish to thank the students of my undergraduate and graduate courses at Brown University, The New School for Social Research, and Eugene Lang College of The New School.

Finally, I would like to thank my parents, Norma and Jaime, and *mis hermanos* Diego e Inés. This book is dedicated to my wife Laura and my daughters Gabriela and Lucia.

The Ideological Origins of the Dirty War

Introduction

FROM FASCISM TO THE CONCENTRATION CAMPS

THE FASCIST IDEA defines the "Dirty War." Fascism provided the background for the principles and practices of the violence that the Argentine government unleashed against a group of its citizens in the 1970s. Under the junta's rule, even a five-year-old knew the name of the dictator. While I cannot remember hearing political discussions in the middle-class Argentine Jewish home in which I was raised, I knew who the leader of the junta was. General Jorge Rafael Videla was a spectral figure with his gravelly voice, stern look, and mustache. My parents later told me that they had considered it too dangerous to discuss the junta in the presence of a child. They knew too many people who had disappeared.

Like many other Argentines, I am still trying to come to terms with the crimes against humanity committed under Videla's rule: the disappearances, the concentration camps, the citizens tortured, drugged, and then thrown into the Atlantic from military planes. Official estimates range from 10,000 to 15,000 murder victims. According to most human rights organizations there were 30,000 victims. There was also the theft of babies born to illegally detained mothers. One of the reasons I became a historian was because I wanted to understand how the so-called Dirty War could have become a reality in a modern nation with a strong, progressive civil society. This task meant understanding the ideological links between politics and death. Quite simply, I wanted to search the ideological factors that motivated killers to kill. This is why I wrote this book.

Today Argentina once again has a strong civil society, an electoral democracy, and a dynamic political culture with no place for the military in politics. The country has moved beyond Videla's efforts at "reconciliation"; it was clear from the reactions to his death in 2013 that in twenty-first-century Argentina almost nobody bought Videla's idea that the military were saviors of the nation. In Latin America, Videla is widely considered the Argentine version of Hitler. But unlike the German fascist dictator, Videla never thought that he was a god-like figure or the sacred leader of a fascist political religion. This does not mean that he was humble: far from it. In fact, he saw himself as God's political representative on Argentine soil. But Videla's God, and his earthly mission, were of a special sort. He became the leader of one of the most murderous dictatorships in history and in this bloodshed he saw a redeemed future for his country, one that would bring Argentina back to Christian civilization. As a leader Videla combined extreme political repression with a wild version of austerity measures and economic deregulation. All these measures were taken in the name of religion. In contrast with many other Latin American countries, the Catholic Church was one of the main backers of the junta. The junta's sacralizing ideology was rooted in a long history of alliances between the Catholic Church and military dictatorships in Argentina.

The basis for this alliance rested on a notion accepted by most Argentine bishops at the time: any condemnation of human rights violations was a threat to the homeland and God. That is, most Argentine bishops either actively or passively, and in public, accepted the actions of the dictatorship. The dictatorship understood these actions as part of a common Christian undertaking against the "atheistic subversion" whose justification was ecclesiastical and whose actions were military. The intimacy between God and the military nation was emphasized at the time, and Pope Francis, who as Father Bergoglio was the most important Jesuit in the country, never spoke out against this. Some human rights activists and victims poignantly presented him as an active collaborator of the dictatorship and accused him of denouncing victims as leftists to the authorities. Father Bergoglio belatedly dismissed these accusations as slander but the fact remains that he stayed silent during the repression. And by this silence the pope played a central role, like many of his peers. It was this combination of ecclesiastical endorsement and indifference that created the ideological conditions for the state killings. Unlike the Church in other Latin American countries, for example, Chile and Brazil, which also witnessed a powerful encounter between Catholic integrism and the extreme right in the last century, in Argentina the Catholic Church was not inclined to defend victims of the armed forces. Both the Church and the military considered the Dirty War a real war, essential to their survival.

The mainstream of the Argentine Church played a long-standing historical role as a theoretical guide for the armed forces, beginning in 1930 with the first military coup in Argentine history and continuing up to the military junta during the "Dirty War." By the time of the 1976 coup the links between the Church and the military were almost structural. They saw themselves as the essence of the nation: the sacred Argentine bond between the Cross and the Sword. Paradoxically this radically conservative Church was and is situated in one of the region's most secular and progressive civil societies. This has been the case since the Uriburu dictatorship in the 1930s when the Argentine Church started to solidify its ideological and political links with key spheres of state power, especially the armed forces. Rather than addressing the most pluralistic dimensions of Argentine society, historically the Church preferred to focus on securing almost symbiotic links with the structures of the state. In Argentina, civil society and state power are often opposed and most Church intellectuals and members of its hierarchy have historically aimed to correct this situation from above.

This book returns to a past that has been repressed. Most Argentines today share with professional historians a view of the dictatorship as having led a devastating attack against one of Latin America's most progressive and secular civil societies. This negative view of the junta was not always prevalent in Argentina. It was in its time highly popular, especially during the first phases of the coup in early 1976 and during the celebrations of Argentina's 1978 victory in the soccer World Cup. The 1982 war with Britain over the islands that Britain calls the Falklands and that Argentines call Las Malvinas generated a great deal of support but ultimately it proved catastrophic for the junta, a military regime that could not deliver victory on the battlefield. When democracy returned to the country in 1983, Argentina was impoverished, defeated, and longing for a society free of the military presence in politics that Videla and his fellow generals represented.

The Dirty War was not a real war but an illegal militarization of state repression. This is a popularized term that needs to be explained in terms of the country's fascist genealogies. From a historical perspective, the Dirty War did not feature two combatants but rather victims and perpetrators. In fact, the state made "war" against its citizens. This state-sanctioned terror had its roots in the fascist movements of the interwar years through to the concentration camps. Argentina is known for its ties with fascism as well as the warm welcome it gave Nazi war criminals after the Second World War.[1] In addition, it was the home of Peronism, the first articulated form of Latin American populism. Finally, Argentina was the birthplace of one of Latin America's most criminal dictatorships in the 1970s and early 1980s, the Argentine military junta. How are Peronism and this military dictatorship connected to the legacy of fascism? How and why did all of these regimes emerge in a country that was "born liberal"?[2]

Why did these influential Latin American authoritarian traits first emerge in Argentina under the shadow of fascism? To be sure, European totalitarian connections with Argentina are significant, and there is validity to the stereotype of Argentina as a refuge of irredeemable European forms of fascism before and after 1945. Argentina is less famous for its homegrown fascism and its conflation of Catholicism and fascism. Ultimately Argentine ideological formations of the fascist kind were much more influential than European fascisms in shaping the history of the nation's violent twentieth century and the country's political culture. The Argentine road to fascism was built in the 1920s and 1930s and from then on continued to acquire many political and ideological reformulations and personifications, from Peronism (1943–1955) to terrorist right-wing organizations in the 1960s and 1970s (especially Tacuara and the Triple A) to the last military dictatorship (1976–1983). These are, in short, the historical avenues of global totalitarianism in Argentina that this book explores and explains.

Paradoxically, while the world was defeating fascism, Argentina was affirming fascism's legacy. United States President Franklin Delano Roosevelt noted this and presented it as the result of the distance between fascist governments and liberal public spheres. He stated in September of 1944: "I have been following closely and with increasing concern the development of the Argentine situation in recent months. This situation presents the extraordinary paradox of the growth of Nazi–Fascist influence and the increasing application of Nazi–Fascist methods in a country of this hemisphere, at the very time that those forces of oppression and aggression are drawing ever closer to the hour of defeat." He added: "The paradox is accentuated by the fact, of which we are all quite aware, that the vast majority of the people of Argentina have remained steadfast in their faith in their own, free, democratic traditions."[3]

For President Roosevelt, Argentina's nacionalista dictatorship was the expression of a global ideology that did not have support among ordinary Argentines. Was fascism never popular in Argentina? If so, how could it be so influential in defining political violence and military dictatorship in the last century? This book explores these questions by showing the ways in which fascism's meaning changed at different times.

At the present time, pundits use fascism to loosely describe an authoritarian regime, international terrorism (the so-called "islamo-fascism"), or repressive stances by the state, but this laxity is problematic from a historical point of view. In Latin America the term has often been used more as an instrument of political criticism than a tool for critical analysis. It has been applied to political figures ranging from Juan Domingo Perón to Hugo Chávez and from the Argentine General Videla to the Chilean General Augusto Pinochet. This use often conflates populist leaders who aggressively used mass politics with leaders who criminally attempted to suppress them. It also conflates democratically elected regimes with military dictatorships that destroyed democracy. This situation is often understandable but in historical terms its use as an adjective is anachronistic.

In Argentine terms, it is possible of course to compare the Argentine dictatorship (1976–1983) with those of Mussolini and Hitler. To be sure, all these regimes suppressed democracy. All of them killed their own citizens. They all promoted war ("internal" and external) as a political instrument, that is, as the continuation of politics by other means. In addition, all these dictatorships repressed labor unions and other forms of opposition to the regime. However, the differences between the Italian and German dictatorships and those of Argentina, or for that matter any other recent political dictatorships in Latin America and elsewhere, are more significant than their similarities. German and Italian fascism was radical in its aim to change the world by conquering it. Italy and Germany wanted to forge a new Roman Empire and a Thousand-Year Reich. They also strove to forget, once and for all, the legacy of the French Revolution by establishing an alternative to capitalism and communism. Finally, Nazis and fascists aimed to achieve a permanent state of war, that is, a total war through which, as Mussolini argued, those ruled by the fascists would become new men. The Argentine dictatorship shared some ideological dimensions with Hitler and Mussolini, but the Argentines were more modest. They wanted to silence and selectively eliminate all opposition, to concentrate economic and political capital, and eventually to win a conventional war in the South Atlantic.

The fascist persecution of its own citizens unfolded into the racial distinction between citizens and then their extermination, either indirectly (fascist Italy's collaboration with the Nazis) or directly (Germany). Italian racism, which included the indiscriminate use of chemical weapons in Africa, eventually became part of the Holocaust.[4]

All in all, Nazism and Italian fascism were totalitarian. They wanted to establish an in extremis form of government, one that seeks absolute control of society. As with fascism, totalitarianism is often used as a political term rather than as a conceptual historical category.[5]

It is necessary for historians to reclaim "fascism" in order to discuss specific historical movements between 1919 and 1945, and later movements dubbed "neofascism," which consciously appropriated the legacies of the first fascist moment. In this sense, fascism needs to be seen as an interwar creation that is characterized by a specific revolutionary politics oriented toward the masses and an extreme form of nationalism endowed with an ideology of its own. In Argentina it represented an extreme amalgamation between the secular and the sacred. Finally, fascism presents the development of a relatively unique public style that emphasized both mass emotion and symbolic action, demanded hierarchic relations and authoritarian policies, and, at the same time, defined in doctrinarian terms the value of political violence and war.[6]

Historians have recently highlighted the fact that the Argentine extreme right understood itself as a form of fascism before 1945 and as a form of neofascism after that date.[7] In contrast with Italian fascism or German Nazism, the Argentine fascists, also called nacionalistas, created a specific Latin American formation with a unique clerico-fascist bent. This political formation bridged European movements and Latin American realities. It included arguments about war, political violence, imperialism, and anti-imperialism. It aimed to revise Argentina's history (including the history of the Patagonian extermination of native populations) with the ultimate aim of changing the country's foundational liberalism. Above all, this ideology was presented as a God-given theory and its practice a reflection of what God wanted for the country.

This book argues that this fascist idea of the sacred represents a central dimension of the long Argentine history of violence in the twentieth century. Moreover, it defines Argentine politics beyond its context of emergence. Specifically, Argentine fascism epitomized central features of one of the first modern South American coups, namely the Uriburu dictatorship (1930–1932). Did fascism encompass the Perón regime (1945–1955) or the last Argentine military dictatorship? Is fascism a key to understanding the recent history of Argentine authoritarianism?

This work contributes to a broader and recent trend of Latin American historians studying the practice and theory of political violence.[8] It examines political violence not only as the outcome of social and institutional matters, but also as a central dimension of political culture. In this sense, the study of violence involves its symbolic and explicit connotations from censorship, notions of the self, and ideological manipulation, to bombings, torture, and killings.

Political violence, and more specifically fascist-driven political violence, needs to be contextualized in ideological and political terms, in order to understand the histories of revolution and counterrevolution that defined Latin American history in the last century.[9] Is it possible to understand populism, a Latin American political movement par excellence, without framing it within this dynamic tension of revolution and fascist and neofascist counterrevolution?

Fascism influenced Peronism but the latter was not necessarily fascist. Perón presented himself as a student of Mussolini. During a trip to Italy he was full of praise for Mussolini and his regime when addressing the fascist press.[10] This excess of diplomacy makes sense in light of the influence of fascist ideologies in an interwar period that was already global in its political exchanges.

The main elements of fascism: extreme and exclusivist nationalism, racism, xenophobia and anti-Semitism, mass politics, the rejection of the legacy of the Enlightenment, "proletarian imperialism" and anti-imperialism, political violence, state terrorism, dictatorship, and the sublimation of war appeared simultaneously in Latin America and Europe. Thus it would be difficult to argue that Argentine fascism was an imported product. There was a great deal of appropriation, reformulation, and distortion in the Argentine reception of fascism, and this reception was already "prepared" by local illiberal ideologies that had predated it.[11]

Fascism and the extreme right became synonymous in Argentina. If Mussolini was the father of fascism as a universal ideology, the Argentine extreme right constituted the mother of Argentine fascism. The Argentine Catholic Church and the army were also "founding fathers" of this ideology. This book tells the dramatic history of the origins and development of an Argentine form of totalitarianism that was simultaneously fascist and religious. Most Argentine fascists understood this ideology as "Christianized fascism." This ideology also included a particular brand of anti-Semitism that conflated sexual stereotypes with theological texts.

The idea of the enemy was a primordial element of Argentine fascism. It also constituted one of its most gruesome and long-standing legacies. The concentration camps of the last military dictatorship were the place of its final consecration in the name of God, the sword, and the homeland. In a telling sermon in 1975, months before the coup, the archbishop of the littoral capital of Paraná in Argentina, Monsignor Victorio Bonamín, asked his audience: "Will Christ not want that one day the armed forces will act beyond their function?"[12] In the audience was future junta leader General Roberto Viola who, like many members of the military, understood this question as a sacred invitation to subvert the democratic order of things. The question presupposed an answer.

Since the 1920s and 1930s, for the Argentine extreme right, its politics was supposed to represent the will of God. Monsignor Bonamín represented the long-standing role of the mainstream Catholic Church as a theoretical vector of Argentine fascism. Originated in the 1920s and 1930s, the fascist idea in Argentina had an essentially Christian and militaristic character in accordance with the nacionalista fascist definition. Prominent Catholic priests acted as agents of transmission of this "holy ideology." Nacionalistas inside and outside the armed forces always acknowledged the central role of these priests as political emissaries of the sacred.

General Cristino Nicolaides, a major repressor in the junta, would later define Monsignor Bonamín as an "authentic soldier of Christ and the Homeland." Nicolaides synthesized the theoretical role of the Argentine Catholic Church in the persona of Bonamín: "[H]is advice definitely secures the proper itinerary for the sword."[13]

In the concentration camps low-level repressors saw their actions on behalf of the "Catholic nation," the sword, and its enemies as part of an internal and sacred war. In this sense, the dialogue between the journalist Fernando Almirón and the former sergeant Víctor Ibáñez, an active perpetrator in the concentration camp of El Campito, serves as an example. A posteriori Ibáñez would "remember" his own indoctrination as "brainwashing" but at the time of the dictatorship he shared with other colleagues the nacionalista ideology that reigned in the camps. He conceived it as an evident truth that explained the logic of repressive torture and violence.

"How did your military superiors tell you to fight the enemy?"
"Towards total extermination. Death, blood. They said that those guys, the subversives, wanted to destroy the Family, that they wanted to impose a totalitarian government, a red plan. They also told us that subversives wanted to destroy our traditions, the national being [el ser nacional]. They wanted to destroy the Church and institutions in order to replace them with a different doctrine, a different way of

life which was foreign and antinational. The homeland [*la Patria*] is
in danger; that was what they said."

"What was the homeland for you?"

"To me, the homeland meant defending my territory; that was what
I believed then. It meant defending our way of life which was
traditional, Catholic, Western. You will hear this in all the army
speeches. Defending the way of life which always was our system
of life."[14]

Like the low-level repressor and the military decision-makers, the hierarchical Catholic Church was also part of the ideological project of the
military dictatorship. As historians Marcos Novaro and Vicente Palermo
discuss, the decisive overwhelming support of the Catholic hierarchy for
the military repression, namely the killing of tens of thousands of citizens,
was a central part of the military plan to eradicate their invented and real
enemies.[15] Another central dimension of the plan was the open denial of
the killings. This denial constituted an attempt to blur the ideology that
made it possible. Rhetorical subterfuges did not always serve this function. Most often they betrayed or made explicit the ideology that motivated
the killers. For the most important members of the clergy during the dictatorship there were no reasons after repression was accomplished for
the military dictatorship to continue addressing the issue. Thus, Cardinal
Juan Carlos Aramburu, the archbishop of Buenos Aires between 1975
and 1990, told the Italian newspaper *Il Messaggero* in 1982: "In Argentina
there are no common graves. A coffin corresponds to every corpse. It was
all registered in the corresponding books. The common graves belong to
people who died without the knowledge of authorities. The disappeared?
One should not confuse things. You know, there are disappeared that are
currently living at ease here in Europe."[16] Denial was given meaning by a
dictatorial clerical ideology with a fascist genealogy.

In a reverse form of "progressive" paternalism different journalists
and researchers tend to present the Latin American case, and especially
the Argentine case, as a transplanted form of European fascism. One
American visitor even presented the Latin America contexts as passive
reservoirs, "jungles of fascism."[17] The French extreme right, Italy's fascism, Germany's Nazis, and Spanish fascism are all presented as the
roots of Latin American intellectual development. [18] For these historians
there is no Latin American agency. For perpetrators, victims, and bystanders, however, the situation was far more complicated. Without proper

contextualization, including the central issue of how the fascist perpetrators saw themselves, it is difficult to provide a subtler account of migrating global ideas such as fascism. Fascism was a global experience but in Argentina it was essentially inscribed in national intellectual and political traditions. It could not have been otherwise insofar as fascism was an ideology that emphasized extreme nationalism. "Christianized fascism" was the Argentine response to democracy, the left, and liberalism. In short, it was a reaction against a central dimension of the Argentine *habitus* and intellectual traditions.[19]

Argentina's unique approach to violence and repression was later exported to other countries in Latin America. This must be explained in terms of the ethnographic, political, social, and economic conditions of that particular Latin American context.[20] However, the state killings of the 1970s also must be understood in terms of the Argentine genealogy of violence that made them possible. In the case of the last military dictatorship, the discourse and practice of death constituted a reformulation of ideologies and practices previously enacted by Argentine fascists in the 1920s, 1930s, and 1940s. To be sure, the ideology of the Argentine junta shared elements with other military traditions, especially those enforced by the United States and France during the Cold War.[21] But in Argentina local practices of torture and national definitions of the enemy emerged alongside transatlantic fascism decades before the Cold War. Arguing against a long-standing stereotypical view of Latin American dictatorships as mere puppets of American Cold War imperatives or French political conceptions, this book contributes to literature on the agency of Latin American perpetrators during the Cold War.[22] To be sure, American encouragement given to perpetrators was a key feature in triggering the Latin American states' decisions to discriminate against, torture, and kill many of its citizens. But the decisions were made at the local level with significant support from local societies. From Argentina and Chile, and from South Africa to Indonesia, the ideology of the perpetrators did not exclusively originate at the center. The killers' motivations were a combination of outside influences and long-term internal developments. In Argentina, these developments were significantly determined by the historical paths of fascist ideology. In its camps the "sacred" ideology of Argentine fascism was made tangible. Other practices from French and American colonialism and national security doctrine and even the experiences of the Holocaust were domesticated in light of Argentine ideological preconceptions and praxis. The book emphasizes the genocidal dimensions of the persecution of Argentine Jewish victims. Proportionately, the last military dictatorship punished Argentine Jews more than other sectors of the population. Although Jews represented less than 1 percent of the population, they were between 10 and 15 percent of the victims of the military dictatorship. The book explains why and how this was the case.

In Argentina, fascism became part of the political ethos of the nation and was continually reformulated throughout the century. This book analyzes this ideological trajectory, namely Argentina's twisted history of political violence from its fascist formulations in the 1920s and 1930s to the practical impact of the ideology in the military concentration camps of the 1970s.

The first part of the book roughly encompasses the years between 1900 and 1945 and traces the origins and development of fascism and anti-Semitism in Argentina. The second part analyzes the intellectual path from Peronism (1943–1955) to right-wing paramilitary groups in the 1960s and 1970s, as well as the military dictatorship, the "Dirty War," the "disappearances," and the concentration camps.

Chapters 1 and 2 analyze the origins of Argentine fascist ideology and the originality of the Argentine form of fascism, which I dub "ecclesiastic" fascism. Chapter 3 focuses on the specific conflation of anti-Semitism, "sacred" violence, and sexuality. Subsequent chapters trace the long-term influences of Argentine fascism. They address the ideological connections between Peronist authoritarianism and fascism (Chapter 4), the neo-Nazi and paramilitary organizations that emerged between 1955 and 1976 (Chapter 5), and the last military dictatorship and its "Dirty War" (1976–1983). Chapter 6 analyzes how fascist ideology became objectified through a set of radical practices and theories, including the mix of post-fascist ideological conflations, religious extremism, neoconservative economics, and the creation of renditional processes of "disappearing people" with a nationwide network of concentration camps. The epilogue briefly analyzes fascist intellectual legacies in the recent politics of history and memory in Argentina.

In the concentration camps of the 1970s, the Argentine fascist "Christianized" ideology created in the 1920s and 1930s became a matter of everyday life for prisoners and perpetrators. In the camps, the long century of political violence and dictatorship created a reality that was entirely ideological. If the Argentine fascists threatened to exterminate their enemies, the last Argentine military dictatorship delivered death with stern ideological impetus. The country's fascist ideological tradition, with a unique Latin American combination of political violence and state repression, suited its peculiar trajectory from liberalism to illiberal populism, dictatorship, and war, with the legacies outlasting any regime.

1

The Ideological Origins of Fascist Argentina

NACIONALISTAS OF THE 1920s and 1930s were the local Argentine variant of transnational fascism. Their shape and substance were rooted in global processes, especially the emergence of mass politics of the extreme right after World War I. However, the history of the vernacular nacionalistas, or Argentine fascists, began with the idea of nationalism itself. The idea that the territory that had belonged to the viceroyalty of Rio de La Plata constituted a single country was the result of a conscious construction by a group of intellectuals. Argentina was "invented." As a country it emerged along with this idea. In this sense, Argentina did not differ from other nations that were also invented, such as France, England, and Bolivia.

What distinguished Argentina was its particular process of state formation and the singularity of feelings, shared identities, and ideas from which it was created. To be sure, nineteenth-century intellectuals such as Domingo Faustino Sarmiento, Juan Bautista Alberdi, and Bartolome Mitre gave national meaning to collective sentiments of belonging to a specific territory. These feelings frequently existed before their intellectual articulation. This collective experience of belonging was related to the fact that the inhabitants of "Argentina" shared a common language, as well as a common political tradition rooted in friendships and enmities. They also shared a constitution that regulated all citizens. Most important, they shared a common history. This history modeled the feeling of belonging and, in time, it created new myths and historical reconstructions.

Mitre, Sarmiento, and Alberdi conceptualized Argentine history in a way that is still read in primary and secondary schools, as well as in the works of popular history. In these accounts, General José de San Martín, the founding father of the nation, and Juan Manuel de Rosas, the nineteenth-century dictator, have little relationship to fascism, totalitarianism, or modern democracy, yet their historical characters are modeled after these tropes in the standard narratives about the history of the nation. The first narratives of the nation conceived it as a contest between heroes and villains, a history that is constantly repeated by Latin American pundits and politicians. Despite strong differences regarding practices and genocidal formulations, nineteenth-century intellectuals like Sarmiento, Alberdi, and Mitre shared an "inclusive" idea of the nation.[1]

As stated in the Argentine Constitution of 1853, every person who accepted the idea of the nation and its norms could be swiftly incorporated into the nascent nation. Argentine historian José Luis Romero highlighted many years ago that different layers of new immigration and new internal migrations complemented each other, along with segments of the original population, creating a more or less open nation.[2] In short, this was the ideology of liberal Argentina. The contrast with fascist-style nacionalismo is evident. Fascist nacionalistas understood the nation in exclusive, xenophobic terms. For them, no "outsider" could become part of the nation. As the fascists of the Argentine Civic Legion during the 1930s would later claim in posters that proliferated on the walls of Buenos Aires, "Foreigners: Welcome to Those Who Share the Greatness and Progress of our Homeland; but Damnation to Those Who Come with Perverted Purposes of Disorder and Anarchy."[3]

At first glance, the nationalism of Mitre and Sarmiento does not seem like an appropriate point of departure for understanding the later twentieth-century nacionalismo of fascist poet Leopoldo Lugones and Dirty War dictator Jorge Rafael Videla. But is this later nacionalismo to be understood as an external influence? This view would render nineteenth-century Argentina free of illiberal genealogies. Those who adhere to this view think that Mussolini and Hitler found imitators in Latin America. For them, fascist ideas had nothing to do with the emergence of the national being, the concept of the nation, or above all the putative, open nature of Argentines that they presented as a fact rather than as a construction or invention.[4]

The relation between the inclusive and open nationalism of the nineteenth- century and the exclusive and totalitarian one of the twentieth century was one of compromise and collaboration, of attachments and elective affinities. Although during the twentieth century many followed the more democratic dimensions of nineteenth-century notions of reason, others preferred to explore its more destructive elements. In this sense Argentina does not differ from Nazi Germany or European genocides and colonial barbarism more generally. The argument of the Philosophic School of Frankfurt—that modernity and enlightenment dialectically carry, in addition to their democratic and egalitarian dimensions, an incubated modern destruction that characterized the last century—applies to the relation between Argentina and genocide.

Sarmiento, a Latin American champion of liberalism and a founding father of modern Argentina, exemplified this situation in 1844. He felt "an invincible repugnancy" for the native populations of the Americas. He saw them as "savages incapable of progress" and advocated for their extermination.[5]

Sarmiento's opinion is consistent with the prevailing beliefs of his time. General Julio Argentino Roca, leader in the war against the indigenous peoples of the "desert," expressed a similar ideology in 1879 when he wrote to his lieutenant Napoleón Uriburu to tell him that he must "cleanse from Indians" the bordering zones in the Patagonian territory of Neuquén. Uriburu disobeyed his orders and decided to invade the southern territories. General Roca did not reprimand him but congratulated him because the "[Indian] race" is "always refractory to the excesses of goodness." By the end of the campaign thousands of Indians were dead and thousands more taken prisoner and deported to Tucumán in northern Argentina to labor on the sugar plantations. Still others were forced to serve for six years in the army or navy, and many women and children were sent to work as "domestic servants" in the households of upper-class families that had solicited them from the state.[6]

This was not just a war of conquest, but an ethnic cleansing. In Argentina, the war of extermination against Patagonian indigenous peoples was undertaken to replace them with white settlers. It was not a war in the sense of two combatant armies, but an internal war, a belligerent conflict in which the state waged war against a segment of the national population, in this case a particular national ethnic group. This would not be the last time.

Later, nacionalistas praised the genocidal actions in Patagonia, arguing that they constituted "a genuinely national enterprise, a work of grandiose significance" identified with the end of the "secular" action of conquest, namely "the occupation of America by the white race, with the spread of Christianity, the establishment of European culture by one of its most illustrious branches, the Spanish, soldiers of the Church." For the Argentine fascists, the conquest of Patagonia implied a republican triumph, a surpassing of the Spanish empire in terms of imposing

"Christianization" and "control": "for if the Spanish triumph over the old indigenous empires was golden and immediate, in the austral Pampas [the republican triumph over them] presented the complementary condition of affirming the dominion of the White race. This belated triumph over the natives [by the Argentines] not only implied more sacrifices but also allowed for its maximum development."[7] As nacionalista politician Manuel Fresco told Roca's son in a private letter, the country was "hugely indebted" to his father for the Patagonian war.[8]

In the nacionalista mentality, true Argentines were supposed to be attracted to the land. They were true settlers. Their lack of movement and migration was thought to be a reflection of their established roots in the land. Their enemies had a nomadic way of life. They were either nomadic in the countryside (as Indians) or lived in cosmopolitan cities (as Jews, leftists, and intellectuals, among other imagined enemies). For the nacionalista Ernesto Palacio, the idea of Argentina did not include Indian elements but was fully white. Repeating global genocidal tropes about the enemy, Palacio conflated Indians' nomadic life with the urban cosmopolitanism of their defenders. The idea that Indians contributed to Argentine culture was, for Palacio, "an invention" of "scholars" in the cities. "I repeat, this polemic invention was never truly felt by the Argentine people of the countryside, who knew the Indians before their extermination."[9]

The genocide of Argentina's native populations was executed by modern Argentines, not premodern conquistadors. Racism and the idea that Argentina must be a laboratory of progress, but only for a European population, was essentially a modern idea. The Patagonian massacres were not a product of fascist Argentina, but of a liberal authoritarian Argentina with destructive dimensions that announced, and engendered, the possibility of the former.

Concurrent with the Patagonian genocide, Argentina's most important newspaper, *La Nación*, announced in 1881 that a group of people arriving from Europe could not be assimilated into the nation because they represented "heterogeneous elements" that could "produce its decomposition." The group in question was the Jews. The serialized publication in the same paper of the anti-Semitic novel *La bolsa* announced a new epoch in Argentine racism.[10]

These anti-Semitic pronouncements, along with the practice of ethnic cleansing in Patagonia, broke with Argentina's tradition of enlightenment as presented in the preamble to Argentina's Constitution. This text, a landmark of cosmopolitanism, made significant references to freedom as practically rooted in the idea that all men, and implicitly all women, of the world could participate in Argentina's nation building. It was based on dogmas that seemed to contradict the emergence of Argentina's genocide, racism, and the increasing "scientific" authoritarianism of the fin-de-siècle.

The emergence of this practical challenge to liberal Argentina was not an inexorable fact. However, it is important to read its genealogy emerging from liberalism. In fact, the very existence of genocide and discrimination are symptoms of the lack of solid democratic structures and/or their instability before the coming of fascism. To be sure, it would be impossible to find a liberal polity devoid of illiberal trends in the fin-de-siècle world. But unlike other countries, Argentina had a particular path from liberalism to illiberalism that was eventually affected by the peculiar combination of fascism and religion.

Argentina combined an advanced degree of critical emancipatory traditions in and through its public sphere, while racism and political repression concurrently assumed new modern roles in societal interactions with the official world of the state. A repression of workers that morphed into a racist pogrom, the so-called "tragic week of 1919" showed how repressive the state could suddenly become in light of the strengthening of both modern revolution and ethnic diversity. The army's brutal massacre of Patagonian workers on strike in the 1920s, along with automatic extraditions, forced exile into a notorious Patagonian penal colony, and generalized repression of workers, are examples of the authoritarian practices of liberal Argentina in the first two decades of the twentieth century. Repressive practices contradicted Argentina's founding ideals. Argentine fascists would later reject this Argentina while continuing some of its most brutal practices of racism and political violence.

From a historical point of view such elements seemingly facilitated the transition from liberalism to nacionalista fascism. Although Argentine liberalism was conceptually contradictory and would seem, in retrospect, clearly antidemocratic and authoritarian, in reality it did not differ from other European and American understandings of liberalism during that period. Nineteenth-century liberalism had symptoms of totalitarian violence. However, fascism, an extreme nationalism, only appropriated the symptoms and denied liberalism as a whole. The political liberalism of the twentieth century, either out of conviction, convenience, or necessity, denied many of its authoritarian symptoms and democratized itself progressively. These symptoms (genocide, racism, repression, and extreme gender inequality, among others) could have gradually diminished, as it did in other places, but they instead deepened in interwar Argentina. In the process, nacionalismo ceased to be liberal.

Origins of the Nacionalista Ideal

Intellectuals like Ricardo Rojas, Manuel Gálvez, and Leopoldo Lugones wanted to be the first Argentines to claim that the country needed renewal through a new form of nationalism. In 1909, Rojas wrote *La restauración nacionalista*, in which he denounced the negative effects of European immigration and its supposedly destructive influence on the nation. He did not reject liberal Argentina as a whole. Gálvez proposed a wider assimilation of differences through education. He also promoted a new type of nationalism rooted in the colonial legacy. While critical of European and Argentine liberalism, he fell short of proposing a change in the political system. Unlike Rojas, Gálvez eventually became a fascist in the 1930s.[11]

In the early 1920s, the Argentine Patriotic League was established as the country's first right-wing paramilitary force. It maintained links with the Radical Party, the police, the army, the aristocracy, and the Church. The League, which attracted thousands of followers throughout the country, was a civil guard that operated to eliminate workers' mobilizations. It presented a nationalism aimed at maintaining social harmony and, as historian Sandra McGee Deutsch suggests, for its members the promotion of Argentineness implied accepting the status quo. However, the League was not fascist and its positions regarding immigration and racism were moderate compared with those of later nacionalista organizations.[12]

Rojas, Gálvez, and the League promoted a nationalism that bridged the nineteenth and twentieth centuries. In all of them, a movement to the right, an increasing displacement from an inclusive to an exclusive idea of the nation, is evident. In short, while Gálvez later supported and Rojas actually rejected fascism, they were its unwilling precursors.

The fear of communism, a disdain of political and social difference, and an emphasis on excessive national legitimacy found their justification in this precocious right-wing nacionalismo. In the early 1920s Argentine nacionalismo was not yet fascism, but it had already begun to conceive of Argentines as Catholic, anticommunist, and increasingly antiliberal and anti-Jewish. A significant group of politicians and intellectuals began to question the benefits that the enlightenment had bestowed upon nineteenth-century Argentina. In short, they stood against modern liberal democracy.

For them the real Argentina was republican. As with most Argentine political traditions, the nacionalista vision was profoundly antagonistic. Argentina could only be identified with their national project. Therefore, the inclusive Argentina of the constitutional preamble was for them an Argentina of traitors to the homeland and foreigners who did not deserve to live in it.

As in every other nacionalista argument, these propositions were an expression of political desires, rather than reality.[13] According to nacionalistas, modern Argentina needed a dictatorial form of government. The fact that it had never had such a regime was not significant. In their sense of the need for an authoritarian change, the Argentine fascist nacionalistas saw themselves as true revolutionaries. Eventually, they argued, like their fascist counterparts across the Atlantic and beyond, for a revolution against the revolution, that is, a fascist revolution against the legacy of the French Revolution.[14] It is not insignificant that all the coups that the nacionalistas promoted, according to the logic of their ideology, were called "*revoluciones.*"

Nacionalismo increasingly became a multi-class movement of varied origins. Even though the groups that represented this new right came from the army, the Church, and other traditionally hierarchical sectors of society, many intellectuals joined them from the socialist left and anarchism, as well as from middle-class conservative groups and the Radical Party. Leopoldo Lugones, the most famous and most influential of these intellectuals, is arguably the father of Argentine fascism. Strikingly, in ideological and cultural terms, he could also be considered the father of Argentine liberalism. How can this be? Lugones was, above all, a powerful synthetic thinker, who could define and unite the major tenets of different ideological formations from left to right. Through Lugones, nacionalismo became synonymous with fascism, militarism, dictatorship, and, at the end of his life, the "Argentine" Catholic nation.

Lugones explored the complexities of the nacionalista universe, rooting it in his own idiosyncratic notions of socialism and liberalism. As a young man, he had first been an anarchist and then one of the early members of the Argentine Socialist Party. At some point he left socialism, critical of its social-democratic moderate tendencies. Even as a socialist, Lugones dismissed the democracy that his peers wanted to promote. He considered himself a revolutionary.

Lugones's subsequent turn to the right was a striking embrace of the authoritarian form of liberalism promoted by important members of the elite such as General Roca, the general and president responsible for the Patagonian genocide. Lugones was very close to Roca and became liberal Argentina's most prominent intellectual. As a spokesperson for the elites, he celebrated oligarchic forms of liberal nationalism, especially in his 1910 centennial celebratory poem where he praised the land of "cattle and corn-fields."[15] He still considered this land to be the potential homeland of all immigrants, including the Jews. But coincidentally with the expansion of political rights in 1912, Lugones, once again, turned rightward, expanding on certain antidemocratic concepts from his leftist period and denouncing parliamentarianism from the point of view of oligarchic liberalism. He also denounced electoral politics and argued that the army was a caste "superior" to the people.[16] Throughout the 1910s Lugones was not, however, a fascist. Similarly, Mussolini did not become a fascist before 1919, also drifting between socialism and antidemocratic warmongering feelings. Lugones was also an ideological drifter but this did not make him an opportunist. Above all, like Mussolini, he based his political opinions on feelings and unarticulated sensations. Both despised systematic ideas and democracy.

Almost simultaneously with the birth of European fascism at the beginning of the 1920s, Lugones announced his revolutionary faith in the sword, the army, and dictatorship on the stage of *Teatro Coliseo* of Buenos Aires. This successful round of public conferences was later published in a book entitled *Acción*. The kind of action he had in mind was announced in these multitudinous conferences of 1923, which were well attended by members of the elite, ministers, and army. Lugones claimed that violence was a great thing if it was for the good of the homeland.[17] "We need to confront with virility the task of cleaning the country." Argentina was in danger of becoming a "soviet colony" and Lugones wanted to get rid of the internal enemy. The army needed to be ready. If in Europe there was a danger of civil war between left and right, in Argentina this war would be a "national war" against its resident foreign leftists. He assured his public that this war would be "more dangerous than a military war because it will be treasonously conducted from within." Lugones wanted Argentines to adopt a military attitude in life.[18] This proposal became a full-fledged program one year later. It was pompously announced to Latin America in 1924 as not only a political proposal for Argentina but also a Latin American program for the continent and beyond.

In 1924 the democratically elected government of radical president Marcelo T. de Alvear sent Lugones as its representative to Peru for the centennial celebration of the Independence Battle of Ayacucho. In front of representatives from all Latin American nations, Lugones famously announced the imminent arrival of the "hour of the sword." This hour signified his project for an authoritarian military dictatorship that he conceived of as a revolution against liberal democracy. The sword that made the nation would replace democracy with "hierarchy."[19]

According to Lugones the sword stood against democracy and socialism, with socialism being the natural consequence of democracy. The sword was the symbol of order and violence, and for Lugones violence was synonymous with beauty. The idea of violence as an aesthetic and ethical end in the political realm was a typical ideological element of fascisms in general and the Lugonean fascism in particular. Providing a stark contrast with Italian and German fascisms, but similar to the Spanish case, Lugones saw the armed forces as the central player in politics. He understood fascism as militarist in nature. All fascisms need enemies, and Lugones identified the internal enemies of the homeland as Argentines who promoted democracy.

Nacionalismo and Dictatorship

Although he presented himself as a solitary and quixotic fascist, Leopoldo Lugones was not alone. In the mid-1920s, young militants who had formerly belonged to radicalism and the left, along with others coming unambiguously from the right, founded two publications. *La Nueva República* had a more secular orientation, while *Criterio* had a religious one, though they shared the same authors and the same opinions. Both were critical of modernity and stood for a revolution against democracy. With an ideological influence larger than their actual circulation, these publications posited ideas that became central to Argentine fascism. Like Lugones, they endorsed dictatorship as a form of government.

One of their most famous authors, Julio Irazusta, stated that "history has recorded several wonderful dictatorships" and that "democracy does not respect nor promote dignity."[20] Months before, Irazusta had upheld the "ugliness" of religious freedom, which, according to him, concealed an anti-Catholic project, obvious in its encouragement of Protestant "sects." Julio Irazusta was considered one of the most moderate ideologues of the extreme right, which indicates the generalized extremism of such positions. In 1931, warning against the possibility of a socialist takeover, Irazusta expressed his preference for "civil war," rather than handing power over to the leftists.[21]

To be sure, many nacionalistas often conflated democracy with dictatorship. What they envisioned was a form of extreme authoritarian government of the majority that could be, if needed, confirmed by electoral majorities, as had been the case with the rise to power of Italian fascism and later with Nazism. For instrumental reasons fascism often used democratic electoral means to destroy liberal democracy in the long run. But the power of this form of dictatorial "democracy" without deliberation did not rely entirely on electoral representation. Popular sovereignty was not based in electoral methods. Its authenticity was rooted in the sacred. In fact, Argentine fascists like Federico Ibarguren came to this idea by citing and reflecting on the writings of the nineteenth-century Spanish Catholic thinker Juan Donoso Cortés who wrote, "The Sovereign is like God: either it is one, or does not exist; sovereignty, like divinity, either it is or it is not. It is indivisible and incommunicable."[22] For Ibarguren dictatorship could be similarly presented as the republican form of absolute monarchy.[23]

Fascism presented a new form of sovereignty, one based on power and violence. For Lugones and other fascists, popular electoral sovereignty was a thing of the past. It was being displaced by what he regarded as a more authentic form of political legitimacy. In fact, this novel structure of political representation depicted a kernel of global fascism. A mixed form of political legitimation, it was a fascist fusion of the sacred and the will that underscored the totalitarian view of an elementary source of authenticity rooted in violent action and the power that it engendered.

For fascists like Lugones, this form of sovereignty was not mediated and did not mirror deliberative and electoral outcomes. Thus individual freedom was no longer a matter of global concern. The world looked for political "domination," either in the form of the "dictatorship of capital, the proletariat or the Army." He claimed that "experience" proved that the solution of the social problem was not based in "concessions" but in the use of force: "Lenin in Russia and Mussolini in Italy have suppressed class struggle through the imposition of authority." Lugones concluded, "[T]he sovereignty of the people ceases to be in order to transform itself into the sovereignty of the nation. The Law becomes again an expression of potency and no longer an expression of reason or logic." For Lugones this new notion of fascist sovereignty implied a formidable return of all that reason has repressed. "We are again in the times of the warrior of force and conquest."[24]

For nacionalistas at large, dictatorship was legitimate when it was the "dictatorship of the people." The fascist leader represented the people's power, the very conditions of sovereignty. This idea of dictatorial democracy was new in the Argentine political system and it was not open to discussion.[25]

For nacionalistas, democratic Argentina was not really Argentine. In a piece published in *La Nueva República* in 1928, Julio's brother, Rodolfo Irazusta, claimed that "The Argentine state is Catholic in its origins and constitution. Democracy is, by nature, anti-Catholic. Therefore, democracy is incompatible with Argentine institutions." [26] Nacionalistas believed in the natural quality of the Argentine national character. The essence of nationality was not a product of ideas, traditions, and creations but of something more intrinsic, like air or blood, a sort of faith that stemmed from what is natural and absolute. Any alternative conceptions of the nation were discarded as artificial or as mere imitations.

The interwar period was an era of essentialist interpretations about the nation, which defined the *habitus* of its members literally as fallen from heaven and not as the historical product of concrete human relations. These were the years in which a peculiar literary nationalism made its appearance, in Jorge Luis Borges's *El idioma de los argentinos* (*The Language of the Argentines*), Raúl Scalabrini Ortiz's *El hombre que está solo y espera* (*The Man Who Stands Alone and Waiting*), and Ezequiel Martínez Estrada's *Radiografía de la pampa* (*X-Ray of the Pampa*).[27]

The originality of these national visions is doubtful and their postulations uncertain. Still, their significance should not be overlooked. In those years, Borges stood clearly against fascism, and Martínez Estrada redeemed himself as a leftist writer, even after occasionally flirting with the arguments of the extreme right. Scalabrini, on the other hand, introduced a left-wing and populist version of nationalism that overlapped with many of the claims of fellow nacionalistas, while disagreeing with others. Scalabrini had gone into exile for his antidictatorial opposition to the Uriburu regime, which was clearly too conservative for him. Interestingly, he chose to live in exile in Italy, where he collaborated with Italian fascist and German Nazi publications. During this period his anti-imperialist thinking took the form of an antiliberal critique of the plutocracy of empire. All in all, the nacionalistas drew clear lines to distance themselves from these writers. Contrary to Borges, Scalabrini, and Martínez Estrada, who saw *criollo* identity as potentially inclusive, nacionalistas deemed Argentina to be a closed nation.

At the same time that they denounced the liberal creation of traditions, nacionalistas contradictorily presented an essential Argentine tradition that transcended history. This denunciation did not imply a vindication of Argentina's position in Latin America, nor identification with indigenous peoples. "*Indigenismo* is for *mestizo* imbeciles," argued the nacionalista intellectual César Pico, for we Argentines "are Europeans in the Americas."[28]

The idea that Argentina was Europe not only challenged the truisms of geography, but racism and faith also explained the supposed virtues of the Argentine "race." Nacionalistas proposed that Argentina represented the tradition of heroic conquest. Argentina, they believed, was the true heir of the Spanish imperial legacy. They did not see this heritage as implying the need for subjugation to Spain, but as a result of the idea that Argentina was more Hispanic than modern Spain and thus more imperial.

In fascist and modern undertones, nacionalistas updated the myth of "the restoration of the Viceroyalty."[29] According to them, the era of independence was the moment in which Argentina's rightful dominions in Chile, Paraguay, Uruguay, and Bolivia were stolen. Presented as anti-imperialism, the rhetorical South Americanism of the nacionalistas was unabashedly imperialistic and inscribed in the notion that Argentina represented Europe's best imperial possibility for the Americas.[30]

In this sense, Argentina represented Europe's glorious and authentic past, in which a facile way of making a living was frowned upon. The alleged solution was "to provide the national character with a heroic sense of life" that evoked the age of empire. Violence would become both means and end, with civil war and coup d'état as its concrete manifestations, for "our spirit has not been forged by pain, which is the only thing that makes men great."[31]

In its view of Argentine history, nacionalismo reaffirmed its rejection of difference. Argentine historical revisionism appeared as the product of a broader nacionalista context that cast doubt on the notion that all good-willed individuals had a right to be included within the nation. "The people" were defined a priori and remained "closed" to those who did not conform to the national Catholic norm. The later success of the nacionalista stance, with its worship of Juan Manuel de Rosas, of *caudillos* and its *montoneras*, was the product of a long tradition that aimed to reformulate Sarmiento's quandary of "civilization or barbarism," identifying the former with European liberalism and the latter with that which is authentically Argentine. Indeed, the nacionalistas did not condemn the genocide of indigenous peoples, deemed by Sarmiento as legitimate. The nacionalista project criticized the notion of public secular education and Juan Bautista Alberdi's policies on immigration. Thus, with Argentine liberalism perceived of as a myth that betrayed the essence of the nation, the break was no less than absolute.

The nacionalista vision identified otherness with artifice, the unusual with being anti-Argentine. The falseness of liberal principles was not something subject to verification, but only presented as a priori truth. In the words of Julio Irazusta, there was a "democratic fiction."[32] Nacionalista constructivism, that is, the notion of political ideas being "unnatural" or "artificial," applied to its liberal antagonist, while nacionalismo came to be seen as inherently natural, as an authentic experience and practice and only later as an idea grounded in reality. For its enthusiasts, nacionalismo was as natural as the grass of the pampas, the Patagonian deserts, and the mountain range. Nacionalismo and territory represented the great homeland.

Leopoldo Lugones's notions of "*Patria fuerte*" (Strong Homeland) came to be seen as an opposition to democracy and the failure of liberalism.[33] In stating that they wished for a "great, strong and free Homeland," nacionalistas advocated the abolition of electoral freedoms, for they deviated from true change.[34] According to Rodolfo Irazusta's view, published in late 1933 in *Criterio*, liberal Argentina was one of "false adaptations," a product of British, American, and Jewish imitations.[35]

Such positions were symptomatic of an ideologically constant characteristic of Argentine fascism. In several publications, such as *Bandera Argentina, Crisol, Clarinada, Choque,* and *Aduna,* an admiration, without outright replication, of certain strains of European intellectual and political thought existed. Fascism, Catholic fundamentalism, and the doctrines of the French extreme right, with all their anti-Semitic, racist, and anti-democratic features, were widely represented. Publications of this sort, along with radio shows, accompanied the formation of political groups sharing members and ideas. Others, such as *Legión de Mayo* and *Liga Republicana,* even functioned as shock troops.

In this early period (1928–1930) the development of these groups coincided with the second term of radical president Hipólito Yrigoyen. Although events advanced more rapidly than these forms of *criollo* fascism, they continued to hew to the notion of civil war as a prescription for the immediate future and dictatorship as prognosis. The coup of José Félix Uriburu caught them in their infancy and, unsurprisingly, they aligned with his new regime on September 6, 1930.

The First Argentine Dictatorship

Uriburu's coup inaugurated the first modern dictatorship in the country. Soon political prisoners, torture, and even executions of anarchists from the opposition abounded. What alternative to democracy did the dictator propose? Many young nacionalistas asked themselves this. Was Uriburu a fascist? For the left, the answer was simple and affirmative. For the conservatives allied with the General (radical anti-Yrigoyenists and social reformists), Uriburu's actions couldn't be considered as such.

A fervent admirer of the German army, Uriburu apostatized the popular will when it expressed itself in radical terms. The General coincided with the Lugonean assertion regarding the absolute necessity of the army's preeminence in the life of the country. A young participant in the coup, Captain Juan Domingo Perón, saw in Uriburu an honest sort but not necessarily a fascist. For the influential General Agustín P. Justo, Uriburu was an instrument to topple the current order and restore the conservative homeland. For the men and women of nacionalismo, Uriburu was assuredly fascist.[36]

Uriburu was an avid reader of *Criterio* and *La Nueva República*, an admirer of Italian fascism, and a personal friend of Lugones and young nacionalistas like Juan Carulla, a former anarchist doctor converted to fascism. Lugones himself dictated the original proclamation of the coup. Military planes threw copies from the sky for all Argentines to read.[37] Lugones turned down Uriburu's offer to become the Director of the National Library and instead dedicated himself to writing the theory of the Uriburu "Revolution." He presented the dictatorship as essentially antipolitical and thereby rooted in a spirit of military conquest, in contrast to European militarism. Lugones rejected the electoral process and argued for a fascist type of corporativism that would be essentially Argentine and therefore diverge from European forms of fascism. He clearly identified the dictatorship with the "current authoritarian reaction in the world" and reiterated his position that the Argentine military should occupy the central role in Argentine politics. He claimed that Argentines needed the "imposition of the military technique at the governmental plane." They needed a process of national military reorganization of the nation, or what he called "an Authoritarian reorganization" [*reorganización autoritaria*] of the state.[38]

Uriburu agreed with Lugones's theories but was not equally idealist about their practical political implications. In the context of the failed radical military revolt of 1931 and without the support of the entire military coup cadre, which also included conservatives who wanted to return to the oligarchic order prior to the electoral reforms of 1912, Uriburu was forced to constantly take intermediate positions between fascism and conservative authoritarianism.

In 1931 Uriburu tried to reform the constitution and create a corporate system. Ironically he called elections in the province of Buenos Aires and lost. As he lost power, Uriburu got closer to fascism, despite its being more costly to implement. One of his actions was creating a paramilitary nacionalista movement, trained and partially subsidized by the state. Named *Legión Cívica*, it had more than 200,000 adherents and included male and female branches. Its members identified with the nacionalista and protofascist project of their leader.[39] Nonetheless, Uriburu's political capital weakened along with his health. The top-down fascist revolution failed with the European "exile" of Uriburu and his death in France months later.

Shortly before leaving the Casa Rosada, the Argentine house of government, Uriburu gave a speech in which he attempted to clarify his ideas. Uriburu explained that the revolution of September, that is, the first Argentine dictatorship, "lacked the necessary time to radiate its thought and form this public conscience" since "the gravity of the circumstances and the imminent danger that threatened the country precipitated the actions and made heroic remedy unavoidably urgent." This situation of internal danger impeded programmatic change, Uriburu justified, because "to expose at that moment new political ideas for our social arena, when the country suffered from all sides, would have been ingenuous and absurd."[40]

Uriburu distanced himself from the government but promised that his disciples would continue the struggle against the "cause of evil." Finally, he recognized his theoretical difficulties in defining the political project of the dictatorship: "I can't express...in this manifesto of farewell my thoughts...on a better electoral system" but, he announced, "I want to anticipate what some of the men who have been by my side will support and develop in political action that should be implemented." Uriburu argued, "We consider absurd the implantation in this country of a monarchic system. This country is based on republican foundations; we prefer to speak of republican foundations not democratic foundations."[41]

The idea of republic replaced the idea of democracy. As Uriburu noted, "The word Democracy with a capital D no longer has meaning for us.... This doesn't imply that we are not democrats but more sincerely how much we hope that at some point a democracy in lowercase, but organic and truthful, replaces the dislocated demagogy that has done us great harm."[42]

The solution for Uriburu, as for Mussolini, lay in the creation of a corporatist system. However, Uriburu highlighted the need for originality rather than merely copying Italian fascism. The dictator argued that for those who want to believe "that the last word in politics is universal suffrage...as if there were nothing new under the sun, the corporations gave greatness and splendor to the Italian Communes of the 12th and 13th centuries and degenerated later by the predominant action of the princes." Uriburu concluded, "The corporatist union is not a discovery of fascism, but the modernized adaptation of a system whose results over a long epoch of history justify their resurgence." Uriburu insisted on abolishing universal suffrage and even doubted the necessity of political parties. In sum, he proposed to repeal the legacy of the French Revolution and the enlightenment supposedly promoted in Argentina by persecuted Jews: "The Argentine revolutionaries of 1930 cannot take seriously the accusation that we are reactionaries with the language and ideas of the French revolution...we cannot take seriously that a few naturalized citizens that have lived the anguish of far-off oppressions scandalize themselves over the supposed purpose they maliciously attribute to us of wanting to import foreign electoral systems."[43]

For Uriburu, the Argentine political dilemma was not between fascism and communism, but rather the juxtaposition of the Argentine and the foreign, which he identified with democracy. "It corresponds to our loyalty to declare, without hesitation, that if we were forced to decide between Italian fascism and Russian and shameful communism of the so-called political parties of the left, the choice would not be in doubt. Fortunately, nothing and no one impose on us this dilemma."[44]

Army and Movement

After Uriburu's loss of power, nacionalistas radicalized their fascism.

They formed new organizations, among them the *Acción Nacionalista Argentina* (ANA), *Acción Antijudía Argentina* (AAA), *Aduna (Afirmación de una Nueva Argentina)*, *Guardia Argentina*, *Partido Fascista Argentino* (PFA), and *Alianza de la Juventud Nacionalista* (AJN). Nacionalismo consisted of a universe of groups sharing names, ideas, and resources, which revolved around the same myths and ideologies, and was defined by a profound militarism and a symbiotic relationship with Catholicism.

The Legión Cívica Argentina, or LCA, for instance, had several thousand members, many of whom also belonged to other organizations. Among the LCA's resources were "civil airplanes" that dropped nacionalista pamphlets over cities. Members received military training in army facilities, dressed in uniforms, and held public demonstrations and parades. The militaristic nature of the LCA is captured in a statement about its ultimate goals: "The Legion aims at creating a permanent and unbreakable link of solidarity with the Armed Forces to give continuity to the 'internal and external state of national defense.'" The LCA endorsed the reimplementation of the death penalty and what today is known as an "iron fist" (*mano dura*) in dealing with crime. [45] Likewise, another nacionalista organization, the *Legión de Mayo*, sponsored street demonstrations and public acts in Plaza de Mayo against "delinquency" and "the liberal laws that allow delinquents to act." [46]

ANA and *Aduna* embodied a strand of Argentine fascism inspired especially by Uriburu and Mussolini. They clearly identified the dictatorship of the former with the ideology of the latter. In political terms, *Aduna* wanted an army that fully identified with fascism.[47] In contrast with Il Duce, they stressed the need for a true nacionalismo that integrated practice with theory, meaning situating fascism within the realm of the sacred. Argentine fascist doctrine was "pure." Those deemed worthy of it needed to be nacionalista in an "integral" way, "by adjusting our lives to the strict principles of Catholic Religion." [48] The leader of *Aduna*, Dr. Juan P. Ramos, claimed that the fascists were soldiers with an "invincible faith" in God's desires, which he equated with those of the Uriburu military dictatorship and nacionalismo.[49] Similarly, in its 1933 "Purposes," *Guardia Argentina*, led by Leopoldo Lugones, posited the centrality of the Army and the Church in the "formation of public consciousness."[50] The *Partido Fascista Argentino* and *Alianza de la Juventud Nacionalista* were the most radical and massive of these organizations, and also identified with the army and the Church. The PFA posted murals that urged "the soldiers of the Patria" to join fascism.[51]

The AJN had an estimated 30,000 to 50,000 members.[52] According to a secret intelligence report, all its members were told upon entering the movement that its main aim was to establish a dictatorship through a coup.[53] By the 1940s, the AJN had slowly mutated into the *Alianza Libertadora Nacionalista*, giving its support to the candidacy of Juan Perón. The ALN stood as a working-class nacionalista force fighting "the battle of the Homeland against the *anti-patria* embodied by foreign imperialism, international capitalism and Judaic Communism."[54] In 1943, the ALN endorsed the military coup of that year and reclaimed its place as ideological beacon of nacionalismo. Two years later it proposed an alliance between labor and capital, as well as "the nationalization of all public services" to achieve "national economic liberation."[55]

The trajectory of the ALN was characteristic of a nacionalista conglomerate that, in economic and social terms, ran parallel to Italian fascism: from Uriburu's moderately corporatist fascist project (1930–1932) to the social fascism of 1932–1945, exemplified in Italy by the Republic of Salò (1943–1945). But Argentine fascists were perhaps more socially radical in their populism than their Italian and Nazi counterparts. According to historian Sandra McGee Deutsch, when nacionalistas found themselves out of power, their fascism became more radicalized. In this context, they resolved the dilemma between fascism and communism that was not confronted by Uriburu. This process was characterized by a deepening of anti-Semitism, rejection of imperialism and the traditional conservative oligarchy, pride in the "Argentine race," belief in social justice, and violent expressions of "masculinity," such as assassinations of socialists and communists and the constant victimization of Argentine Jews.[56]

Between 1932 and 1945, Argentine fascists and nacionalistas, fanatical followers of the late Uriburu, tried to take advantage of their outsider status to plan a new start in their pursuit of political power. They formulated an *Uriburista* founding myth that, in its emphasis on the figure of their dead leader, distorted political reality and guaranteed an imaginary future similar to the contemporary European realities of Italian fascism and German Nazism.

Uriburu's myth was a central aspect of the nacionalista imaginary future because it defined their political objectives. It featured the stereotypical virtues of the "Argentine nacionalista macho" and the Lugonean idea of the "hour of the sword" that was the expression of divine will. In this context, nacionalistas constantly redefined their ideology as a social Catholic fascism and maintained the need to apply fascism to the army.[57]

Despite their subsequent move towards uniformity, the armed forces of the 1930s were not fully nacionalista. Nacionalismo became stronger in the army at the beginning of World War II. [58] The defense of the homeland implied the defense of the exclusionary national project. For nacionalistas, the armed forces could not stand by passively in relation to the political system but must play a primary role. A majority of Argentine army officials admired European fascism, and Argentine nacionalistas gave them the theoretical framework to articulate it. They argued, as Lugones had before them, that the armed forces were the true representatives of the country's interests. Soldiers with dictatorial tendencies heard this message and, swords in hand, waited for their moment. The overtly nacionalista coup d'état of 1943, and in large part those that followed it, was justified in these fascist terms.

The mythical figure of Uriburu and his coup d'état became the basis for the nacionalista justification of later military coups. The myth reflected the fascist ideal of "the movement" that had to hijack the state by violent means in order to realize revolutionary change. Here "revolution" was defined as both "national" and "socialist," that is, as a proto-populist, non-pluralist combination of the social postulates of the left and the totalitarian politics of the right. It is not coincidental that all military coups of that era defined themselves as revolutionary. In short, nacionalistas represented the revolution against the century of revolutions and stood for a notion of being Argentine that they defined in their image and likeness.

The military state found its perfect incarnation in 1943 with the second Argentine dictatorship, which for nacionalistas was the product of the ideological hegemony that nacionalismo "inculcated in the Army's conscience."[59] The military and spiritual Argentina that nacionalistas promised was not just a reaction against liberal Argentina. The idea of social reform was contained in the nacionalista reading of the socialist tradition and, likewise, in the recuperation and subsequent fascistization of the social Catholicism of the Church. The idea of fighting against monopolies to obtain "economic independence" allowed for an Argentine capitalist class that yielded to the state the administration of certain activities that could not be in private hands. The social nacionalista reform was similar to other fascist experiences, especially those of early Nazism and Italian fascism before its rise to power in 1922 and later in 1943–1945. In contrast, Argentine fascism, putting forward the central role of religion in its political equation, was closer to Franco's experience, which was conservative and not as socially radical as Argentine nacionalismo.

Ideas of agrarian reform in a capitalist countryside devoid of feudal colonial remnants were also unique to this Argentine variant.[60] In sum, nacionalismo combined the anti-Semitism of the Nazis, the corporatist, imperialist "proletarian" and aestheticized violence of Italian fascism, and the ultra-Catholic militarism of Spanish fascism. Argentine nacionalismo represented the most sacralized articulation of fascist ideology on either side of the Atlantic.

This anti-Semitic, anti-imperialist, Christian, and violent nacionalismo also presented itself as the champion of a vertical combination of "social justice" and militarism.[61] In 1941, General Juan Bautista Molina, the so-called "First Soldier" and "supreme leader" of the *Alianza de la Juventud Nacionalista*, underscored the centrality of "social justice" for this confessional and militaristic nacionalismo and claimed that the core objective of nacionalismo was "national liberation."[62]

The nacionalistas defended the idea of a Catholic and right-wing Argentina clearly anchored in transatlantic fascism. Like Mussolini and Hitler, they wanted to change "the consciousness of the people."[63] This meant eliminating the mentality of liberal Argentina and creating a militaristic dictatorship that would last for many years. As nacionalista Bonifacio Lastra argued, they wanted "an Argentina without materialism, with a mystique of renovation, a restoration of Christian content and a distinctively Argentine hallmark." This social and popular Argentina would not accept dissent: "[W]e feel it deeply and we will make the half-hearted feel it too.... We reserve punishment for the sell-outs, because this new-found State will not stand for the weaknesses of pity, but for the severity of justice."[64]

2

Catholic Fascist Ideology in Argentina

IN ARGENTINA FASCISM was at once a transatlantic ideology and a national religious experience. It combined global totalitarian connections and local Christian dimensions. It was transnational in its reification of violence, war, and empire; its radical combination of xenophobic nationalism with an extremist idea of the enemy; and last, but not least, its stated desire to destroy democracy from within in order to create a militaristic totalitarian dictatorship. It was more specifically local in the sense that the fascists of Argentina believed fascism had to be rooted in Catholicism.

This Argentine emphasis on the Catholic nature of their fascism did not affect the dissemination of an international understanding of fascism. In fact, they believed that fascism was a universal ideology with distinctive local adaptations. Thus, nacionalistas often stressed that fascism had different names in different countries. In Italy, the place where it had first attained power it was called Italian fascism, in Germany Nazism, and in Argentina nacionalismo. In contrast to the European cases, they also considered the Argentine variant's sacred distinction to be the essential feature of their movement, one that placed them above the more profane dimensions of the political. Their ideology was not only a radical form of political religion but also an extreme fascist political theology.

Like its European counterparts, this Latin American variant of fascist ideology was not structured in terms of rational programs, textbooks, or academic definitions. In Argentina, fascism was also rooted in affect: "[N]acionalismo is not a political party, and it must not be; it is more than ideology, it is an emotion."[1] According to the journal *Alianza*, it was this specific transcendence of reason and its replacement with the intuitive forces of the sensory world that made nacionalismo a radical force in Argentine politics: "On being extremist, it speaks of a certain faith on top of purely intellectual conviction, a fervor and a 'pathos' that transcend the limits of cold reason, a passionate will to open new frontiers for the Homeland, saving its perennial identity. Therefore, there is no doubt that nacionalismo is extremist and glorifies itself in so being."[2] Enrique Osés, in his book *Medios y Fines del Nacionalismo* (Means and Ends of Nacionalismo), reiterated this idea of nacionalismo as a "collective feeling," a "spiritual state," and a "movement of souls. It is an ideal convergence in a dagger of Argentine aspirations." [3]

While Argentine fascists imagined this collective agreement of souls and minds as the natural emanation of the Argentine spirit, they also thought that this "ideal convergence" had international political implications. It was part of a global movement of fascist warriors fighting against democracy and communism. They all shared elective affinities rooted in their respective bloods and soils. In this respect Argentine nacionalistas saw the goals and ideas of their particular movement as applicable to cases around the world.

Nacionalistas were well informed about the universal dimensions of fascism. Many, including famous nacionalistas such as Manuel Fresco, Matías Sánchez Sorondo, and Juan Carlos Goyeneche, traveled to Europe to see Mussolini and other fascist leaders. Their meetings confirmed the relevance of their ideological quest. For example, in a private interview in 1943, Il Duce promised Goyeneche and his Argentine fascist allies that the "Argentine republic will have to play a vitally important role in the future world order." [4]

The fascist's leader confirmation of a premier ideological partnership with the Argentines reiterated a paramount belief in Argentine fascism: the existence of transatlantic fascism as a clear and present danger to Latin American liberalism. For Mussolini, Argentina was a leader of the new order in South America and he made clear that Italy would be a strong ally on the world scene. He gave Goyeneche his support for the neutralist campaign—which was in fact an Argentine fascist attempt to support the Axis by complicating American hemispheric attempts to present a Latin American front against fascist powers—led by nacionalistas and the Argentine army. Moreover, in a key concession that would cement the relationship, he announced that "Italy recognized Argentine sovereignty over the Falklands/Malvinas islands."[5] Many Italian fascists also visited Argentina during those years and Nazis and fascists contributed money to Argentine fascism, secretly subsidizing the fascist press and other activities.[6]

The nacionalistas openly expressed their reverence for Mussolini and admiration for the extreme right-wing nationalist movement he had engendered.. They saw in the Italian leader a source of inspiration. In his book *El fascismo y nosotros* (Fascism and Us, 1933), the nacionalista Felipe Yofre argued that fascism could be applied outside of Italy since it was a "spiritual state" of being. Fascism was a "conception of life."[7] In the same way, the nacionalista Carlos Ibarguren argued that fascism was born out of a context of global "unease" and represented an illiberal response.[8] Luis Gallardo also recognized fascism as "the interpreter of our century" but highlighted the need for Argentine fascists to shape their fascism in Argentine fashion.[9] According to Yofre, nacionalistas had to identify with the "great Argentina" of Lugones and with "the example" of Uriburu. However, he also stressed the need for a reformulation rather than an emulation of fascism. Nacionalismo "does not embody the blind and unconscious imitation of the Italian regime, but rather our movement and the birth of the fascist organization are the consequence of analogous situations and analogous necessities." Fascism was a global ideology but it also had local premises.[10] As Juan P. Ramos, the leader of *Aduna*, argued in a famous speech at the *Coliseo* theatre in Buenos Aires, the fascism that would be "implanted in Argentina" would have Argentine characteristics without forgetting that Mussolini's fascism sounded like a "clarion in the night."[11] The members of the Argentine fascist party (PFA) also shared this view in 1933. They were inspired by Rome in their attempt to fully dominate the life of the country up to the point where "fascism and the Argentine state will constitute a single entity."[12] They regarded their fascism as being better than the other fascisms insofar as it connected sacred bonds across the Atlantic.

Moreover, they thought of themselves as warriors of Christ and bearers of the imperial traditions of Europe and Latin America. [13] They saw their ideology as clearly rooted in local political traditions, as "essentially national. It is influenced by historical revisionism and it reclaims the majestic empire of the Hispanic tradition. It joins the Latin cultural legacy and the perennial light of Rome. It joins the Cross of Christ. Nacionalismo without being a movement of refraction aligns itself with the New Order."[14]

As the members of the PFA from the port city of Rosario argued, fascism had clear universal implications even as it represented a specific nationalist response to local contexts. For them, its main premises were "unitarian and totalitarian," which meant that fascism was rooted in "the concept of universality" while it responded individually to the needs of every nation. Fascism was socially concerned, unlike "old oligarchic nationalism." Thus, at the national level it promoted class collaboration rather than class struggle. They argued that the old conservative nacionalismo was ceding to the "new universal nacionalismo." In fact, for them fascism was just the name that Italian nationalists had chosen to represent the new nacionalismo and it had ceased to be uniquely Italian as its creator had previously defined it. Instead, it had transcended political frontiers, linking Europe and Latin America. Fascism "has initiated its world expansion as a redemptive crusade."[15] If the notion of crusade called to mind Christian medieval warfare, in Argentina another term taken from Europe's past was similarly used, *Reconquista*. The fascist reference to what they saw as an epic struggle between the Cross and the Crescent helped them to equate Argentine liberalism with Islam, and they mobilized this orientalist trope to insist upon liberalism's foreignness to the spirit of the nation. "In our Patria, we Argentines must reconquer, because what is ours is owned by the others [*los otros*]...the fascist idea starts to be undeniably felt by the people." They believed that the constant popular repetition of the idea that "Argentina needs a Mussolini is an evident symptom of this need [of the fascist idea]." Fascism had a "redemptive mission" and the Argentine fascists had a "secure faith in its victory."[16] Nacionalistas equated their future political victory with the supposed will of the entire nation.

If the idea of Mussolini as a global icon of fascism was pervasive in Argentine fascist circles, other fascist leaders were also presented as the ideal incarnation of the will of the people. To be sure, nacionalistas agreed with European fascists that the presence of the fascist dictators replaced the need for elections insofar as these leaders organically expressed, and even intuitively anticipated, their people's best desires. In this sense nacionalismo, like fascism as a whole, did not put forward a populist authoritarian democracy but a popularly supported dictatorship. However, nacionalistas also thought that popular sovereignty was not the exclusive source of modern political legitimacy. In their view, a divine notion of sovereignty also played a role in determining the legitimacy of their politics. Thus, unlike their European counterparts, nacionalistas put some limits on the fascist sacralization of the leader as a godlike figure, insisting on the subordinate role of fascism in relation to the divine. For them, fascism was the political instrument of God.

On another level, the fascist leaders were believed to be the epitome of a new era where politics was decoupled from projects, platforms, and ideas.

It was the transformation of politics as usual into the "politics of action" that the leaders embodied. They were thought to personify, express, and even create fascist theory through their actions. Violence played a central role in defining what constituted action. It was the preferred tool to force reason, an outmoded form of thought, to cede its unearned place of privilege to occult and mysterious forces. Nazi violence particularly represented a perfect metaphor for this general trend of transnational fascism, as the antifascist writer Jorge Luis Borges so aptly illustrated in his contemporaneous Holocaust story, *Deutsches Requiem.*[17]

In this context, hatred of democratic Argentina went hand in hand with admiration for violent leaders like Hitler. Thus, nacionalistas like Juan Carulla would later call this extended ideological trend the "Hitlerian hypnosis."[18]

Hitler acquired the aura of a leading man of action as well as, more surprisingly, that of a leading intellectual who combined theory with its praxis. Julio Irazusta shared this profound admiration for the Führer. In a revealing text written for *Nuevo Orden* in 1941 and titled "The Personality of Hitler," he argued that the reasons presented by the Spanish fascist Ramiro de Maeztu to define Hitler as the "political genius of the 20th Century" had "increased considerably" over the years. Without being a "political philosopher," the German dictator had presented in *Mein Kampf* "a treatise of practical science, for German use, based on the most solid general ideas." The "general ideas" were available to all, part of the common matrix of transnational fascism. For Irazusta, Hitler was characterized by his "brilliant career," his "effective action," his "flexibility," his "modesty," and his "range." Hitler was, in sum, "an eminently sensible man, the complete opposite of the intolerant and presumptuous megalomaniac that his detractors paint him as." [19]

Hitler's attack on liberalism and democracy was also a source of admiration. As Nimio de Anquín, the fascist leader from Córdoba, argued in 1941: "[B]y the work of the great Hitler, liberalism and ugly democracy have died."[20] The admiration for Hitler was inscribed in the framework of global fascism. The members of AJN in Córdoba and Santa Fe felt a special sense of appreciation for the Nazi victories. Hitler was one of their own.[21] Political criticisms of Hitler were seen as direct attacks on Argentine fascism itself. For example, in 1940 the exiled French philosopher Roger Callois argued at a Buenos Aires conference organized by the liberal magazine *Sur* that Hitler "is an inspired man whose only function consists of brandishing lightning and running blindly toward a catastrophic destiny."

The nacionalistas of *Nuevo Orden* answered, "[W]e've laughed a lot" at this "insolent foreign tongue." [22]

What was the reason for the nacionalista laughter? In terms of Argentine fascist ideology, Hitler could not have had supernatural attributes since only the divine "master" of nacionalismo possessed them. In fact, Callois had presented a solid critique of the sacralizing dimensions of the Nazi myth of the leader. But Argentine cleric fascists disagreed with the antifascist characterization of Hitler as a wild pursuer of crazy dreams. They believed Hitler played a positive role in the divine order of things.

For nacionalista priests like Julio Meinvielle or Gustavo Franceschi, the "paganism" of the European fascisms was related to their belief in the all-powerful humanity of the leader. This was not an observation based on democratic thought, but rather on the idea that, knowingly or not, fascisms fought for the kingdom of God on earth against traditional superstitions. As fascist intellectual Alberto Ezcurra Medrano commented: "[E]ven if we are mistaken, even if Hitler is the monster that you believe he is, a precursor of the anti-Christ, neither will we fear him as much as we fear you...disciples of Judas." Among those disciples Ezcurra named Protestantism, liberalism, Judaism, communism, and Freemasonry. "Thank heaven. Let Hitler fight against all anti-Christian sects and let him be for them the terrible executioner that they have built up and deserve. We know that at the end, whatever happens, the jaws of hell will not prevail against the Church and Jesus Christ is enough to save the Christian civilization."[23]

Nonetheless, the idea that Hitler or Mussolini could turn out to be contrary to Christ and their nacionalismo caused considerable anxiety for Argentine fascists who had to reckon with the fact that ideological gymnastics might not be enough to reconcile the anticlericalism of the most important luminaries of European fascism with their Church-centered variation. If Mussolini promoted an imperialism of "proletarian" peoples, what could nations poor in military might like Argentina hope for in the face of a complete Nazi/fascist victory? To a certain extent, nacionalistas participated in more extended Argentine fears about being overwhelmed by more powerful Eurofascists. Would Argentina become part of the "vital space" of fascist potencies that the Argentine antifascists denounced? Goyeneche also asked Mussolini about this:

Goyeneche: Do you believe in the fear, very pronounced in America, that a total victory by the Axis would endanger the independence of the diverse countries that have individuality and their own histories; and that it would try to impose ideologies contrary to the Catholic essence of Latin countries?

Mussolini: I declare categorically that this fear is completely unfounded. The Axis potencies have never had in their program, much less in their objective of war, the repeal of the independence of minor states and the imposition of foreign ideologies on nations full of history and tradition.[24]

Mussolini's reference to "minor states" could not have been appreciated by the Argentine nacionalistas. Despite their respect for these European fascist leaders, as good Argentine nacionalistas they believed they were better than the Nazis or the Italian fascists. This belief was justified by faith. For them, the *führer* of nacionalismo was Jesus Christ. In integral Catholicism nacionalistas found a source of knowledge and inspiration. At the final reckoning, even in politics, it was God, and not Mussolini or Hitler, who alone was all-powerful.

Already in 1928, the nacionalista César Pico had presented the supposed failure of democracy and the alleged danger of communism as examples of a fascist direction that was impossible to avoid. Far from proposing to copy concrete aspects of fascism, Pico concluded with what for him was synonymous with theoretical action and practical guidance: "Seek ye first the kingdom of God, and his righteousness, for all these things shall be added unto you."[25] As Ezcurra maintained, "Catholicism and nacionalismo should march united."[26] Similarly, for the nacionalistas of *Crisol*, Catholicism was the hinge that defined "what we want and what we don't want."[27]

In 1933, the nacionalista Catholic journal *Criterio* endorsed the fascist movement *Aduna*. The fascists of *Aduna* claimed that they stood for God and homeland and against socialists and Jews whom they considered "enemies of Jesus." They presented their sacred understanding of fascism as a "supreme and eternal ideal of the transcendental overcoming of life."[28] Nacionalistas believed they were the political vicars of God on earth. This idea is noteworthy considering that the most important Catholic priests of the ecclesiastical mainstream, the principal referents of Catholic orthodoxy in interwar Argentina, participated in the nacionalista movement. Priests like Franceschi, Meinvielle, Virgilio Filippo, Leonardo Castellani, and Gabriel Riesco, to name the most famous ones, were key members of the Church and at the same time nacionalistas on the front line.[29]

It is not difficult to understand these ecclesiastical affiliations to fascism if the crusade the Church undertook against liberal Argentina, a struggle that resulted in the Church's cultural hegemony in alliance with the nacionalistas and the army, is taken into consideration. To be sure, the idea that the cross and the sword could be the emblems of a fascist project, at once extremely nationalist and xenophobic, had already been explored in the nacionalista experience with the Uriburu myth. However, it was also related to a sacred re-inscription of the Argentine past in world history. As the nacionalista César Pico signaled, "[O]ur history, that of Christian civilization, was forged by the cross and the sword." [30] For Pico, Argentine nacionalismo had to be "Christianized fascism."[31] In this sense Pico, like the rest of the nacionalistas, did not promote a product of foreign importation but an Argentine variant of the universal fascist constellation. But how could fascism be logically defined if it was one thing in Italy and another in Argentina? This was a question that the nacionalistas discarded in the sense that they saw fascism as an ideology based on feelings and not on books, logic, or programmatic constitutions. For them, fascism could not be understood through reason.

For Luis Barrantes Molina, a leading columnist of El Pueblo, the principal Catholic newspaper of the 1930s, the defense of nacionalismo and Italian fascism as equal examples of global anti-enlightenment reaction was part of a broader Argentine effort to downplay Eurofascism's more revolutionary dimensions. He mirrored wider fears among the Argentine fascists that their ideology would be seen by Catholic dogma as blameworthy innovation. In this respect, their ideological work was as much aimed at moving the movement forward and destroying their enemies as it was focused on protecting themselves from the secular tendencies of their European fascist friends.

El Pueblo was partly subsidized by Italian fascism and included prominent nacionalistas among its contributors. For Barrantes, even though fascism was difficult to define, it constituted an example of a universal dictatorial tendency. This meant that Mussolini's conflicts with the Church could be ignored, because "the Duce is not totalitarian since…in practice he recognizes the spiritual and temporal sovereignty of the Pope."[32] In other words, Mussolini was who Barrantes wanted him to be, a "good Catholic" and a fascist.

For Argentine fascists, the existential dilemma put forward by Uriburu between communism and fascism legitimized the choice of the latter. Father Julio Meinvielle saw this dilemma as based in dichotomies that jointly defined the national being and its enemies. Eventually, true fascism would become Christianized fascism: "Will we form an alliance with fascism or with democracy? Will we favor the modern conquests of women's suffrage? Will we try to Christianize liberalism, socialism, democracy, feminism? It would be healthier for us to Christianize ourselves."[33] Meinvielle understood Christianization as a way of doing nacionalista fascist politics.

Meinvielle's comments reveal a political view rooted in all-or-nothing political binaries. It was not so much a result of the antagonism between friend and enemy in politics (theorized by authoritarian thinker Carl Schmitt) but more precisely the idea that the enemy must be expelled from the political realm. Less than constituting a nacionalista conception of the political, this antagonism indicated its violent and messianic resolution.[34] The interlocutor had to disappear.

To defend the nation against its enemies also implied the promotion of an "Argentine imperialism" that was understood as the rebirth of an Argentine viceroyalty.[35] According to this view, Latin American countries like Uruguay or Bolivia would also be somehow liberated under Argentine imperialism. The nacionalistas of *Guardia Argentina* rejected "the void Americanism" promoted through liberalism and instead supported the "unity of La Plata." They put forward an Argentine-led consortium of five nations (Argentina, Uruguay, Bolivia, Paraguay, and Chile) whose territories made up the old viceroyalty of the River Plate. For Leopoldo Lugones, the author of the political "purposes" of the *Guardia*, achieving this "unity" represented "our manifest destiny." This destiny symbolized a second independence: "Our fathers brought about emancipation. We must sustain and complete it."[36] "Argentine imperialism" was understood as a political regeneration of a Hispanic American Empire under nacionalista hegemony. Stressing national independence was conflated with the development of a Latin American form of neo-imperialism. Argentina was still grappling with the "remaining colonialism of our national political sub-emancipation."[37] In short, for nacionalistas like Ramón Doll, the Argentine postcolonial situation meant that the country was not truly free. Ignoring the fact that Argentina had become a nation only after it ceased to be part of the River Plate viceroyalty, nacionalistas redefined the colonial experience of pre-independence Argentina and advocated for its fascist reconfiguration. Thus full "decolonization" was impossible under the liberal regime; only a fascist-led undertaking would restore Argentina to itself.

For Doll, Rosas's dictatorial had already begun this task since "he had a vast program of reconstruction of the viceroyalty" and had defended

Argentina from European imperialism, as well as from the supposed Brazilian, Bolivian, and Chilean forms of imperialism. Thanks to Rosas, Doll argued, Argentina did not become *Argelia* (Algeria), referring to the North African country's colonization by France.[38]

While positivists such as José Ingenieros announced in 1910 that there were scientific reasons to think about the "evolution" of Argentina's history as a path from "barbarism to imperialism," for nacionalistas, imperial Argentina emanated from the cross.[39] The need for an Argentine empire was thought of as an obvious consequence of the futile nature of the class struggle. In the nacionalista and fascist imaginary, the class struggle was replaced with a new struggle between nations, the liberal "plutocratic" nations and the "proletarian" peoples.[40]

Here the Argentine nacionalistas worked through a conceptualization of state expansion first offered by Italian fascism. Mussolini had maintained that there were two different forms of imperialism, liberal and fascist. But in Argentina more than in Italy, Mussolini's form of imperialism was also integrated with the Latin American tradition of anti-imperialism. Thus the Argentines proposed a new form of imperialism: linking European fascist understandings of empire with the Latin American struggles against the Hispanic empire. In other words, although Argentine nationalism was rooted in the struggle for "national liberation" from the Spanish empire, it took the Catholic dimensions of this first imperial moment and tried to reanimate it for the twentieth century as "Argentine" imperialism.

Argentine fascists presented this tradition as a manifestation of popular sovereignty. Typically they also added theological motifs to this view. For them, traditional secular empires (i.e., England, France, and the United States) were pagan, while they saw fascist imperialism as an anti-imperialist God-sanctioned negation of the secular liberal empires. This was, for nacionalistas, "the dialectics of empire" which they understood as an Argentine popular regeneration of the imperial legacies of the Spanish and Roman empires.[41] However, nacionalistas did not think of the imperial legacy as a mere return to the past, because the Cross and the Sword had to be at the service of the "new order."[42] In contrast with other Argentine fascists who equated totalitarianism with paganism, communism, and liberalism, Pico, Ezcurra Medrano, and many others tried to recuperate the concept of totalitarianisms for clerical fascism. The totalitarian nature of Argentine fascism was supposed to be rooted in its integral Christianity. As Ezcurra Medrano put it, "only a Catholic totalitarianism can secure Catholic freedom." This sacred integralism was a

"Totalitarianism of the Truth."[43] To be sure, Mussolini had similarly appropriated the term totalitarianism from the antifascists. If the former had presented fascism as tyranny, Il Duce himself presented fascism as an integralistic form of politics. But for the nacionalistas, imperialism and integralism were part of totalitarianism because they were Christian. In other words, imperialism represented the jointly popular and divine legitimacy of the Argentine nation.

For Pico, imperialism demonstrated a superior destiny for Argentina and Latin America. Those who criticized imperialism were affected by "the analytical tradition of Freud and Marx, [who] in explaining the superior by the inferior, distrust all the splendor of the temporal city."[44] Defending the fascist notion of sovereignty as jointly rooted in popular and sacred sources of legitimation was an example of the "superior" might and potency of the movement. For Argentine nacionalista Ernesto Palacio to "adopt from fascism only its authoritarian shell when its essence is mystical, and when only this constitutes the architecture of the State, is insanity.... Popular support is what makes fascism strong, and it will lose it when it is lacking."[45] For Palacio, a fascist dictatorship had to be part of a hegemonic project marked by a common history (understood by him as antiliberal, imperial, and Hispanic) and religion. Nacionalismo would then allow for the realization of the fascist Kingdom of God on Earth. Therefore, the nacionalista "action" was seen as the confirmation that nacionalismo in Argentina was fascism as God wanted it.

Nimio de Anquín, who as "chief" of fascism in the province of Córdoba had thousands of followers, defined nacionalismo in 1939 as a political thought that "is a clear Christian ideal" although formulated "for the temporal order in perfect coincidence with the celestial state."[46] De Anquín included this project in the framework of the similarities between nacionalismo and Mussolini's fascism. Therefore, in a massive mobilization in 1936, the Argentine fascist leader proclaimed the superiority of the right in a growing minority over the weak majority. Noting the importance of having achieved unity of action and doctrine, he urged young nacionalistas to join the struggle as "a norm of action and life," reminding them of Mussolini's words, "If I advance, follow me, if I fall back kill me, if I am killed, avenge me."[47] The fascists of Córdoba, like Argentine nacionalistas in general, did not distinguish among fascisms because they understood, perhaps better than Mussolini, the nacionalista particularities of each in the framework of universal fascism.[48] This last point was defined by a collective structure of feelings that became "norms of life" for the individuals and the nation as a whole. But in Argentina, more than in other places, feelings and actions were connected to the perceived will of God.

The nacionalista poet Leopoldo Marechal expressed the nacionalista connection to the sacred in even more dramatic terms. In the pages of the Catholic nacionalista magazine *Sol y Luna* in 1938, the poet presented his peers with an ultra-messianic reading of the past and the future. He even argued that Argentina was potentially placed at the terrestrial boundaries of the celestial domain. As the ultimate site of redemptive politics, it occupied a place in between the most sacred frontiers, those of life and death. Marechal noted that there were peoples who "have a mission" according to the designs of God and lift "the singing voice of history." "Is our country one with a mission? I believe it is: mine is a faith and a hope, nothing more, but it is great." The poet maintained that if the "designs of God" were followed, Argentina would become not only a "great province on earth" but a "great province of heaven."[49]

Marechal summarized a shared belief among Argentine fascists. Their Argentine imperialism was an outcome of a broader fascist plan to reshape secular Argentina in sacred terms. Their view of the enemy was also shaped by this extremely antagonistic political theology that brought back to politics a transcendental religious fight between good and evil. For example, the nacionalistas of *Clarinada* declared that Catholics must organize to combat communism, and must never think of joining the communists, since the followers of Stalin were the incarnation of the devil.[50] Precisely because they identified political adversaries with demonic forces, they believed they were the political emissaries of God. In sum, Argentine fascism can be defined by its stated political imperative to "expand the kingdom of God, adorning the emblem of the Homeland."[51]

A Fascist Religion

Believing themselves to be God's warriors, nacionalistas constituted more than a standard version of the so-called modern "political religions." In short, they did not only mimic rituals and language from traditional religion as most modern political religions do. Nor were they were simply a secular movement occupying the traditional public spaces of religion. Argentine fascists conflated their movement with Christianity and they were in a state of becoming a fascist religion. While they used religious practices and metaphors in profane political contexts, they also fused fascism with more traditional spheres of religion. In practice, they brought fascism to the churches of Argentina, proselytizing in and out of religious sites. In theory, they fused political ideas with the more proper domain of Christian theology. In this context, they equated God's violence with their own violent actions. In *Clarinada*, Eugenia Silveyra de Oyuela, one of the most extreme nacionalista intellectuals, argued that a "totalitarian government is not against Catholic dogma." She believed that the nacionalista regime of the future needed to be subordinate to Christ. In this context, violence was legitimate as a result of God's war against the internal enemies. For her, this was the situation in Argentina where "red hordes" had invaded the country. "[W]e have the invaders in our midst, and we are, in fact, in a state of defensive war. This is a licit war for the Argentine who needs 'to defend the rights of the threatened homeland.'"[52]

In fascism, violence was presented as essentially preemptive. In other words, fascist violence was conceived as a response to the (imagined) violent actions of the enemy. A mechanism of projective identification played a key role in this context, propelling fascists to ascribe violent desires of war, torture, and extermination to the enemies. The legitimation of "preemptive" violent desires was actually central to fascist ideology. Fascism conceived political violence as the collective expression of inner authenticity, the best expression, and the ideal outcome, of a nation of warriors.

Given the theological nature of Argentina's *fascismo criollo*, the call for "preemptive violence" was full of messianic implications. The perceived immediacy of future violence opened the gates to a sort of fascist self-realization. This violence allowed for a regeneration of the people at the time of a "gruesome and penitential hour." It was in short, the hour for national redemption. Nacionalistas claimed that only after the "dark night" of violence would nacionalismo see the "light."[53] The notion of redemptive violence was not exclusive to Argentine fascism but especially in this context did thinkers find in violence a source of sacred ethical legitimacy, a "moralizing" force. Fascists saw their own violence as an emanation of the divine. As Yofre claimed, "violence distinguished the charlatan from the apostle."[54] Divinely sanctioned violence represented the crystallization of fascist theory. "Superior violence" was made tangible by the word of God. It was a "defensive violence."[55] Or, as *Clarinada* put it, emphasizing the practical implications of their ideology, "Praying to God and punishing with the stick [*A dios rogando y con el mazo dando*]."[56]

Sacred violence was the premier Argentine way to synthesize fascism and religion. For Meinvielle, fascism as it was known in Europe was objectionable, but conceived for the Argentine context and in terms of the nacionalista religious crusade it was not only possible, but sound.[57] In *Criterio*, Father Gustavo Franceschi displayed his nacionalismo and presented it as the Catholic political movement in times of internal war.[58] He also criticized the anti-Church tendencies of the Italian dictator, but finally explained that even Il Duce had been the only salvation against civil war. After his visit to the fascist front in the Spanish Civil War, Franceschi was strengthened in his conviction that Argentina would experience similar events. For him, God was on the side of fascism.[59]

Nacionalista clerico-fascist propaganda penetrated throughout the country, and priests played a significant role in its distribution. While Father Filippo defended Argentine fascist ideas on the radio, Father Castellani addressed three radically different audiences with his writings. The first was his nacionalista readership, the second the conservative readers of the mainstream paper *La Nación*, where Castellani, along with Lugones and other nacionalistas sometimes wrote. Children constituted the third audience. Mobilizing children was new in Argentine politics, and in this sense also preceded its better-known manifestation in Peronism. Father Castellani was not the first nacionalista who wrote fascist literature for children. Nacionalista A. H. Varela wrote a children's book in the format of a totalitarian fable, with communist-espousing cats that were predictably overthrown by an Argentine fascist feline.[60] In turn, Father Castellani presented stories of the "pampa and mountain" for adults to read with their children. In these stories, the Father acted as a sort of clerico-fascist antithesis to Horacio Quiroga, the liberal Uruguayan author who had written stories about the Argentine northeastern jungles. Castellani warned that the readers should be "the men who really love the children, who suffer and die for them. Those who don't love them strive to imitate them not in the purity of their hearts but in the irresponsibility of their actions." The "fables, legends and stories of this collection are for boys who don't want to grow up to be girls and for men who see in every boy the image of the son and not a species of semi-god beyond good and evil."[61]

Castellani's metaphors were clear and violent. Perhaps in his conversation with the many liberal stories of the jungle (from Rudyard Kipling to Horacio Quiroga), marshes represented lust for the priest and in them, for example, an "English man" met his death. In this context, animals were the object of political suspicions. In this way, Castellani communicated to Argentine children that, like the parrots, the *pirinchos* (a type of bird typical of Argentina) had become communists.[62]

In one of his most notable fascist stories, Castellani told of the plague of locusts that desolated the Argentine countryside during the 1930s, an event that allowed him to deploy biblical allegories to advance fascist politics among his young readers. This story is highly symptomatic of the key dimensions of Argentine clerico-fascist ideology, especially in terms of the ideas of the fascist leader, liberalism, and the enemy. The insects represented communists and the unassimilable others whose presumed racial differences made them objects of victimization in fascist ideology. Castellani narrates how an immense swarm of flying *langostas* assaulted a rural colony of immigrant farmers and how the colony surrendered and abandoned itself to the "omnipotent and malicious will of the scourge." But suddenly a farmer named "Benedicto Mulosini" proposed to burn a little field to incinerate the insects.[63] The transformation of the name of Mussolini into a Catholic version of fascism is very clear in the story. The metamorphosis illuminates the synthesis of fascism and Catholicism that Castellani and his clerico-fascist peers put forward.

During those years, Castellani published an article in the nacionalista newspaper *Cabildo* in which he told the true story of an old Italian immigrant who on his deathbed worried about the criticism that many Argentines directed against Mussolini. Castellani complained that in liberal Argentina this immigrant had lost his Catholicism, which made the dying man an incomplete fascist.[64] In this context, one could read the story about the plague of insects as a projection of Castellani's wishes vis-à-vis the country's immigrants. In contrast with that real secular Italian immigrant, in the imaginary colony of his story, the protagonist "Benedicto Mulosini" is an immigrant who happens to be a fervent Catholic and acts as God's representative on earth.

The little field that "Mulosini" wanted to burn belonged to the civic commission, that is, "it belonged to everyone but also to nobody." Here, the commission represents a clear example of a liberal institution as Castellani imagined them. After many hours of deliberation and while the insects continued their destruction of the land, the commission told the "energetic and violent Italian" to burn his own field if he wanted to do so.

"Benedict, who was the only one who had never ceased to fight [the plague] at his farm, raised his arms to heaven and swore an imposing malediction. The next morning the communal field and some nearby fields burned with fire. A terrible outrage emerged among the people and some even spoke of killing the Italian but the burning of the fields caused the insects that had not died with the fire to leave and saved half of the harvest."[65]

Castellani stressed the analogy between the field and the country. He commented that someone said that the community needed to thank Mulosini for incinerating the invaders. This was not to be. Castellani concluded the story by informing his young readers that some members of the community accused Mulosini of being an arsonist and beat him to death. One of the assassins was the president of the commission. Members agreed that Mulosini had been wrong to proceed through illegal means, and they referred the case back to the review of the development commission, "and talking and talking at length they reached the conclusion that maybe all had been a fluke and that the insects were gone by the decision of God, so the matter was settled and they did not thank him. The story ends with the following preemptive words: "That is why I say that it is better to kill the locust when it is a little bug."[66]

The metaphor of vermin and plagues as enemies of the country belongs to the usual rhetoric of fascism. The commission represents parliamentarianism and liberalism. The little communal field is the common good and the Italian immigrant simply stands for fascism as the Argentines understood it. He does not rely on reason or logic. His actions are rooted in the experience of the sacred, raising his "hands to heaven."

Castellani's children's stories were meant to fill the void of the national secular schools that nacionalismo presented as corrupt. Along with the hierarchy of the Church, nacionalistas proposed that religion be imparted in Argentine public schools. This was one of their principal political propositions. More generally, Argentine fascism proposed the dissolution of the secular boundaries between church and state.

The recurrent insistence on the primary role of Catholic religion as the vector of the fascist future was a defining feature of nacionalismo. According to Federico Ibarguren and his nacionalista collaborators, it signaled the path that led from the "hedonistic shit" of the liberal context to nacionalista politics.[67] The young Ibarguren was a student of Castellani and Meinvielle at the *Cursos de Cultura Católica*, which would later become the Argentine Catholic University. As a faithful servant of his ideological mentors, Ibarguren defined in a poem the political path to God as a vital illumination of the senses: "I have found in God/The lantern."[68] Ibarguren's God was, in effect, a torch that illuminated his fascist experiences. This light was less metaphysical than political. In nacionalismo, faith legitimized the political authenticity of the self.

This "recognition" of the supposed divine truth of the paths of nacionalismo was a driving force of its war against liberal Argentina. For the nacionalista Father Juan Sepich, one of Ibarguren's "masters," a fundamental task was that of resisting cultural "hybridization."[69] Sepich, like other priests, didn't theorize about politics, but rather urged the nacionalistas to action. In a characteristic dialogue with the young nacionalista Felipe Yofre, Sepich told him that the "tranquility in which we live is really an artificial state maintained by the enemies of God and the Homeland." The enemy did this to fool the people and to work in the "shadows." Sepich informed nacionalistas about the immediacy of a catastrophic future and warned them about "the dangers that threaten us if we don't react.... The communist network is building throughout the country and waits for none other than the order of Moscow to put in motion the colossal machine they have mounted to squash us like cockroaches."[70]

The idea that the nacionalistas could become despicable animals was scandalous for fascists. It constituted a clerico-fascist projection of the enemy's designs. For the fascists, the war against the internal enemy had clear Latin American implications. Anarchy and civil war were closing in, promoted by a "vast conspiracy of leftists that fight on all fronts to finish at once with God, the Homeland, and with family in Argentina and all of Spanish America." In these types of dialogues, and in their writings, nacionalista priests like Father Sepich confirmed the legitimacy of their violent and pro-coup ideals to their young followers. In the absence of a program, the preemptive practices of the latter actualized the ideology of the movement, making it tangible to the believers and providing them with a full-fledged sense of ideological certainty. Action and speed were valued in the context of a fascist development of defensive measures against the imagined internal war promoted by the left. In Father Castellani's assessment, nacionalistas "don't know where they want to go, but they want to get there quickly."[71]

This nacionalista eagerness to act violently implied having no patience for established political and legal norms. They worked with certainty about the divine nature of their actions. For the nacionalistas of *Clarinada*, recent events demonstrated "very clearly that God chooses the nacionalistas to manifest his kingdom on earth."[72] Argentine nacionalistas thought that their violence was not the consequence of a functional ascription by the sacred (as in Italy or Germany) but rather the expression of God's most prevalent desires.

According to the Argentine nacionalista Father Meinvielle, violence was justified when it had a sacred sanction. He proposed the use of sacred violence to change the country: "If fascist violence is not implemented, the people begin to fall rapidly into communist chaos. The example of fascist violence is inevitable."[73]

Nacionalistas contrasted their intuitive celerity in theory and practice with a supposed democratic and bourgeois political stagnation. The critique of the bourgeoisie was a shared motif for all nacionalistas, who also shared with Meinvielle the idea of purifying the bourgeoisie of their liberalism. In *Sol y Luna*, for example, it was promised in 1939 that the bourgeoisie would be dethroned and restored to the subaltern functions that were incumbent on them: "[T]he reactionary movements, generically fascist, are already elaborating the bases of a new aristocracy."[74]

The idea of a new aristocracy of soldiers of Christ was presented as a reason for celebrating the supposedly purifying virtues of violence. For Meinvielle, if violence didn't achieve the establishment of a stable regime, it would serve at least to "prepare" future generations to face the battle of the "two final camps," that of God and that of the godless.[75] In sum, the nacionalista concept of a war between believers and infidels represented a metaphor for future state-sanctioned terrorism. Nacionalistas justified this terrorism theoretically before it actually became a reality some decades later.

For them, the political nacionalista solution, besides being accepted in the populist sense of the leader as the best incarnation of the people, also had to be dictatorial, violent, and rooted in the sacred. Violence represented a purifying end in that it was thought of as being called for by God, who was also conceived of as Argentine. In the context of an internal war, profane politics were displaced by political theology. The result was a war for the nation, war made in the name of the Father. As the fascist Juan Carulla put it, nacionalismo "will fight a holy war for the sake of the country."[76] The sacred war called for extreme measures, including torture and executions. The Uriburu dictatorship's repressive practices had included the *picana*, the fatefully famous electric rod to torture victims. The *picana* transcended its role in the memory of repression and became for nacionalistas a symbol of the politics of the future: a war to cleanse the imagined dirt of the nation: "We, the nacionalistas, let's gather the '*pichana*.' [sic] With it we will create the most patriotic broom. We will use this broom when the day of final cleansing comes."[77]

But who were these dirty enemies who could not be accepted and therefore had to be "stabbed" and "cleansed"? For the fascists, they were all those thought of as being against God. Father Filippo argued as much in a poem whose poor stylistic pathos makes it no less important as a symptom of nacionalista ideological simplicity. Its simplicity erects the binary conception of the world in which the historical and the national represent the sacred, while the other, the distinct and the abject, is actively opposed. Projection reigned supreme, and the nacionalistas attributed their own intentions to the enemy, here characterized by his dreams of insanity and death:

> The learned man admires
> That in our glorious Homeland
> To a religious phalanx
> The brilliant turn is owed,
> See how they conspire
> Against tradition
> An anarchist gang
> Of expelled foreigners
> That rashly try
> To leave us without religion.[78]

The answer in Filippo's poem relates to the nacionalista idea of the extreme enemy, the radical otherness that cannot be a part of the national being. These enemies included not only Jews, gays, and people from the left, but also everyone who doubted the nacionalista ecclesiastic creed. The majority of Argentines who acquiesced or hid their dissent could be accepted in the fascist world of the future. The excluded were thought of, as the nacionalistas of *Combate* stated in 1943, as "true apostates of the Homeland."[79] Their presence was objectified in real subjects who would later suffer the consequences of this literalization of racist fiction and discrimination in their bodies. All of these elements were, in effect, alien to the Argentina of the Cross and the Sword. In their mere existence, they could subvert the sacred image of the Catholic nation, its armed forces, and its Christianized fascism.

3

Anti-Semitism, Sex, and Christianity

IN AN ANONYMOUS report on the "Jewish Question," Nazi diplomacy reviewed what anti-Semitism could expect to encounter in Argentina. This document features the typical elements of the modern anti-Semitic conspiracy theory. In Argentina this form of anti-Semitism already had fervent adherents and defenders.

The Nazi report shares many anti-Semitic fantasies with the Argentine fascists, especially the notion that the economy was controlled by the Jews, who also had great power in political circles. It commented on the infiltration of the principal newspapers, like *La Nación*, whose owners were "probably Jews," *El Mundo* "that finds itself in Jewish hands," and *Crítica*, whose "proprietor, a Mr. Botana, certainly would not be Aryan." In fact, none of these papers were owned by Jews. The high degree of identification of Argentine Jews with their country was seen as problematic by the anonymous Nazi interpreter of Argentina. This writer agreed with the nacionalista view of the role of liberalism in Argentina: "The Jewish immigrant could, thanks to the liberalism that gains power and presents itself throughout the world, not only maintain awake that mentality in Argentines, but deepen it as much as possible." For this reason, before 1920 the Jewish community in Argentina "had no other antipathy against it than that of the Catholic Church, omnipotent and very influential in this country." For the Nazi observer, the dictatorship of General Uriburu was responsible for the links between communism and Judaism having been exposed: "Thanks to the censorship to which the newspapers were submitted, the government could locate the Jews at the center of the communist disturbances. Since then, anti-Semitism has taken a step toward the heart of Argentine patriots."[1]

In highlighting the role of Uriburu and the Church, the Nazi report presented the double genesis of the anti-Semitic phenomenon in the "theories" of the Church and in the paramilitary and fascist groups created by Uriburu's government. Men and women close to the Catholic Church, alongside nacionalistas, propelled anti-Semitism, giving it a legitimacy it had never enjoyed before. Anti-Semitism represented a strong ideological affinity between a sizable group of Catholic priests and nacionalistas. In this context, the fascist memory of the Uriburu dictatorship defined what they saw as a strong anti-Semitic legacy. However, the history of Argentine anti-Semitism did not begin with Uriburu. The liberal daily *La Nación* had traces of anti-Semitism toward the end of the nineteenth century. Nor was liberal President Sarmiento free from anti-Semitism, although his intolerance was meager compared to later fascist Argentine anti-Semitism.

During the so-called Tragic Week of 1919 Argentine anti-Semitism went beyond racist writing to become a victimizing practice. With the fascists of the 1930s and 1940s anti-Semitic nacionalismo begun to occupy a prominent place in Argentine society.

Outside of the nacionalista and Catholic contexts, the effects of this anti-Semitism were less prominent. But they were not marginal, and they were connected with other forms of racism, authoritarianism, and xenophobia that characterized the political culture of the country.

A Racist Faith

During the 1930s, famous Catholic priests like Gustavo Franceschi, Julio Meinvielle, Leonardo Castellani, and Virgilio Filippo, together with writers from the Argentine Catholic world like Gustavo Martínez Zuviría (Hugo Wast), played a central role in the definition of the stereotype of the enemy. Their message was financed by the embassies of Hitler and Mussolini. Their intellectual efforts redefined the image of the Jew such that it could link traditional Catholic anti-Semitism to new forms of racist and pseudo-biological anti-Semitism.[2] The legitimacy of their discourse—partly due to the fact that they were acting representatives of the institutional Church, which gave their writings official imprimatur—was a major factor in their widespread influence on the many Argentine fascist publications. Many Argentine fascists read Argentine reality through the anti-Semitic Catholic prism that these "theorists" offered them with their writings.

In this way, principal actors from the nacionalista and Catholic worlds legitimized anti-Semitic propaganda through an original take on the "Jewish problem" that borrowed from the traditional anti-Semitic definitions of the Church and fused them with an often unrecognized racist and pseudobiological definition of the Jew.

Priests like Franceschi explicitly rejected the idea that their discourse was racist, but didn't deny the possibility of thinking of Jews in racial terms. Similarly, Barrantes Molina argued in *El Pueblo*: "[W]e cannot deny that we find a great similarity between the racial psychology of the anti-Christian Israelites and the character and mentality of those people currently affiliated with communism."[3] Franceschi, who was director of the most significant Argentine Catholic journal, *Criterio*, maintained that the necessary public exclusion of the Israelites was due to their political and cultural behavior and not their racial character. Franceschi charged the Jews with living in every nation but identifying themselves with none; economically exploiting the country in which they situated themselves even though "no other economic regime could be more favorable to the triumph of Israel than our capitalistic system"; and building "the social solvent by antonomasia" through revolutionary movements.[4] For Franceschi, this was enough to explain the persecution of the German Jews during what would later become known as the Holocaust, and justified the necessity of rejecting the new refugees who tried to enter the country after the German invasion of Poland in September 1939. These thoughts were shared by those in power.

By the end of the 1930s, the nacionalistas fantasized that the cause of anti-Semitism was found in the very actions of the Jews. They proposed to solve the "Jewish problem" with the "Christian solution": separate them from Christian society and maintain them in a place of subordination.[5] For Leonardo Castellani this "Christian solution" was rooted in the segregation tradition of the ghetto, and he advocated the full separation of Jews from other Argentines.[6] Father Franceschi did not exclude more radical solutions. He suggested that the idea of the expulsion of the Jews and their violent victimization were possible in the near future. According to the Catholic priest, Argentina was crammed with "the relentless Semitic penetration" that monopolized industry, impoverished "non-Hebrews," intervened in "extremist movements," and distributed "pornographic propaganda" with impunity.[7]

In Franceschi's account, the racist violent solution at times seemed to replace the need for the traditional Christian solution of segregation. Franceschi did not reject the need for racist violence. In his view it constituted a legitimate "reaction" to the "catastrophe" the Jews were bringing the country: "What until very recently was judged to be impossible in

Argentina, an assailant anti-Semitism...that demands the elimination of the Jew by whatever means, is manifested with each step and gains day by day new and enthusiastic supporters. Let's be real: a great pogrom is no longer improbable among us."[8]

For Argentine cleric-fascists the "Jewish problem" was not merely theological but also racial. Like Franceschi and Castellani, for Meinvielle the solution to the "problem" in Argentina had to be Catholic and not what eventually became the Final Solution of the Nazis.[9] He saw Nazi anti-Semitism as being detached from superior political interests. And yet he also regarded Nazi violence as an outcome of God's global plan against the left.[10] Given that Meinvielle accused the Jews of everything he didn't like, nacionalista violence could only be an anti-Semitic remedy. But this violence could not be pagan. For Meinvielle, there existed "a pagan mode that will reject the foreign because it's foreign; a Christian mode that will reject it in the measures in which it could be detrimental for the just interests of the country. A pagan mode that will reject and will hate the Jew because he is Jewish; a Christian mode that, knowing the solvent mission which the Jew occupies in the heart of Christian peoples, will limit his influence so that it doesn't cause harm."[11]

In this way of thinking, Judaism, as a millenary race, tried to dominate the world through the exaltation of the corporeal and the material in Christian societies. Meinvielle established a historic dichotomy in which Christianity and Judaism represented an eternal battle between the spiritual and the ethereal, represented by the former, and the low and carnal represented by the latter. Christians represented God and the Jews the Antichrist.[12] According to the nacionalista priest, Protestantism, liberalism, and communism were entities dominated by the "carnal Jew" who promoted sin, through which they enslaved Christians.[13]

The relationship between this way of thinking and the Argentine reality of the 1930s was evident to Meinvielle. In his 1936 book *El Judío* (The Jew), Meinvielle tried to prove the Jewish domination of politics, the economy, education, and the press, and warned about the perniciousness of "the mixture of Jews and Christians." One of the most worrisome aspects for Meinvielle was that related to the most grave of Jewish characteristics: the extreme emphasis on corporeality and sexuality. He understood both as the antithesis of Christian spirituality.

The establishment of "Judaic molds" in the Argentine mentality confirmed Meinvielle's fears about the advent of sin through a popular culture that he identified with Jewishness.[14] He saw Jewish contamination as not just ideological but also economic, political, and cultural. He blamed the Jews for forms of bodily or sexual behavior supposedly "propelled" by them through a strong apparatus of propaganda in which the cinema, theater, sports, and the radio played a central role.

Perhaps the lack of conceptual depth or the attempt to simplify the anti-Semitic arguments even further made the priest Virgilio Filippo one of the most important and dangerous anti-Semites in Argentine society. Like Franceschi and Meinvielle, Filippo saw the Jews as a race that strove relentlessly to maintain their "purity." He ascribed to them his own desire to create a homogenously pure Argentine race. He claimed, "The principal caution of the religion of Israel is to maintain the purity of the race. It is not true that the Jews constitute in the first place a religious community. They are a race."[15]

Through his famous radio transmissions, articles in *Clarinada*, and anti-Semitic pamphlets, Filippo reduced Jews to a physical stereotype that could easily be recognized: "Upon seeing this type of Jew, I see the whole of his race, as you all also distinguish them by their physiognomic traits. No one can move the lines of their nose and the undulations of their mane."[16] This stereotype coincided with those elaborated by European racists but Filippo's discourse maintained a vernacular specificity. He denounced the secularizing effects of Judaism in Argentina on religious grounds. In his view, these effects were specially related to the spread of abnormal forms of behavior. Due to their "degenerative" and viral character, the Jews were the historical epitome of the "most agitated, restless, and nomadic herds."[17]

For Filippo, the public expression of sexuality was a primordial element of the "ignominy of this century." He grouped the psychoanalytic theory of the "Jewish propagandist," Freud, with the "Jewish theories" of Marx, Lenin, and Trotsky as a set of "Jewish-Masonic-Communist discoveries." For him, Freud was the prototypical Jewish intellectual who brought secular contagion to Christian society and achieved ubiquitous and hidden Jewish designs.

In the mind of the Argentine priest, Freud was an important exponent of the dangerous Jewish sexual degeneration that he saw as particularly alarming in Argentina. According to Filippo, with psychoanalytic theory the lower dimensions of the Jewish "ego" were going to take the place of the higher doctrines of the Church. This replacement, if not prevented, was supposedly going to promote racial degeneration, especially in schools and among the younger segments of the population: "...the youth (will find) pleasure in unrestrained carnal joy...forgetting their traditions, denigrating their race, shadowing their foreheads with the cloud of ignominy...and killing their superior part in order to give free rein to the inferior part, to the animality that is only useful when bridled by the laws of the spirit."[18]

Fascist Fictions

Argentine fascists, following in the line of Filippo, Meinvielle, and Franceschi, shared the biological discourse on this "fearsome destructive ferment" that could only motivate an anti-Semitic reaction in the population, understood as an "inevitable reaction of the country against a foreign and disruptive element."[19] Argentine fascism, at least discursively, understood anti-Semitic action as a scientific and planned cleansing of "the Hebrew infiltration" of Argentine society and state and was unlike traditional anti-Semitism: "Our nacionalismo does not persecute the Semites nor does it dream of organizing bloody 'pogroms.' The only thing it does is scorn them due to reasons of racial anaphylaxis." A discursive dehumanization of the victim accompanied this new form of racial anti-Semitism: "the ptomaine of fish makes some people sick: the ptomaine of the Jewish race sickens us."[20] The animality of the "bearded microbes" was defined in a dubious poem as a characteristic of "a sordid zoological species" that had to be eliminated because it represented a "racial pest" to Buenos Aires:

> Buenos Aires, my beloved land
> Dominated by a racial pest
> Drowns at Lavalle and Junín [the Jewish neighborhood].
> And those good *porteños* of yore
> Curse Motherfucker,
> Pounding the nearing end of the pest.[21]

In publications recommended by Filippo, Jews appeared in pornographic caricatures, hanged or impaled through the abdomen by an Argentine flag.[22]

In *Clarinada*, the traditional Catholic images of Jews as God killers were fused with representations of them as naked, sick, and ready to pass on their contagion sexually. The publication was cited by the Nazis of *Der Stürmer* as an ideal example of anti-Semitism because it had proposed to bury the Jews alive.[23] In contrast with German Nazism, these images were combined with a clerico-fascist ideological framework. Thus the charge of deicide and the stereotype of the Judas type of traitor were fused with Nazi-style racism: "With a kiss, Jews sold and betrayed Christ; that is why today they are not ashamed to kiss the flag of the Homeland, to sell and betray her while in their pockets they finger the dollars of treason."[24]

Jews were also described as engaged in the "corruption of the youth."[25] In another caricature, a "Jew" tried to rape a woman with the word "Argentina" written across her dress, who exclaimed that there appeared no real Argentine man "to free her from this filth."[26] In the nacionalista's view, real Argentine men had to be with the authentic female expression of the country. The "Argentine woman" was deeply religious, the formulaic "woman of the home" who was "the mother, the employee, the worker."[27] For them, the nacionalista woman had to be "on par with men" but without abandoning their "natural" subordinate position.[28] Women who thought like men were disqualified as *"marimachos"* and men who agreed with them were presented as *"los feministas"* and *"maricones."*[29]

In short, the enemy was construed in terms of very traditional gender roles and fascist notions of so-called abnormal sexuality. The image constructed of the racial enemy, who was drawn as "feminine," in addition to being naked, old, nervous, and sexually degenerated, expressed, according to the nacionalista Catholic ideology, a moral disorder as well as physical disarray. Central to this ideology was the idea that the physical aspect was a reflection of the inner self and emotions. For Argentine fascists, "Liberal democracy has come to its senile plenitude, and leaves us as corollary, its illegitimate produce of chaos, disorder, unemployment, and Judaic communism."[30]

The idea of democracy as a senile but also a hypersexualized female subject worked in tandem with the fascist connection between homosexuality and antifascism. Father Gabriel Riesco presented "lack of virility" and "feminization" as characteristics stemming from a general lack of Argentine consciousness that would impede "self-control."[31] If "feminization" was the mark of the enemy, hypermasculinity was the main feature of the self. For Father Meinvielle, the fragmenting effects of both Judaism and communism had to be combated "with valiant masculinity."[32] Similarly, for Argentine fascists, the homeland was infected with a virus that had to be combated: "Young Argentines who study and work!

Fascism offers you a hatchet you must brandish virilely to cut the weeds that infest our homeland to the root."[33]

The fear of the future was instilled by the paranoid notion of social infection. In 1928, Juan Carulla wrote as a fiction of futurology in *La Nueva República* a "history written in 1940 by order of the North American inspector." In this version, Carulla made the radical politician Leopoldo Bard "minister of foreign affairs." According to Carulla's imaginary future, Bard "brought half a million Jews in two years and had considered adding a Star of David to the national flag that would figure together with the sun." The idea that Judaism would come to power was characterized as a terminal crisis. Like a fascist Nostradamus, Carulla promised his readers that in the near future, with Jews in the government "the depreciation of currency was alarming and after the 'great withdrawals' of October and November 1928, the city of Buenos Aires had been left almost destroyed."[34]

The fiction of future Jewish domination through total destruction was clearly rooted in a religious view, which rested on the existence of an all-or-nothing conflict with the liberal secular world. In Argentine fascism, the idea of the Catholic nation was presented as the antithesis of the enemy: "the star of Zion against the Cross of the South." [35]

In actual history, Bard, the first president of the prestigious River Plate soccer club, was tortured by Lugones's son, who commented, with evident sadism, on Bard's supposed lack of virility when he succumbed during the interrogations.[36] The torture sessions attempted to actualize the racial fictions about the Other. Fascists ultimately did not distinguish between literature and reality in their fictional works. Among the racial fictions of Argentine fascism, the writings of the National Library's director, Hugo Wast, were especially influential in demarcating the boundaries between normal and abnormal sexuality.[37]

The publication during the 1930s of *Kahal y Oro* signaled the definitive consecration of Hugo Wast's commitment as nacionalista and Catholic intellectual.[38] An adaptation of the universal Jewish conspiracy theory to the Argentine context, Wast's novel revolved around nineteenth-century Jewish immigrants to Argentina forming a secret lodge or "*Kahal.*" They gradually dominate the country's finances and marry their descendants with the daughters of well-known aristocratic and Catholic families with the intention of eventually dominating the state. The novel features Jewish characters who, with suspicious lewdness, are sexually attracted to Catholics, along with Catholic characters who explore the limits of the nacionalista conception of sexuality. For example, the hero of the novel, the future president Fernando Adalid views his converted Jewish niece with ambivalence and is surprised to see in her possible asexual corporeal traits that do not correspond to the fascist stereotype of the Jews: "Adalid discovered in this instant something that seemed novel to him: Marta's eyes were not cruel, nor feline, but rather sweet, deep, and visibly sad."[39]

In the novel, Wast traces the intersections between modern racism and more traditional Christian ideas about conversion. He is peculiarly interested in whether a Jewish body such as Marta's can acquire a proper Argentine Catholic mold. The narrative ponders Marta's harmful and anti-Christian sexual attributes, reducing them to the point where her body acquires for Adalid, uncle and recipient of Marta's erotic encounters, a "new grace" only when she "remained quiet, with far-off thoughts."[40] The perverse and ambivalent attraction that the figure of Marta, Jewish and Christian at once, arouses in Adalid presents him with the opportunity to affirm his Argentine masculinity, when he is compared with the doubtful and numerous "*muchachos* of Buenos Aires" incapable of conquering her.

Adalid's position with respect to the character of Mauricio Cohen is clearer. Cohen is presented as a Jewish member of the global conspiracy. As a fictional account of the Protocols of the Elders of Zion, the novel stands as the fiction of a fiction. In Cohen, Adalid recognizes evil personified: "Mauricio Cohen, circumcised in the Synagogue, baptized in the Cathedral, tenacious enemy of Catholicism."[41] The "miserable Cohen," as the narrator calls him, also converts to Catholicism. But Adalid appreciates this conversion only in ambivalent terms: "[T]hey weren't friends, but they saw each other often, and were mutually appreciative."[42] This is even after the *converso* Cohen, a flamboyant new anti-Semite, argues before his interlocutor that Judaism has died.

The anti-Semitism of the Jewish *converso* who ends the novel rambling about the scriptures with his bride, the *conversa* Marta Blumen, has a strong quasi-sacrificial appearance, in the sense that the regeneration of the outsider, seen as a threat to the community and the individual, is only possible through the dissolution or elimination of this constituent outsider's identity. The fascination with the victimization of the outsider combines, as historian Dominick LaCapra argues, attraction and repulsion. Anti-Semitism, he contends, was a crucial form of a discourse and practice that was full of sacrificial dimensions.[43] In the case of Wast's novel, the sacrifice of the identity of the characters and their marked self-hatred entails an ambivalent degradation of the "Christian solution" to the "Jewish question" proposed by priests like Franceschi, Castellani,

Meinvielle, and, above all, Filippo. All of them at least partially continued perceiving Jews, even *conversos*, in racial terms assigned by the degenerate biological character of the "Jewish race." This assessment was not unrelated to earlier images of the Christian anti-Semitic tradition, in particular the experience of the Spanish Inquisition in relation to the so-called "new Christians."

The many Catholic interpretations of Wast's novel shared the writer's preoccupation that there "exists in our young country a secret organization, estranged from the Argentine tradition," "the *Kahal*" that, according to him, was the local branch of the "international Jewish conspiracy."[44] Father Franceschi defined this society as an Argentine "Hebrew bloc" with "aspirations of domination." For Castellani, Wast had been "generous with the Jews" by showing them the "Christian solution to the Jewish situation." [45] Father Chumillas, who reviewed the book in the daily *El Pueblo*, found in the novel "the reason why among all peoples the cry 'die Jew!' has almost always been synonymous with 'long live the homeland!' "[46] For Barrantes Molina, Wast's novel went beyond the greatness of writers like Victor Hugo in its combination of literature with a formidable philosophy of history. The book provided a "transcendental teaching" about the Jews in Argentina and beyond. Writing in the most important Catholic paper, Barrantes once again put forward the basic tenets of Argentine clerical fascism. For him, as for many other nacionalistas, anti-Semitic fascism and religion were part of the same global concern about the enemy. In fact, Barrantes was sure of the "universal interest" generated by Wast's anti-Semitic work and he augured its future success in "European Catholic countries where religious problems are still worthy of consideration and in the protestant nations where the Jewish octopus has extended its financial tentacles as it is the case in Germany, the United States and many others."[47]

While nacionalistas supported Wast and publicized his book in magazines, newspapers, books, and pamphlets, Argentine antifascists decried Wast's work.[48] Among the most notable critics were two Argentine Jewish antifascist intellectuals, Lázaro Schallmann and César Tiempo. They stressed the links between religion and sexuality, especially the fear shared by the author and other Catholic nacionalistas of the "infiltration" of Jewish racial and sexual contamination.[49] Significantly, for the members of Argentine Anti-Jewish Action or (AAA), the "infiltration" was related specifically to "the straight connections that exist between these disgusting hawkers and opulent bankers who make their sons marry to the sound of drums and cymbals the daughters of the crazy and proud Buenos Aires aristocracy." [50]

The construction of anti-Semitic stereotypes and their relationship with the anti-Semitic practices that were articulated during the 1930s and 1940s constituted a principal genealogy for the intellectual activities of Argentine neofascists and nacionalistas after 1945. The discursive actions of priests like Franceschi, Meinvielle, and above all Filippo in the public projection of the racist Jewish stereotype occupied a central role. Beyond defining and issuing warnings about the contaminating and constitutive otherness of the "internal enemy," they established a canon of social and cultural readings that were at once markedly racist and Catholic.

The establishment of a mimetic relationship between Judaism and popular culture allowed them to signal the existence of an enemy of another mimesis that was equally conceptual and imaginative, that of the nation and the Catholic religion as two indissoluble units. In the anti-Semitic fantasy of these priests and their nacionalista peers, the Jews as a people were participants and even leaders of an anti-Argentine conspiracy that originated in the same country.[51]

In *Clarinada* they illustrated the idea that the Jews represented and were architects of everything that was not desirable from the nacionalista point of view. "The enemies of nacionalismo" were divided into two branches, "Judaism" and "Conservatism." The branch of Judaism was composed of Marxism (socialism, communism, anarchism), Freemasonry (liberalism, democracy, leftism, atheism), and Capitalism (trusts, merchants and industrialists, English and North American imperialism). The Conservatism branch spanned Liberalism (politicians, journalists and writers and professional lecturers), Democracy (conservative, radical, and democratic politicians), Freemasonry (political parties, public functionaries, magistrates), and Capitalism (foreign and national trusts, landowners and estate holders, commercial and industrial exploiters, and imperialism).[52]

In the nacionalista mind, Jews were even at fault for drug trafficking, an idea that would later be repeated in nacionalista circles in the 1990s and 2000s. For example, in 1938 a cover caricature was drawn of a "Jew" with Argentina in one hand, and silver, morphine, and cocaine in the other. The caricature read "I am a poor Jew, Great Rabbi, great trafficker, pursued by nacionalistas from all over the world, because I spread religious prayers of Palestine ... with a bit of heroin."[53] The reference to the "nacionalistas from all parts of the world" reinforces the idea of a transnational theory and practice of racism in all fascisms, including Italian fascism. Argentine racism, in contrast to Italian or Nazi fascism, was less based on an exclusively racist idea than on a combination of racism with traditional Catholic anti-Semitism: "*Clarinada* does not combat the Jews because they are Jews, nor aspires to provoke religious or racial struggles. *Clarinada* combats the Jews because they are the inventors, organizers, directors, and sustainers of communism throughout the world. *Clarinada* combats the Jews because the Jews, complying with the directives of the 'Sages of Zion' corrupt Christian morality, and stimulate human vices and defects, to destroy the spiritual conquest of humanity made by Jesus, first victim of the GOD-KILLING JEWS."[54]

The internal enemy, because it was conceived of as an enemy of God, was an enemy of the homeland. For Argentine fascists, the presence of a racial enemy, who was also a religious enemy, justified the sacred relevance of nacionalismo. As Franceschi, the most moderate of the priests analyzed in this chapter, argued, "[W]e find ourselves in a distinct case: the probabilities of aggression on the borders are practically null. But there is another threat from the internal enemy, and the significance of that amply justifies the shock of patriotism in our country that is called nacionalismo." This "justification" was related for Franceschi to the bankruptcy of liberalism and the Argentine system of government in combating this "internal enemy" that endangered "our nationality": "Going to the root of the problem, it can be seen that neither the parliamentarism nor the general liberalism of our institutions will permit an effective defense against communism, the Judaic spirit, and the Marxist disorganization and general ruin of the economy."[55] For this spokesman of the Argentine ecclesiastic hierarchy, shoring up and supporting the struggles of the nacionalista formation was a task of collaborative development, since the "future of the nation" depended on it. For Franceschi, the definition of the internal enemy included the elaboration of a religious anti-Semitic stereotype.

For the nacionalistas, the "final solution" to the "Jewish problem" in Argentina represented one of the most original aspects of their fascism. This Argentine anti-Semitism coincided in discursive terms with that of the Nazis, although its double genealogy, Catholic and nacionalista, equipped it with a supposedly theological base and gave it greater longevity. After World War II and the Holocaust, Filippo, more adept than many of his fascist comrades, would reproduce his racist and anti-Semitic discourse under Peronism. For him, the Jews would no longer be only enemies of the Catholic nation, but enemies of the Peronist regime as well.[56]

Jews represented for nacionalismo the archetypical internal and irreconcilable enemy.[57] Eventually their destiny had to be total elimination, as argued in 1942 by nacionalistas in *Clarinada*: "What a great homage the extermination of these squids would be for our Homeland!"[58] How to do it? What would happen on "the day on which nacionalismo triumphs as a regime" and on which the "good Argentines" knew "to give the cry, 'God, homeland and family'"? In a portent of the future of the enemy under the aegis of global fascism, disappearance and the ocean were the answer: "The day when the Jews disappear from this Earth, swept by the broom that pushes them into the ocean...without mercy so that in its crystalline immensity they vomit the slobber that gave them their sinister and repulsive lineage."[59]

4

Peronist Populism and Fascism

THE RELATIONSHIP BETWEEN Peronism and fascism is central to the understanding of Argentina's political history. If the question is asked if Perón was a fascist, the answer is no. But fascism did play an important role in the ideological genesis of Peronist populism This chapter analyzes the contextual difference between these two concepts.

The clerico-fascist anti-Semitism, a *criollo* blend of biological racism and Christian theology, particularly characterized the Argentine strand of fascism. This aspect of Argentine nacionalismo was not, however, a general characteristic of Peronism.[1] After the 1943 military coup brought the nacionalista alliance of the Cross and the Sword to power, a new, unexpected strand related to the incremental leadership of Perón in the context of that military dictatorship began to emerge.

In its complex reformulation of the past, the Peronist phenomenon, especially in terms of its cultural, socioeconomic, and ideological genealogies, rethought the fascist legacy while not denying it entirely. Although fascism was a central genealogy of Peronism, Perón's coming to power signaled a break from diverse traditional precedents, including fascist nacionalismo. However, the ideological continuities between Argentine fascism and Italian fascism are notable in Perón's military junta between 1943 and 1946 and the first Peronist regime (1946–1955).

Many nacionalistas saw in Perón and the movement that bore his name the continuation of imperial and vernacular Argentina, heir of Rosas, and the Argentine history of "religion or death" and the "Holy Federation," the nacionalista union of the Cross and the Sword. But nacionalistas also complained that Perón had stolen their slogans, their social program, their hegemonic plan of Catholic and military education, their state corporatism, and their defense of fascism's legacy. They saw in Peronism an appropriation of fascism.[2] On the other side of the political spectrum, in the eyes of the Argentine antifascists, Perón and the military dictatorship, of which the Argentine colonel had been architect and participant, were clearly totalitarian and even Hitleresque.[3]

Peronism also had a significant reception in Europe. The Italian fascists saw in Peronism a worthy successor to Mussolini's ideas in the postwar world, while many Italian antifascist partisans described the Argentine military government of 1943 as a Latin American fascism similar to those they had fought against in Europe.[4] Even a major critical thinker like Hannah Arendt apparently saw in Peronism the continuation of the seeds planted by fascism.[5] Shared by left and right, the fascist genealogy of Peronism is clear. Less clear are its consequences.

Peronism was the unexpected result for everyone, including its creator, of an attempt at fascist reform of Argentine political life. Fascism was always the model Perón had looked to. But, as historian Tulio Halperín Donghi has suggested, "[I]f the example of fascism couldn't give concrete orientation to the Peronist movement, instead it contributed very effectively by disorienting it."[6] The fascist model tended to focus on objectives that didn't coincide with Argentine and global postwar realities or with the vertical and horizontal contradictions of the leadership and bases of the Peronist movement. While Argentina appeared to be ripe for fascism, the world showed itself to be too ripe for it.[7]

In the journey traveled by Peronist ideology and practice, from the messianic idea of fascist leadership to the profound transformations of unionized Peronism, from Perón's inspiration in fascism to the worker's movement, a dynamic interaction was created that limited the former at the same time as it mobilized and transformed the logic of the latter. The structural reforms of the social base accomplished by Perón and the dictatorship of 1943–1946 were not accompanied by democratic advances. This couldn't have been done without delegitimizing an authoritarian coup that sought popularity. Perón resolved this contradiction by calling for elections to legitimize his leadership, up until then based on dictatorship. The result was a democracy that combined the expansion of social rights with the limitation of political rights. This novel form of politics later became the classic form of Latin American populism. An authoritarian version of electoral democracy, populism invokes the name of the people to stress a form of vertical leadership, to downplay political dialogue, and to solve a perceived crisis of representation by suppressing democratic checks and balances. It does so in order to assert a direct link between "the people" and the leader. It relies on a form of vertical leadership that might be best described as "religious," and it conflates the mandates of electoral majorities with the will of the people of the nation as a whole. Populism buttresses social and political polarization in the name of the people. Fewer spaces are left for the expression of political minorities, who are presented as traitors to the "real" will of the nation or, worse, as mere puppets of foreign powers plotting against the country. Finally, populism conflates state and movement, enforcing forms of clientelism that feature the leader as the incarnation of the people. Indeed, Perón saw his leadership as the eternal link between the people of the nation as a whole and the security apparatus of the state. As he argued in an early third-person reference to himself in the famous speech of October 17, 1945: "In this historical hour for the Republic, let Colonel Perón be the link of union that would make indestructible the brothership between the people, the army and the police. Let this union be eternal and infinite so this people will grow in that spiritual unity of the true and authentic forces of nationality and order."[8]

In contrast to classic fascism, which used democracy to destroy itself and establish a dictatorship, Peronism originated in a military dictatorship, but established a populist authoritarian democracy. The second military dictatorship in the history of the country lasted only a few years (1943–1946). While it was the closest the Argentine government would come to a classic fascist regime, it changed the history of the country. While in economic terms the dictatorship, and afterward Peronism, deepened the autonomy of the state regarding traditional property sectors, the most fundamental changes were ideological and social. In social terms, the most important structural changes are clear as much in the country (statute of the peon) as in the city (industrial projects and labor reforms).[9]

The dictatorship of 1943 constituted a full-front attack on Argentine secularism. The coup of 1943 "nationalized" Catholic education (making it mandatory in public school) and brought about other measures proposed by the United Officers Group (GOU), officials united to achieve a nationalist agenda. As signaled by the anti-Semitic writer and the dictatorship's minister of education, Gustavo Martínez Zuviría (Hugo Wast), the agenda intended to "Christianize the country," decrease immigration and increase the birth rate, and eradicate secular doctrines.[10] More importantly from the Peronist point of view, the democratically chosen government of Perón maintained, and sometimes deepened, the social reforms applied during his term as the secretary of labor of the military dictatorship (from improving working conditions and enforcing labor laws, significantly expanding the power of unions, restricting the conditions under which workers could be fired, to paid holidays and vacations).[11] Perón also maintained an active racist immigration policy that discriminated against Jewish immigrants and encouraged white, Catholic immigration from Italy and Spain.[12]

In political and ideological terms, the coup of 1943 announced the power of the military inspired by an ideology that was nacionalista, neutral (that is, pro-Nazi and pro-German in an anti-Nazi hemispheric context), authoritarian, anti-imperialist, and clerico-fascist. The Church supported the coup as a sacred cause.[13] The nacionalista priest, Juan Sepich, named by the military as rector of the Colegio Secundario Nacional de Buenos Aires, thought of it as the defense of national sovereignty and suggested that abandoning the position of neutrality was to be a traitor. Speaking to his students in 1944, Father Sepich told them: "You can say proudly that you enjoy an honor and a tradition that was never interrupted, from the first day on which the inhabitants of this land comprehended the greatness of the Cross and the dignity of the Sword."[14]

Father Franceschi, the principal ideologue of the Argentine Church between 1930 and 1950, endorsed the dictatorship in the Catholic journal *Criterio* and the military president General Pedro Pablo Ramírez responded by confirming the centrality of the Cross. In his support of Colonel Perón's social policies, Franceschi even denied that they were totalitarian. He insisted that the dictatorship was clearly respectful of the sacred.[15] Beyond the declarations of the nacionalista general and the nacionalista enthusiasm of Argentina's most famous priest, the dictatorship was quickly dominated by the GOU. The GOU continued the clerico-fascism proposed by the Argentine fascists a few years before and set a program intended to eliminate the last vestiges of liberal democracy.

The history of the GOU and the military dictatorship is, in large part, the odyssey of Perón to appropriate their commands. These changes were realized in the context of what scholars call a "revolution within a revolution," in which young officers led by Perón took advantage of the opportunity put forward by the coup to redesign the institutional bases of the country in anticommunist and religious terms.[16] During this period ideology was constantly reformulated to adapt to the multifarious demands of different social and political "Peronist" actors, from the fascists within and outside of the military to the left-leaning unions and the working class at large.

The vicissitudes of Perón have been compared with those of Stalin. Similar to the Soviet dictator, Perón began from the right, supporting the more nacionalista sectors of the army, and later moving away from them

in order to support the rupture of diplomatic relations with the Axis powers.[17] Outside of the GOU, Perón played to the left and the right among
members of the military, trade unionists, and other political sectors.

Despite the leader's adept maneuvers, central parameters of Perón's
political philosophy can be seen in the "*Nuevas bases para la organización y
funcionamiento del GOU*" ("New Bases for the Organization and Operation
of the GOU"). In this "confidential" document, probably dictated by Perón,
the young nacionalista officers proposed that "neutrality is the symbol of
national sovereignty."[18] This equation revealed the importance of supporting fascisms by the only means possible on the external front, while
simultaneously combating communism on the internal front. Another
nacionalista element is the anti-imperialism characterized by the claim of
sovereignty over the Malvinas/Falkland Islands. Influenced by Leopoldo
Lugones, the various documents of the GOU, which also contain elements of anti-Semitic paranoia, identified the army with the homeland
and the "Catholicism of the people."[19] The idea of contamination, a central
element of the fascist and anti-Semitic tradition, was also central to the
GOU. The army was represented as a center of purity, "not yet contami-
nated... it has found the immunizing vaccination that must save us from
calamity."[20] Later, in his famous speech on the *Bolsa de Comercio* (Stock
Market) of 1944—when he presented himself as a staunch anticommunist and a "defender" of businessmen and capital—Perón also referred to
the communist infiltration as leading to calamity and civil war, to "social
cataclysm" and "absolute ruin."[21] The enemy is identified in the document
of the GOU as a "vulgar meeting of communist elements with loyal politicians in service of Judaism." The military men must govern to "cut evil to
the root."[22]

From Dictatorship to Populist Authoritarian Democracy

The genealogy of Peronism is rooted in dictatorship but unlike classic
forms of fascism that had originated in democracy and later established a
dictatorship, destroying democracy from within, Peronism did the opposite. Peronism used the state to promote its democratic authoritarian
reforms. In Argentina the popular movements are helped from above. If the
Radical Party came to power in 1916 thanks to the electoral reforms of 1912
(decided with naiveté by the old conservative regime that radicalism came

to replace), Peronism came to power in 1946 thanks to social reforms that, while later confirmed by democratic electoral means, had been imposed by a dictatorship. Perón effectively updated the nacionalista agenda, giving it a widely popular context as historian Sandra McGee Deutsch argues.[23] The military dictatorship engendered Peronism but it eventually became a highly hierarchical nonpluralistic form of democracy. Notwithstanding these significant structural differences between Peron's dictatorship and his elected administrations, there were also meaningful points of ideological convergence.

The military dictatorship of Perón and the GOU dismantled the political parties, established religious propaganda in the secondary schools, and attempted to curtail the freedom of the press. Religous intolerance and the censorship of the press would continue once Perón became democratic by early 1946. But the three measures reflect the success of years of indoctrination in the nacionalista mindset in the military and in Perón's own mind, particularly influenced by his mentor, nacionalista general Francisco Fasola Castaño, his ties to *Liga Patriótica Argentina*, his own experience in the coups of 1930 and 1943, and the ideas of Leopoldo Lugones. Fasola Castaño was, according to some nacionalistas, the "Argentine Mussolini."[24]

General Fasola Castaño was a friend of the first Argentine dictator, General José Félix Uriburu, who governed the country between 1930 and 1932. After denouncing the conservative restoration (1932–1943), Fasola publicly recuperated the legacy of the Uriburu dictatorship, becoming one of the main proponents of the Uriburu "myth." As expert on Peronism Juan Carlos Torre remembers, Perón agreed in 1936 that Fasola had a point, since the legacy of September, that is, the military coup, had been "twisted." "Enlightened men like you, they will surely permit us to revert to a more nacionalista path than the present one." In 1936, Fasola, a confessed admirer of Hitler and Mussolini, was the leader of an Argentine fascist organization, the *Grupo Concentración Popular Argentina*. Torre indicates that Perón made the rhetoric of the nacionalistas his own. He also thought that the military should lead the nacionalista Argentine political project. On this point Perón hoped to escape the errors of the Uriburu dictatorship. Perón wanted to establish a national movement that gave him a populist means with which to create a strong homeland with an equitable state. Like Lugones, Perón thought that this was impossible in a liberal democracy. In a letter from 1939, he maintained "there will not be peace until a truly nationalist government takes the reins of the nation."[25]

Even though after 1943 Perón tried to distance himself from fascism, his ideological links with it were evident.[26] In his rhetoric, *Justicialismo* was similar to Italian fascism in that it put an extreme emphasis on a totalitarian notion of society and the state and also displayed a vertical and hypermythical charismatic leadership. The rights of citizens had less value for Peronism than their supposed obligations to state, leader, and movement. Peronist populist ideology was based on the idea of an organized community in which the individual would obtain personal happiness through his immersion in a harmonious collective.[27]

The Peronist *third position* had few differences with the national and social synthesis between left and right of Italian fascism, as well as with the Argentine fascists that preceded it. Like Argentine fascism and unlike that of Mussolini, Perón proposed this synthesis in Christian terms. In 1944 he announced "the representatives of capital and labor must adjust their relations to more Christian rules of coexistence and respect between human beings."[28] If the fascist synthesis fused in the idea of the fascist state an anti-Marxist gaze of the left with the nacionalista ideal of the extreme right, Perón's populist synthesis emphasized the role of that ideal, making explicit its relation to social Catholicism but, understandably after 1945, covering up its fascist genealogy.

Perón went further than the fascists and nacionalistas in his economic nationalism by nationalizing the Argentine central bank, gas, telephone, and railroads. He was closer to Mussolini in his search for an elusive economic autarky that for Il Duce was above all an agrarian ideal but for Perón was industrial in nature. Regardless, in this terrain Mussolini was closer to Perón in his rhetoric and closer to General Uriburu in practice, but neither nationalized as did Perón. Many authors have affirmed that the influences of Fuerza de Orientación Radical de la Joven Argentina (FORJA) and the nationalist group of the left, headed by Raúl Scalabrini Ortiz and Arturo Jauretche, can be seen in Perón's economic nationalism and social program; however, the links between these nationalists and those of the extreme right were closer than previously believed.[29] Scalabrini was in close contact with the nacionalistas and collaborated with Italian fascist and Nazi publications.[30] From the late 1930s on Scalabrini's journal, *Reconquista*, which like other nacionalista publications received Nazi subsidies, included contributions from Ernesto Palacio and notorious anti-Semites like Rodolfo Irazusta, among many other nacionalistas who overlapped extensively with the nationalist "left" in their nationalist anti-imperialist sympathies for the Axis powers. They were fellow travelers in the crusade against the liberal democracies. In sum, nacionalismo, the "Christian fascism" invented in Argentina, represented a fundamental dimension in the genealogy of Peronism.

The First Populist Reformulation of Fascism

If nacionalismo was a key factor in the origins of Peronism, another key ideological factor came directly from Italian fascism. From a comparative perspective, Peronist Argentina seemed to be behind in relation to the Italian historical process. Despite presenting notable divergences in their social structure and political history, the two countries presented similarities that gave way to two different forms of authoritarianism. Fascism and Peronism came to power as a result of the failure of liberal-democratic regimes that were thought to be solid or well-established. Both regimes gave a totalitarian answer to the crisis that modernity had provoked in the public perception of laws, the economy, and the legitimacy of the state. Both regimes were clearly anticommunist and antisocialist. Finally, both regimes mobilized the population "from the top," through their propaganda and various actions, promoting mass politics and convincing majorities that the regime represented them and the nation as a whole. But while fascism mobilized the middle classes, Peronism rallied the working class. While fascism gave war, imperialism, and racism to Europe and the world, Peronism never provoked war.[31]

Historians of fascism agree that fascism was three things in distinct moments and countries: an ideology, a movement, and a regime. Argentina, with its fascist groups of the 1930s and its ideologues, represents only the first two elements: whether Argentina ever had a fascist regime is for many an open question. The regime installed by Uriburu in 1930 and the military regime of 1943–1946 constitute two moments in which attempts can be seen to establish fascist and totalitarian regimes in the sense that Mussolini used the term. However, both attempts failed and Juan Perón, an active participant of both coups, was for many the Argentine heir of fascism. Early Peronism, a confusing phenomenon for its contemporaries, and even its principal actors, increased the Argentine peculiarity and defined it in nacionalista and populist terms that have to do with fascism but distinguish themselves as well. Clearly Peronism, and its leader in particular, maintained a greater degree of rationality than classical fascisms. While the rejection or destruction of realities that lack political value constitutes the principal trait of classical fascism, Peronism was marked by a continual interaction between reality and the integralist ideological tendency of Perón to modify it.

While the Argentine nacionalistas shared an apologetic fascist identity with their European counterparts, Perón tried to learn from the "errors" of Hitler and Mussolini and, at times, he was even highly critical of them in public. Nonetheless, the Argentine leader could never escape a fascist way of thinking, an ideological frame of reference, that in concrete terms wanted and often achieved through totalitarian methods, the minimization of his social actions and redistributive practices. [32] In other words, Peronism combined and often did not integrate two different sets of expectations: those of Perón and those of the majority of his followers. Ideologically, the leader was rooted in the fascist tradition but as a cunning politician he often betrayed his fascist roots to please the majority of his working-class followers. At different times in the history of Peronism this mutual deafness regarding different ideologies and expectations within Peronism was arguably mutually beneficial to all the members of the movement. In an age of increasing ideological polarization the muting of differences between the military leader and his popular base increasingly solidified the movement. It promoted vertical loyalties and opportunities to simultaneously enjoy material benefits and symbolic victories. But the fact remained that, despite many assertive claims by both Perón and his followers, the leader remained anchored in the revolutionary totalitarian synthesis that stemmed from the anti-enlightenment. This is why the original Peronist populist movement was not fascist but Perón's "mentality" was.

In practical terms, the result of this interaction between nonfascist political needs toward and from the base and Peron's fascist mentality was the creation of modern Argentine populism. This populism was defined by the marriage of social reform, state interventionism, nationalism, and anti-imperialism with the logic of single-party rule, social polarization, clientelism, censorship of the press, ostracism, and the persecution of opponents up to, in some cases, prison and torture.[33] However, Peronism was not unique in the modern Argentine history of repression and violence. In authoritarian terms, the dictatorships and even some civilian governments after 1955 exceeded it in political violence and antidemocratic proscriptions.

Peronist authoritarianism was not exclusively linked to fascism but it was related to a broader totalitarian conception of the truth, the integralist idea of the country. The ideology of Perón, also influenced by the Lugonian notion of a great and regimented homeland, had breaks and continuities with both Argentine and Italian fascism. For Perón, the great homeland was the result of the nationalist and corporate subordination of class struggle whose conclusion was "the Great Argentina" (1949).[34] The "*Marcha Peronista*," created by Oscar Ivanissevich, the future minister of education in the 1970s Peronist regime, articulates the Lugonian concept of *la Grande Argentina* and links it with the vision of Perón:

> For this great Argentina
> that San Martín dreamed of
> is the reality and effect
> that we owe to Perón.

The great homeland is synonymous with the greatness of its leader:

> Perón, Perón, how great you are!
> My general, how great your worth!
> Perón, Perón, great conductor,
> you are the first worker! [35]

Perón recognized the legacy of nacionalismo but also the limitations of the first coup that the nacionalista poet had glorified. Lugones declared in 1933 that if independence had promoted national emancipation, Argentine nationalism should "support it and complete it."[36] Perón argued that, despite independence, lack of a "firm doctrine" meant Argentina hadn't "been able to achieve over many years its economic independence, that should have complemented its political independence." For Perón, the coup of Uriburu of 1930 and his own of 1943 were motivated by an absence of economic independence. [37] Equally important was the need to overcome a "demoliberalism" that he had always considered to be "intimately connected" to international Marxism. This antiliberal anticommunism, the fear of a leftist revolution motivated by liberal democracy, is a central element of the ideology that justified the "revolutions" of 1930 and 1943. These authoritarian military dictatorships aimed at creating nondeliberative corporative democracies. Uriburu attempted it in the elections of 1931 and failed. Perón succeeded in the elections of 1946. Perón's brand of populism was rooted in the post-fascist critical view of secular liberal democracy as the source of communism. In Peronism, this authoritarian view of democracy presented the need to update, and legitimate with the popular vote, the synthesis of nationalism and non-Marxist Christian socialism.

In his memoirs, Perón clearly identified Italian fascism and Nazism with this "socialism with a national character." Making reference to his visit to fascist Italy, he stated: "I chose to do my military assignment in Italy because it was where a new national socialism was being tested. Until then, socialism had been Marxist. In constrast, in Italy socialism was sui generis, Italian: fascism."[38]

Perón's *Bolsa de Comercio* speech of August 1944 is, in this sense, equally revealing. Its message to the business owners was that it was necessary for the state to intervene as arbiter of the relations between capital and work in order to avoid a revolution and eliminate class struggle. Perón warned in his speech that if nothing was done, "these inorganic masses" were "susceptible to be manipulated by foreign professional agitators."[39]

As Torre signals, in public defense of his social policies, Perón legitimized them by invoking the social doctrine of the Church while privately recognizing his debt to fascism's example. The nacionalista strategy of co-opting the workers in order to avoid foreign communist manipulation was at the center of Peron's anticommunism.[40] Perón thought that "civil war" was entirely avoidable but also left it very clear on which side he would be in the eventuality of this "cataclysm."

While anticommunism defined Perón's ideological posture, he had a new postwar choice: capitalism reformed (corporate and authoritarian, although not fascist or racist) or communism. In this sense, Peronism is perhaps one of the first ideological products of the Cold War in that it adapted the remains of fascism to a novel context that impeded its complete application.

The Cold War, like Peronist populism, was also born of a reformulation of the relationship between fascism and communism. But if American McCarthyism neglected to recognize the context of war that carried the allies to a conclusion contrary to that planted by Uriburu between fascism and communism, Perón was always on the side of the Uriburu option. Yet, like Uriburu and in contrast with the nacionalistas, Perón proposed that it wasn't necessary to choose between fascism or communism because in Argentina a politically decisive moment that would justify this type of decision was not a given. While Perón returned to the Uriburu dilemma without resolving it, his schematic was not that of agitated ambivalence between conservatism and fascism but rather a populist development of the "equitable State" of Lugones to which Lugones himself would, toward the end of his life, add the Cross as complement to the Sword. As José Luis Romero suggested, the influence of nacionalista ideology in Peronist philosophy is overwhelming, for example in Perón's recurring mentions of "the Cross and the Sword" united once more in "a single will." To this was added the rhetoric of "*los muchachos peronistas*," [the Peronist Guys] which exemplified the proletarian appeal of nacionalismo.[41] The result was the proposition of a state that could transcend class struggle and promote the "uniform feeling and thinking of its human material." The state organization was supposed to be the organic reflection of a homogeneous community.[42]

The idea of Perón as transcending the traditional ideological questions also served to avoid the accusation of fascist or totalitarian, an accusation that would be more difficult to logically deny. Perón was the leader of a nacionalista military dictatorship that sought popularity. In Perón, the dictatorship found its savior, while Perón saw in it a base from which to launch himself to the top.

A novel use of popular culture was a key feature of Perón's populist strategy.[43] Perón transcended the nacionalista dislike for tango and soccer and in 1945 defined the political question of his time in soccer terminology. "In our homeland, the conflict between 'liberty' or 'tyranny' ... 'democracy' or 'totalitarianism' is not the real debate."[44] In fact, the arguments against Perón were simply hyperbolic. In a leaflet of the *Union Democrática* one could read that if Perón was elected, the "tragic experience" of Nazism, with 22 million deaths, would be repeated in Latin America. Others argued that Perón's pathological mind could be only treated by psychoanalysis.[45] A proclamation of the "Feminine Democratic Group" of the city of Avellaneda warned Argentine women that if Perón and the dictatorship continued, "your partner will populate the concentration camps." All antifascists agreed that the continuity between Peronism and fascism was a simple matter. He was, as a leaflet put it, "the Argentine Hitler." [46] Another dimension of this intense anti-Peronism is that it conflated nacionalismo with Peronism. To be sure, anti-Peronists had reasons to believe this. In fact, during the electoral campaign, nacionalista men and women actively, and violently, identified Perón with nacionalismo and against democracy and the Argentine Jewish community. But Perón never allowed nacionalismo to encapsulate his emerging populist movement.[47]

Without recognizing the fluctuating nature of early populist Peronism, both local actors and the US government constantly accused Perón of being a Nazi agent of barbarism, especially after the publication before the 1946 election of the so-called "Blue Book" by the State Department on links between Perón and the Nazis.[48] To be sure, Perón several times had stated, "I am not a Nazi" and he also clearly identified his electoral program of 1946 with a continuation of the dictatorship that he, like all its military and nacionalista supporters, called a "revolution."[49] However, Perón did not want to discuss fascism or to address the contrast between military dictatorship and democracy. He understood clearly which role corresponded to him and his military dictatorship in this uncomfortable discussion and argued that what was really being debated in Argentina "is a championship match between social justice and social injustice."[50]

In Perón's view social reform was almost opposed to contemporary issues of democracy, political rights or repression. Perón argued that this social contest was rooted in anti-imperialism and it represented a quest to incinerate the "remnants of feudalism" in Latin America. It was a contest between the American Blue Book and the Argentine White and Blue Book that Perón promptly published in response to the United States. As every Argentine reader knew, Perón's book represented the colors of the Argentine flag, and more specifically a defense of the military dictatorship and Perón against the "violent campaign of opposition to the legitimate government of Argentines." In fact, Perón also accused the United States of supporting the oligarchy, the fascists, and the communists against the military dictatorship and his candidacy.[51]

By identifying the critics of his "legitimate" dictatorship as foreign and imperialistic—posters around Buenos Aires posed the question "Braden or Perón," that is to say, the American ambassador to Argentina or Perón—the leader was simply repeating classic arguments of Argentine fascist nacionalismo and of fascism in general. They all shared a view of the enemy as an alliance of capitalism and communism, as an imaginary amalgamation of both against the country. Or as Perón signaled before the presidential elections of 1946: "Those who vote on the 24th for the formula of the oligarchical-communist collusion, should know that with this act they deliver their vote to Mr. Braden."[52] The idea of the antinational alliance of communism and foreign capitalism removed all possible Argentineness from the opposition to Perón and the military dictatorship. They were simply sell-outs and traitors to the nation.[53] Perón repeated the nacionalista discourse but he did it from the state and with a populist social practice that legitimized it and eventually led him to win elections. In fact, this idea of the enemy would become a trademark of Argentine populism.

Like the fascism of Mussolini and other Argentine nacionalistas, Peronism was inspired by an antibourgeois logic that was above all rhetorical, while at the same time clearly partisan and implicitly violent and messianic. Perón argued that his social policy and those of the 1943 military dictatorship would have phenomenal historical proportions, "as a magnificent bridge, from the evolution from the dominion of the bourgeoisie to that of the masses." During this period of successful intent to popularize the military dictatorship, he maintained in 1945: "All bourgeois prejudice has died and a new era is born in the world." [54] Eva Perón represented this antibourgeois logic to the maximum.

To be sure, Eva and Juan Perón's complex legacy includes the creation of the female branch of the Peronist party and the electoral enfranchisement of women. But especially in Eva Perón's thinking and practice, the antibourgeois discourse was mixed with the anti-imperialism of the right, a patriarchal vision of gender relations, an exacerbated machismo, and a new understanding of national identity that came from the period between the wars.[55] The domestication of official religion played a central role here.

Perón was perceived of as a godlike figure. At times he presented himself as a sort of vicar of the Lord or, as he put it in 1953, God had allowed him to do his works and he always started by "preaching." [56] Here, as elsewhere in Perón's thought, the divine presented a validation of his own sacred agency. Or, as he also said with ironic understatement, things were accomplished not only because "God is great and merciful. We are also helping God in these things." [57] Perón worked in tandem with God. Traditional religion was simply conflated with the Peronist universe. As Eva Perón stated when she announced the coming of a Peronist Christmas in 1946: "I come from the people, like General Perón, and I am delighted to have arrived in this Christmas of the good *pan dulce* [sweet bread] of Perón and the *sidra* [hard cider] of Perón, to all the homes that Perón has reestablished to their Christian heights."[58]

Perón also represented the ideal of Argentine masculinity. He established clear boundaries between women and men and warned against "promiscuity" and the inability to establish proper gender distinctions. He highlighted the central civic duty of women as mothers whose task was to educate the men. The nationalist Peronist Oscar Ivanissevich declared: "The Peronist is a person with a defined sex who admires beauty with all his senses."[59] The idea of Peronist beauty was defined by a traditional and baroque view of culture that avidly assimilated popular elements and at times transformed them. Ivanissevich was responsible for the conversion of Peronism into a political religion that combined the ethic of the absolute reflected in the word of the leader with conservative, and often nacionalista, aesthetic values. This nationalist turned Peronist, admirer of Hugo Wast and protector of escaped Nazis, was also the author of the "*Marcha del trabajo*" ("March of Labor") whose lyrics reflected Argentine social nacionalismo and mixed the belated proto-populism of the Italian social republic of Mussolini with the Cross of the former. The "march" declared:

> Today is the celebration of work
> united for the love of God
> at the foot of the sacrosanct flag
> we swear to defend her with honor[60]

National defense was identified with social reform but also with God and the cause. A nacionalista fascist genealogy was also evident in the continuities between nacionalista governor Manuel Fresco's social fascist politics during the 1930s in the province of Buenos Aires and the activities of Eva Perón for "the poor," whose affinities with the practices of nacionalista women also constitute genealogical antecedents of the Peronist populist movement.[61] With Peronism, the fascist social nationalism of *Choque* that, for example, demanded in 1941 that "public services must be nationalized," was reformulated in a Cold War context.[62] New populist notions of the sacred were central in this reformulation.

If Argentine nacionalistas wanted a "Christianized fascism," after 1946 they began to speak of a Peronist Christianity. While committed Peronists highlighted the "profoundly Christian" dimension of the doctrine, party dignitaries were concerned about subversive attempts to "Christianize the Peronist party."[63] In Peronism, Christianity was subsumed under the totalitarian aegis of the leader. The boundaries between state and movement increasingly disappeared. The same pattern not only applied to the borders between the movement and formal religion but also to those between "fiction" and reality.

Peronism created its own political theology. The hyperbolic nature of the metaphorical dimensions of Peronism expressed the ultimate truth of the ideology of the leader. The religious dimensions of the doctrine were intimately linked with the alleged religious nature of Perón's leadership. At one point, Peronist ideology identified a kernel of truth in these exaggerations. The constant blurring of the profane and the sacred was pushed to its limits. As Eva Perón told her close advisor, the hard-core cleric-fascist Father Filippo, and others in 1951, "Perón is a God for all of us, to the extent that we do not conceive of the sky without Perón. Perón is our sun, Perón is the water. Perón is the life of our country and the Argentine people." Father Filippo, a Catholic priest, ecclesiastic advisor of the presidency, and Peronist representative in Congress, did not see a problem, theological or political, with her statement. In fact, he had proclaimed in 1948 that Perón "had put the homeland in the hands of God" and that "God had put [Perón] as head of the social Christian movement." Other Peronists simply claimed that "God is Peronist." Peronism created its own syncretic approach to the sacred. Catholicism and nationalism were effectively "Peronized," that is, they were presented as a perfectionism of Catholic and nacionalista principles.[64] In fact, the Peronist doctrine was presented as a supercession of both. Peronism resecularized the myth of the Catholic nation; now, the Cross and the Sword were represented by a man and a people.[65]

The emergence of Peronism was a sort of lesser evil for the Church, which supported it in its first years, but never pardoned the movement for having relegated it to a subaltern place in the ideological tutelage of the country. The same happened with the Army and nacionalismo. If the Peronist notion of Argentineness shared with nacionalismo the idea of the temporal power of God and his Church in the land of Argentina, the leadership of Perón cast doubt on the main clerico-fascist tenets of nacionalismo. If, from the nacionalistas' point of view, God had destined them, together with the Church and the military, to be his Argentine political vicars, for Perón leadership could not be shared, not with God nor with his nacionalista crusaders. If, for nacionalistas, God was the true leader of the movement, for Perón, as for Mussolini, the leader was the temporal analogy of the sacred. The conductor was the political leader on earth, not God. These differences of interpretation, in sum, the totalitarian vocation of Perón, go far in explaining the ecclesiastic and military coup against the Peronist regime in 1955.

In contrast to the relative practical interchange of totalitarian ideas among nacionalistas of different veins, Perón insisted on and carried out the ideal of "doctrinarial unity," understood as the idea that the thought of the leader represented a collective sentiment. Peronism took its ideas very seriously. They were supposed to shape Argentine behavior, from homes, to schools, to the workplace. Representations of the main idea of the movement, Perón and Evita were the actual parental figures of the nation for students and state employees alike. For example, children learned to read and write their first words in primary school with sentences such as "Evita me ama" or "Perón loves the children."[66] State employees of the National Ministry of Technical Affairs were compelled to attend weekly "doctrinarian lectures" with topics such as "The Word of Perón. The Integral Formation of Man in the New Argentina," "Esprit de Corps in the Peronist Organization," and "Life and Work of Señora Eva Perón." It was mandatory that pictures of the Peróns adorned the lecture hall during the "indoctrination." Watching propaganda movies about the Peróns and their work was also mandatory. There were also mandatory readings of Eva Perón's book, *The Reason of My Life,* as well as the multiple speeches by General Perón and other readings published in the magazine *Mundo Peronista* (Peronist World).[67]

The compulsive explicit repetition of the words of the leader by himself and many other "little Peróns" displaced the need for more complex articulation of his ideas. Additionally, followers of "proven loyalty to the movement" were asked to engage "in a permanent action of vigilance" against critics as well as work of "affirmation" for Juan Perón and Eva Perón.[68] From the perspective of the leader, the doctrine was there to root out the unbelievers, and eventually correct them. The realizations of the leader were more important than abstract theory. The doctrine existed to affirm a solid belief in whatever Perón said or did. He constantly actualized the ideology of the movement.[69]

Historian José Luis Romero has cogently insisted on the connections between the nacionalista doctrine of "moderate fascism" and the Peronist doctrine.[70] But what constituted this doctrine? Did Peronism have a systematic ideology in the sense of rejecting perception and empirical evidence, while constantly repeating its own postulates and eventually converting them into realities? Totalitarian ideologies combine the extreme individualism of the leader, his radical capacity to interpret the world, with the interpretive passivity of the masses who follow him.[71] In practice the Peronist movement was much more complicated and its members combined passivity with resistance. Moreover, the political attraction of Peronism was centered on its redefinition of the citizenry, in its amplification of the political base of the country.[72] Besides enjoying the economic and social benefits of the first years of the regime, the Peronist base actively experienced the appropriation of an ideology that granted them a principal role in the life of the country.

But this appropriation had its limits. The political culture of Peronist populism was the result of a combination of spontaneous mobilization

and incremental political and intellectual demobilization, a demobilization articulated through ritual, emulation, and repetition, and characterized by the adoption of a mystical faith in the leader. For example, Edelma
Arauz, a dedicated follower, stressed complete identification as the defining trait of the "soldier of the cause." She stated "a Peronist is the one that
permanently behaves and thinks in accordance with the mystique of the
inspirer of the movement."[73]

As historian Carlos Altamirano suggests, in terms of political thinking,
Peronism didn't permit more than paraphrasing, the timid adaptation of
the leader's thinking to concrete politics. This was similar to the ideological
development of Mussolini's fascism, especially after 1925 and the declara-
tion of the totalitarian dictatorship. Like Mussolini, Perón had a clear sense
of his role as the only ideological and political authority when he argued
"the best and most authentic expression of an idea is that of its creator."[74]

Driven by ideology, a conscious sense of belonging that went further
than one's own personal finiteness replaced all alternative viewpoints,
including that of personal observation. The ideological argument itself
proved that what it said was correct. The doctrine was an objectification of
the ideology, a rationalization of this self-faith in which ideology sacrificed
thought.

The Doctrine

In movements like fascism and Peronism, the doctrine was established (although not definitively) after various ideological marches and
counter-marches. In the case of fascism, it was not released until a decade
after the foundation of the movement. Peronism emerged in 1943–46, but
not until 1949, in Perón's famous speech at the Congress of Philosophy
of Mendoza, was the leader compelled to present his doctrine as a closed
body of citations and thought. In this cloying "academic" discourse, the
nacionalista ideological roots of Peronism were made clear, as well as its
will to go beyond its nationalist "mentality" in the fascist sense that the
Argentine nacionalistas gave the term. In the Andean city of Mendoza,
Perón gave an official version of Peronist ideology.

The importance of the Congress of Mendoza cannot be overstated.
It represented the Peronist will to establish a third ideological path that
overcame the Capitalism-Communism dichotomy of the Cold War.
Among the international attendees were well-known antifascists like

Rodolfo Mondolfo of the University of Tucumán and Karl Löwith of The New School for Social Research in New York. Fascists such as the Italian Ugo Spirito and the French member of the SS Jaime María de Mahieu ("exiled" in Argentina) were also present. While not in attendance, Martin Heidegger, Jacques Maritain, Benedetto Croce, Karl Jaspers, and Bertrand Russell, among others, sent in their presentations. The Argentine attendees were represented above all by clerico-fascists including the secretary of the congress, nacionalista priest Juan Sepich and notorious Argentine fascists César Pico, Nimio de Anquín, and Father Julio Meinvielle.

Perón's speech must be analyzed in the context of fascism, nationalism, and even antifascism. Similarities and differences with all of these can be seen. Perón signaled the contradictions of liberal modernity and reiterated his previous critiques from December 15, 1944, when he had argued that "liberalism is the worst evil," and from February 24, 1947, when, doubting the legacy of the enlightenment he had denounced "the extreme tendencies that derive from the philosophical currents of the 18th century."[75] In the congress speech of 1949, the caudillo lamented the modern loss of authenticity faith, and ideals: "Man has been persuaded of the convenience of jumping without gradations from a rigorous idealism to a utilitarian materialism; from faith to opinion; from obedience to incondition."[76] It was clear that for the leader, theory detached from reality as he understood it was a problem. A year before, in 1948, Perón had asked, "What is Peronism?" and answered, "Peronism isn't learned, nor is it said: it is felt or not felt. Peronism is a matter of the heart more than the head."[77]

In 1949, Perón arrived at the Mendoza cloister with the bulk of his populist theory on point. With the anti-intellectualism typical of his nacionalista predecessors, the president criticized theoretical thought and accused it of separating theory from action:

> It's possible that the action of thought has lost, in recent times, direct contact with the realities of the people's lives. It's also possible that the cultivation of great truths, the unflagging persecution of the latest reasons, have converted an abstract and educational science by its nature into a technical virtuosity, with the consequent distancing from the perspectives in which man tends to develop.[78]

"The truth" had been lost in technical discussions, "tendencies, alien to the eagerness for knowledge to whose satisfaction one should consecrate all creative force. In the absence of fundamental theses, defended with the owing perseverance, arise the little theses, very capable of planting uncertainty." Perón set out the Peronist doctrine as the truth, a "solid truth for a lifetime," that destroyed confusion. Perón understood the confusion between the individual and the collective, between the ideological and the material, as "the owed relationship between oneself, moderator of everything, and the encircling world, object of fundamental changes."[79]

Perón's speech was intended to establish a history of thought from the Greeks to Perón. Criticism of Darwin was mixed abundantly with quotations that ranged from Spinoza to Kant and from Saint Thomas Aquinas to Martin Heidegger. Far from having written the text himself, Perón identified his ideology with it and this made it relevant as a self-representative look at the political theory of the first Peronist term. It was a text to give luster to relatively simple concepts. The motive of historical novelty was a central element. Perón proposed to define a new moral for the new man of a new epoch. In contrast to the nacionalista vision of the sacred, and closer to that of Il Duce, Perón argued for the primacy of politics complemented by the moral and the liturgical. This allowed him to limit, through repetition and compulsion, the idea of permanent revolution that, despite its diverse origins in radical fascism and socialism, or perhaps because of this, was well established in the Peronist masses.

To accept the new order, "the new Argentina," was to accept a new lifestyle in which, according to Perón, liturgy works in tandem with morality and both are renewed and established:

> Politics is incumbent on winning rights, winning justice and elevating the levels of existence, but it's necessary to other forces. Moral values must create a climate of human virtue that is apt to compensate at every moment, along with the conquered, the owed. In this aspect, virtue reaffirms its sense of efficacy. It will not only be the continual heroism of the liturgical prescriptions; it's a lifestyle that permits us to say of a man who has completed with virility the personal and public mandates: he gave who was obligated to give and could do it, and obeyed what he was obligated to obey.[80]

Politics, when experienced through the populist movement, transcended the individual. "The individual becomes interesting as a function of his participation in the social movement, and it is his evolutionary characteristics that demand preferential attention." These policies "overcame" class struggle because of the social project. This supercession implied a transition in that "the transit from I to We doesn't operate meteorically like an extermination of individualities, but rather like a reaffirmation of them in their collective function."[81]

This collective function opposed liberalism but was not communist. In traditional terminology, fused with orientalist elements, Perón understood the new as a subordination of the material to the spiritual: "[T]he struggle to suppress the rebellion of the material and subordinate it within the spirit as the practice of Yoga assumes, and its tendency to liberate the soul from cravings and bodily pains, signals to us that the question has been energetically planted from the dawn of civilization."[82]

For Perón, as for many nacionalistas, human beings couldn't lose themselves in the city that surrounded them: "The life that accumulates in the big cities offers us with distressing frequency the spectacle of this danger to which some awakened minds have given the terrifying name of 'insectification.' "[83]

Before such questions, such as men becoming insects and thus being stripped of their authentic selves, Perón strongly warned that "the happiness of men" in the modern sphere could not adopt "rhetorics of escape." He proposed that the authenticity of the "internal" could be achieved through the "organized community," which was not necessarily theoretical, but rather a product of the reality imposed by Perón. In it, "the We" acquired "its supreme ordination." In the organized community, "Thought put to the service of Truth spreads a radiant light, from which, like a spring, drink the disciplines of practical character."[84]

Peronism was founded on this absolute idea of freedom, on the centrality of the collective above individual rights: "Neither social justice nor liberty, motors of our time, are comprehensible in a community founded over insectified beings, unless by way of painful solution the ideal is concentrated in the omnipotent mechanism of the State." For Peronism, the doctrine was, in sum, a theoretical justification of the emergent Peronist reality: "Our community, to which we should aspire, is one where liberty and responsibility are cause and effect, where there exists a joy of being, founded on the persuasion of one's own dignity."[85]

The populist break with fascist idealism was evident. Fascists wanted to kill "insects"; Perón wanted them to stop being "insects." Hitler was more idealistic than Perón. The absence of anti-Semitism from Peronism—despite notorious anti-Semites and Nazis that swarmed around Perón, and despite the continuation of the previously mentioned racist immigration policy—was symptomatic of the differences with respect to the idea of the enemy. To be sure, Perón often threatened the opposition with retributive furious violence. In fact, the Peronist idea of the enemy was highly partisan. Perón often invoked the need to defend the nation against "visible and invisible enemies of the homeland."[86] He explicitly warned that if the enemies wanted war, the Peronists would hang them with a rope.[87] The idea of the enemy was so extreme that Perón engaged in verbal fights with the absolute enemies (internal and external) whom he never named or clearly identified: "[T]hey should know that they will pay a high price, if they forget that in this land when it was needed to impose what the people wanted it did not matter how many Argentines should die."[88]

War was connected with these imaginary enemies of Peronism and the nation. Perón carefully delineated the notion of an absolute enemy but he never actualized it. He warned that at one point political adversaries turned to "enemies of the nation." When this was the case, he said they were no longer "gentlemen that one should fight fairly but snakes that one can kill in any way."[89]

The leader's theory of the enemy remained distant from his practice. He displaced the total war of destruction to an imaginary future. His position was reactive, even heroic, as an imaginary response to the violence of the enemy but it never came close to adopting war as a normative definition of ideology or national strength. "If they want war they will get a war. And above all, they should know if they choose war, its outcome will be that they or we will disappear."[90] Total war was safely relegated to the Peronist rhetorical horizon and was far from reality.

The populist organized community was not a community for war. Nationalism appeared to be a resource for winning elections, for example with the Peronist presentation of the fight as "Braden or Perón." With the symbolic conflagration of nationalist Peronism and North American imperialism, Perón knew how to capitalize on US willingness to meddle in internal Argentine politics.

Perón's nationalism was the complacent neutralism that had favored the Axis powers, but he differed practically from those nacionalistas who had planned what to do after what they assumed would be the certain victory of Hitler and Mussolini's armies. The South American and anti-imperialist aims of Perón's government can be seen as attenuated by the continual postwar limitations imposed by a United States that didn't want to pardon his past pro-Axis sympathies. Perón was more anticommunist than anti-imperialist and more "Peronist" than nacionalista. Anti-imperialism was defined as a denunciation of imperialist internal meddling but not as a substantive denunciation of the global colonial order.[91] Perón himself ironically told Ambassador Braden in their last meeting that he understood the reasons behind the US administration's apparent desire to play a central role in Argentine politics and economics. He was even sympathetic as he ironically told Braden that he understood the American need to give priority to US interests over Argentine ones, but there was one difficulty: "[I]n my country everyone that does that is called a son of a bitch."[92] To be sure, anti-imperialism was a central element in Peronist speech but the problem was not imperialism per se but rather the fact that politically, as a populist leader, he could not give up Argentine autonomy vis-à-vis the needs of American leaders. Theoretically, Peronism opposed "the Bolshevik insectification and the capitalist colonial exploitation."[93] In practice, capitalism, communism, and the nation were less important than the fluctuating political needs of the populist leadership.

All in all, Perón did not understand the nation in exclusively territorial terms. As the leader evinced in 1958: "My son, I am like a fakir in India. Wherever I am, there is my country."[94] The general's narcissism didn't change over time, so secure was he in his own leadership. The idea of the fakir defined the principal element of the form in which he understood his leadership. The metaphor developed the populist idea of enchantment. Perón was owner of the masses. In his own words, his personal wealth was not monetary but rather "rich in followers." The idea of Perón as conductor references the titles of fascist leaders. In Peronism the conductor didn't save the homeland by war and violence but rather through a consecration of a new social order that eliminated communism forever.

As much as personalism is central to Argentine history, Perón was a revolutionary narcissist in the sense that he erected his persona as mythic articulator of his ideology. The Peronist ritual strengthened the image of Perón as a charismatic leader and emphasized his monopoly on power. [95] This was no less true for Mussolini or Hitler, but with Perón it didn't represent the exclusion of the chosen enemy but the inclusion of those who accepted the conductor and followed him uncritically.[96] Those who didn't were excluded within a logic of sedition that labeled them traitors opposed to the interests of the nation.

In Peronist populism, the leader was not democratic in the broader sense, although he was in the technical sense: he was elected to ritually confirm his messianic role and not to realize the particular wills of his constituents. He had a militaristic view of the followers. They were "the soldiers of Peronism" in "permanent fight against treason" and the traitors to the nation.[97] At one point in 1946 he boasted of his ability to make revolutions or coups at any moment if he wanted to do so. He stated that he "had" at will "500,000 Peronist followers and, as Napoleon said, with myself as their leader we will count as one million."[98] The "followers" were not seen by the leader as rational actors but neither were they "insects" nor automatons. Their condition as members of the populist organized community was based on their emotional recognition of the conductor as the best of them.

In Perón's telling, the genesis of the movement was less related to ideas, or electoral American "technical methods," than to his own persona. He had started "alone" and created a movement with millions of followers and "preachers of this doctrine in our entire country and in a big chunk of the world." It was exactly as "Christ has done."[99]

Perón didn't hesitate in 1946 to call himself "first descamisado" and said, "I don't want to command over men but rather over their hearts."[100] According to its leader, the ascription to Peronism was based on emotions, not on rational decisions.[101] Organic harmony was achieved through the acceptance of the conductor's ethereal wisdom with the "heart." It was during the dictatorship, in 1944, in which he played a central part, that Perón first articulated his belief in this innate and sacred nature of the leader: "The people should know...that the conductor is born. He is not made, not by decree nor by elections." The art of political conducting was not learned with "recipes" or "booklets." "It is essential that the conductor find his own molds, to later fill them with a content that will be in direct relation, according to his efficiency, with the sacred oil of Samuel that the conductor has received from God."[102] Perón declared this as the justification for the military dictatorship of 1943 and for his persona. If the Argentine fascists had defined themselves as the political representatives of God, Perón pruned the field of reception of the sacred back to only himself. If any doubt remained as to whether the generalizations about the divine support of conductors of the masses applied to Perón himself, he declared, "The masses are conducted with intuition; and intuition is only given by God. Sure of these truths we have tried to make rational government, seeking to get closer to perfection in the conduction of our people. Strength is confessing that up until now we haven't done so badly."[103]

Perón reiterated here the centrality of divine will in his leadership, although he still didn't replace the first-person plural with the third-person singular, as he would later.[104] He called himself a "big brother" of the people.[105] He even presented the supposed passivity of the masses in accepting his leadership and doctrine as a metaphor of sexual inexperience. "We had taken the people when they were virgin."[106] In this and other instances, the conductor was the *first Argentine*. Equally, Eva Perón, who in more spontaneous terms also became a mythical figure, erected this figure of the leader as first in everything: worker, master, director of collective destinies.[107] In a famous speech of 1951, the wife of the general elevated him to the political messiah of a people:

> I haven't done anything; everything is Perón. Perón is the Homeland, Perón is everything, and all of us are at an astronomical distance from the Leader of the nationality. I, my general, with the spiritual plenipotency that the descamisados of the Homeland have given me, and before the people vote on the 11th of November, I proclaim you, the president of all Argentines. The Homeland is saved, because it is in the hands of General Perón.[108]

Eva Perón's speech was symptomatic of the populist disrespect of democratic norms and institutions. Evita maintained that before the election the leader had been elected by her personal acclamation. This was possible because the organized community was a reflection of the thought and practice of the leader, not the reverse. The leader was owner of the truth. In fascist Italy, the propaganda repeated in newspapers and murals "Mussolini is always right." In the case of the Argentine populist leader, the effect was perhaps more intimate, as Eva Perón said. In its organized community based on the nacionalista and fascist critique of individualism and collectivism, Peronism proposed itself as a universal "third way."[109]

This organized community was national but not specifically Argentine; rather, it was like a globalized model for all. Peronism was presented as a product for exportation. As the march "Captain Evita" proposed:

> *Justicialista* flag
> our flag will be
> for the Peoples of the world
> flag of love and peace[110]

The title of the march emphasized the subordination of the wife in the military ranking of the husband. It was a metaphor for the hierarchical characteristics of the movement. The lyrics distanced the leader from its military origins in order to emphasize the sentiments and a more con-vincing desire for peace than the original pro-fascist neutralism of Perón during the early period of the GOU.

Was Peronism really for export? To be sure, the export arguments were meant for internal consumption but Peronism took its arguments seriously. Peronist worker attachés promoted it in Argentine embas-sies throughout the globe.[111] Perón presented the Third Position as an Argentine gift to all peoples on earth.[112] The reception and idealization of Peronism ranged from the Indians Ché Guevara found in his Latin American travels as a middle-class anti-Peronist, to the admiration of Khieu Samphan, a close associate of Pol Pot and head of state at the time of the Khmer Rouge regime, who wrote in his doctoral dissertation about the possible application of Peronist theory to Cambodia.

Clearly aware of the movement's international appeal, Peronists even joked that US President Harry Truman needed to visit Buenos Aires and receive Peronist indoctrination.[113] More seriously, Eva Perón argued that if Peronism became a global phenomenon capitalism would be "definitively defeated."[114] Addressing international capitalism and communism, Perón argued that the movement "was a dangerous example that we have given to the world, that is why they do not forgive us and they call us thieves, fascists and communists."[115]

However, as in Italian fascism, the national leadership found it extremely hard to become transnational. Perón presented his movement as a national response to foreign doctrines and at the same time claimed its legitimacy as a world ideology.[116] In his universalism, conceptualized as the transcendental Peronist proposal for the world, Perón intended to pursue the global ideal that Mussolini had pursued, although it eventually required overcoming Il Duce's unsolved contradiction between extreme nationalism and fascist universality. Like Mussolini, Perón presented his regime as greater than the French and Soviet revolutions. Also like Mussolini, Perón maintained in 1953 that the doctrine was the "catalyzing element of the movement." He provided it with "a unity of conception and unity of criterion" and yet it was in permanent "evolution." It couldn't be fixed but rather had to adapt because doctrines were not only thought but also movement and action.[117] More explicitly, Perón maintained that "we are not sectarian...we obey actions....If there is something in com-munism that we can take, we take it, names don't scare us. If fascism, anarchism, or communism have something good, we take it." Borrowing from the left and the right, Perón took the accusation of eclecticism as a compliment.[118] This "eclecticism" that Perón shared with Mussolini distanced him from the Italian in practical, and later theoretical, terms.

Fascism sustained itself in the ideal of violence and war as sublime values of nationality and the leader's persona. In military terms, it mobilized the masses but tended to demobilize them in social terms. Peronism inverted the terms of the fascist equation. In doing so it distanced itself from the nacionalista and fascist models and became a political ideology sui generis. That Peronism reformulated fascism was a matter of foundational significance in the broader history of Latin American populism.

The Argentine nacionalistas, who thought themselves transatlantic peers of Hitler and Mussolini in their zeal for violence and extermination, were fascists. They were also fascist in promoting the idea of the radical enemy that global fascism proclaimed. In his first regime, Perón broke with this violent tradition, which would be followed by the nacionalistas of Tacuara, by the Peronist Triple A of his late regime, and by the last military dictatorship (1976–1983). While after 1945 the Argentine fascists and neofascists continued their identification with transatlantic global forms of fascism, in a circular fashion early Peronists regularly stated that they were only identified with Peronism. Perón didn't see a model to be followed in those defeated in World War II, but neither did he identify with the victors. As he maintained in 1945, little had changed with the "imperialist capitalist" victory and the Nazi–fascist defeat: "[J]ustice and liberty were hardly changed by it and the world continued almost as before."[119] He saw little difference between Hitler and Roosevelt. According to Perón, the postwar world was the world of "capitalist and communist imperialism." This is notable given that Perón shared enemies with the defeated fascist powers and wanted to avoid the same fate.

Presenting himself as the student who learned from the errors of the master, Perón went on to create something new. He had lived in Italy under Mussolini and had visited Nazi Germany. During his stay, he not only expressed to the fascist press his admiration for fascism, but years later remembered that in Mussolini he saw an "autocrat of the soul" who, "in spite of having elevated his country economically and socially, giving it an organic structure model and laws of advancement, during the relevant period of his economic management, what happened to him and to poor Italy for not being able to stand the weight of the purple!"[120]

For Perón, the fall of fascism wasn't due to its lack of leadership but rather to its ideological exhaustion. Fascism was "an unrepeatable phenomenon, a classic style to define a precise and determined epoch."[121] Fascism was not a model to follow or to imitate; for a new epoch a new truth was needed. And the leader thought of himself as the owner of this new truth, as he argued during his electoral campaign on January 1, 1946:

> What is an organic government? It is an aggregation of solidly united forces that has at its head a man of state, who needn't be a genius or a sage, but rather a man on whom nature has bestowed a special condition to span a complete panorama that others don't see.[122]

The organic nature of the movement would lead to political supremacy in the long term: "Our aspiration is not to rule for six years but to secure sixty years of government."[123]

Perón understood the importance of simplifying to the extreme the political equation. Like war, politics is the "clash and the fight of two wills against each other." As Perón said, for a Peronist there was "nothing better than another Peronist." In the end there could be "only one doctrine: the Peronist; only one flag: that of the Homeland; and only one greatness: that of this flag and this Homeland."[124]

The originality of the first Peronist term was marked by its authoritarian tendencies, and even its totalitarian vocation. At the same time, Peronist populism stood out in the history of political ideas for its social applications, especially the redistribution of wealth, that despite their "national socialist" tendencies, the nacionalistas never were able to put into practice. The distributive tendencies that its bases demanded moderated the fascist sympathies of Perón. In this way, Argentina, against the flow of postwar Western Europe, underwent a truncated process of populist modernization that paradoxically broadened the political and social participation of the citizenry as much as authoritarianism.

5

Bombs, Death, and Ideology

FROM TACUARA TO THE TRIPLE A

FROM ITS INCEPTION Peronism had a close but conflicted relationship with Argentine fascism. This is not hard to understand: they were both heirs to a military dictatorship; they were both against liberal democracy, American and British imperialism, and the left. For Argentine fascists, Perón was a guarantor of the "New Order" that had not yet lost the global war against liberalism and the left: Mussolini and Hitler's war. But in the Argentine context this ideological war that the nacionalistas supported was, above all, a war against democracy. In Perón, nacionalistas saw "the great conductor" that the country had been waiting for. [1] He was a new Argentine example of the transnational fight for fascism.

The idea that Perón would safeguard the antiliberal corporatist Revolution of 1943 is not hard to understand; after all, Perón had been one of its main architects, starting with the creation of the GOU, the secret group of military leaders that held the dictatorship together. Many nacionalistas, like Carlos Ibarguren, would see the continuation of the military regime as legitimizing the 1943 military movement. According to Ibarguren, "only now" could the revolution really get underway.[2] The nacionalista and anti-Semitic publication *Ahijuna* agreed: it identified elected Peronism with an "integral recuperation." It was a "national revolution."[3]

After the election of Perón, the extreme right was divided between two distinct camps: the intellectuals and politicians who supported the regime included Virgilio Filippo, Ernesto Palacio, Hugo Wast, Manuel Gálvez, Bonifacio Lastra, Leopoldo Marechal, Ramón Doll, Delfina Bunge de Gálvez, and Carlos Ibarguren, as well as the young members of the *Alianza Nacionalista* (successor to the AJN); the other group was composed of nacionalistas who opposed Peronism because it was not anti-Semitic enough, because it was too radical in social terms, or because Perón considered them "piantavotos," that is, politicians who

ultimately undermined the populist movement by scaring potential vot-
ers and whom he largely ignored, despite having met with them on several occasions. [4] Perón flatly downplayed them and many of them even
abandoned politics after 1945. However, some nacionalistas kept trying to
steer Peronism toward fascism.

Of those nacionalistas who continued in politics, most were co-opted
by Perón, though not granted any real political power outside the cultural
sphere. They took over universities that had been purged of intellectuals
and serious academics.

The nacionalistas accepted Perón as an undeniable reality. Among his
opponents, silence reigned supreme. The reason for this silence was in
part related to the Peronist populist curtailment of freedom of the press,
which also affected the Argentine fascists who disliked the Peronist
regime. As in Romania and Brazil and many other places from Hungary
to Mexico, fascists regularly failed when they had to face an authoritarian government. Paradoxically, fascism triumphed in democratic contexts
(Weimar Germany and democratic Italy) that fascism was able to use
against democracy itself. Once in power it eliminated these freedoms. The
primary reason it took so long for nacionalista fascist opposition to Perón
to fully appear was the fact that Peronism was not fully democratic beyond
its populist ascription to electoral politics and, hence, it did not hesitate to
quash its opposition from left and right. Indeed, only after Perón moved
away from his alliance with the army and the Church, the mainstays of
nacionalismo, did nacionalista opposition to Perón truly take hold. Before
this happened, nacionalismo was politically dormant.

The conflict between Perón and the Catholic Church—a conflict
that led to the Peronist burning of churches in 1955—would move most
Peronist-sympathizing nacionalistas (Father Virgilio Filippo, among others) away from the Peronist movement. Nonetheless, like undying cham-
pions of a lost cause, the young nacionalistas affiliated with the *Alianza*
steadfastly resisted the fall of the Peronist regime. Thus, when Perón fell
in 1955, Argentine fascism was, once again, deeply divided.

After 1955, many nacionalistas openly expressed what many thought
but hadn't dared express: Perón and his ideas had rendered the legacy of
the Revolution of 1943 too radically populist or worse. As Father Meinvielle
stated in 1956, "The Revolution of 1943 was appropriated by a demagogue
who seized and corrupted the flags raised by the generation of 1930 to 1943."
Even more explicit, Argentine fascist Marcelo Sánchez Sorondo would
write in his memoirs, "Perón displaced us as agents of policy, but he was

also heir to a good deal of the ideological capital that we had developed: he was, in fact, the one who took advantage of the message of nacionalismo."[5]

After the fall of Perón in 1955, nacionalista support for Peronism waned. There were some who even dismissed the Peronist years altogether. For example, in a pamphlet dated 1955, Jordán Bruno Genta condemned Peronism as communist and repeated his cleric-fascist thinking from the interwar period. "Only a Catholic and military politics can control the Masonic and communist decay of the Homeland."[6] Genta, like many others, wanted to return to the symbiosis of Church, army, and fascism that Peronist populism had structurally reshaped. However, for most Argentine fascists, it was futile to ignore the sea change that Perón, Evita, and their movement had created.[7] In sum, in its early years, from 1943 to 1945, many nacionalistas saw Peronism as representing exactly what all nacionalistas had wanted: a strong antiliberal movement with a strong military leader and an astonishing new feature, namely a working-class base. From 1946 to 1955 many of them became wary of the idiosyncrasies of Perón's brand of populism. But now that the Peronist regime was gone, the partisan configurations of two irreconcilable Argentinas that Perón had helped to shape presented some nacionalistas with a new political opportunity.

For most nacionalistas, the idea that real Peronism had corrupted Argentine Catholic fascist theory did not mean that the legacy of Peronism or its power bases should be denied. Many nacionalistas supported a fascist-leaning Peronism without Perón and thereby anticipated what would later be a left-wing practice of joining Peronism in order to move it to the left. This strategy, eventually called *entrismo*, or "enterism," was used by the right before the left. It is no coincidence that the leaders of the Peronist guerrilla movement (Mario Firmenich, Fernando Abal Medina, Carlos Ramus, as well as well-known fighters like Rodolfo Galimberti and many others) shared a fascist and anti-Semitic past.[8] From that position they "entered into" Peronism. Once again, the *serpent's egg* was nested in the (militaristic and authoritarian) Montonero leadership—which largely learned how to do binary politics in a far-right, anti-Semitic, and paramilitary organization, Tacuara.

Tacuara

Tacuara represented young nacionalismo in the period after the Peronist regime. Its theoretical basis was rooted in the nacionalista idea of the

Cross and the Sword taken from Meinvielle and from the historic example of Argentine fascism during the interwar period. Its practice was based on the idea of an all-or-nothing struggle against a domestic enemy, the traitor to the homeland. Joe Baxter, who later would become one of the heads of the *Ejercito Revolucionario del Pueblo* or ERP (the Marxist revolutionary guerrilla), was a founding member of Tacuara. The fact that Tacuara was the political cradle of future guerrilla leaders helps explain their subsequent militarism, which so differed from the originally left-wing ideology of the majority of its followers. Their idea of a hierarchical contest of revolutionary soldiers fighting for the new order gave violence a central role in politics. Also rooted in past ideologies of violence was the idea of a chosen elite that messianically believes in its warrior type of leadership.[9] This is not to say that the intellectual origins of Argentina's "Dirty War" presented a genealogy with "two demons," but just one: the ideological legacy of Argentine fascism. As Argentine scholar Hugo Vezzetti has pointed out, according to this militaristic vision, politics is a single conflict with only one possible solution: a holy war of annihilation.[10]

This fascist legacy was not limited to the genesis of the Montonero leadership (let alone its rank and file on the left, which had very little, if anything, to do with Tacuara and the mixed traditions of fascism). The most relevant dimension of this legacy of Argentine fascism is not that of its remarkable influence in the genealogy of the guerrilla leadership. The kernel of the murderous itinerary of the fascist idea in Argentine history is the continual right-wing reformulation of the long-standing alliance between nacionalismo, the army, and the Church. These alliances eventually led to the formation of the Triple A and the state-sanctioned terrorism of the most recent military dictatorship (1976–1983).

There was a substantial difference between the left-wing guerrilla movement and state terrorism. By their own definition, the guerrillas were against the law. They were affected by a poorly theorized, fully partisan revolutionary process. State terrorism, on the other hand, undermined and appropriated the law, often making it disappear entirely, as nacionalismo had always intended. The guerrillas wanted a new normative order, whereas state terrorism desired a state of exception for its actions which were then positioned above the normative order of things. For nacionalismo, and for fascism at large, there was never a solid link between legitimacy and legality. Under the dictatorship nacionalista ideology was attached to the state apparatus and the law became its mere instrument.[11]

The dictatorship's radical brand of political violence was less a result of French and North American concerns about national security—these concerns provided the dictatorship with an international framework and even legitimized it—than a product of the historical genealogy of fascist Argentine nacionalismo.

The basis of ideological fascism lay in the factious previous traditions of Argentina. Several *caudillismos* and civil wars preceded fascism. Equally influential was the synchronic emergence of transnational fascism. However, when justified by religion, Argentina's fascism found a source of holy legitimacy that went beyond the sacralizing nature of fratricidal political struggle to establish what was to be considered the political kingdom of Christ. God was, so to speak, the Duce of Argentine fascism. Peronism challenged this clerical notion of fascism but once its regime was gone the Argentine world was not the same as before. With the military coup against Perón in 1955, the nacionalista right was reconstituted and even held some posts in the new military government of 1955–1958. Fathers Filippo, Castellani, and Meinvielle, for example, kept publishing texts and gaining followers. Tacuara, which appeared after the anti-Peronist coup of 1955, was crucial to post-Peronist nacionalismo.

Tacuara was an organization of young people inspired by the work of their nacionalista elders. Like their elders, Tacuaras regarded Catholicism as an essential part of the nacionalista project. Tacuara was initially energized by the antisecular campaign to defend religious education after 1955 but it increasingly became an outlet for young Peronist sectors of the lower-middle class, "the young Peronists who wanted to fight." Other members of Tacuara were, like the three Tacuara cousins of Ché Guevara, members of an impoverished aristocracy.[12] Tacuara was related to fascism insofar as nacionalismo was fascist in Argentina and Tacuara continued and reformulated its legacy. In other words, Tacuara was related to a historical "Christianized fascism" almost perennially supported by the country's leading Catholic intellectuals and priests. Like its predecessors, it was also part of the networks of transnational fascism after 1945. In sum, it was clearly a neofascist organization.[13]

Tacuara got its name from a rod used as a spear by Indians and federalist *Montoneras* in the nineteenth century. It presented itself as a lance to be used against the traditional enemies of nacionalismo. Once again nacionalismo identified itself with the nation and the nation with God. In the words of its leader, Alberto Ezcurra, the choice was simple: "Either the red flag, with its hammer and sickle, or the blue and white flag under Christ's

Cross." [14] Tacuara had a "vertical loyalty, that as in our whole conception of life, begins with the loyalty to 'Comrade Christ.'" [15]

Through its rituals and militaristic practices Tacuara intended to make tangible the mythical ideological narrative of fascism. Typically, Tacuara members, whose average age was 17, would do the fascist salute in different situations: when passing in front of a Church; in front of their leaders; or when facing their perceived enemies. They would engage in military training in "camps" distributed throughout the country. When the police raided one of these training camps in 1963 in the littoral province of Santa Fe, it found youngsters behaving like military commandos. The police also found Nazi emblems and portraits of Heinrich Himmler and the nineteenth-century Argentine dictator, Rosas. Colonel Kurt Brenner, the police chief who interrogated them, said that they defined themselves as nacionalista and Catholic. Brenner seemed to be troubled by their ideological opaqueness. The police found books by Thomas Aquinas, the Argentine nacionalista intellectual Manuel Gálvez, the Spanish fascist Primo de Rivera, Charles Maurras, and Ché Guevara. Tacuaras were not averse to reading the global partisan revolution from primary sources. The radical right and left continued to read each other throughout the 1960s.

Father Luis V. Dusso, who taught them "religion," said about these Tacuaras from the province of Santa Fe: "They are guys who are really morally sane. They have the ideals of the Falange. God, Homeland and home." Father Dusso added that Tacuaras defended the country against sexual and political threats: "One can trust them. Santa Fe is full of *prostíbulos* and communist centers.... Tacuara wants to defend us from communism and immorality." Tacuara continued the fascist ideal of masculinity in Argentina. It emphasized the idea of its men as ideal machos, male warriors who were intimately linked to violent celestial desires. For Patricio Collins—the brother of Santa Fe's Tacuara leader, Juan Mario Collins—"spitting against Tacuara would be equal to spitting against the sky." He asserted that Tacuaras were preparing for the incoming Argentine war of the future, a civil war that Tacuara would fight along with the armed forces and against Jews and communists.[16]

Although Tacuara was a neofascist, or even neo-Nazi, organization that defended fascism and Nazism, as well as Francoism and other brands of transatlantic fascism, it primarily considered itself heir to Argentine fascist nacionalismo from the interwar period. They regarded Argentina's nacionalismo as a national expression of global fascism.[17]

However, in typical nacionalista fashion they did not consider nacionalismo a form of fascism but rather saw fascism and Nazism as forms of nacionalismo.[18] Many of the young militants of Tacuara were the children of famous nacionalistas but others were middle-class newcomers to fascist politics. Of its two leaders, Ezcurra and Joe Baxter, the first was related to General Uriburu and the son of Alberto Ezcurra Medrano, the famous clerico-fascist theorist, while the second was a middle-class student with no previous political nacionalista background in his family. Tacuara was founded as a continuation of the long established right-wing activities in high schools, and its members were highly influenced by people like Juan Carlos Goyeneche (Mussolini's Argentine interlocutor), Jordán B. Genta, and Fathers Meinvielle, Filippo, and Castellani, as well as many other veteran nacionalistas.

Initially around 1955 and 1956, Tacuara's ideology was almost identical to the ideology of interwar nationalism, but over time it changed, leaning both to the right and to the left.[19] Tacuara was a bridge by which youth came into contact with larger political traditions, from the slightly reformed Catholic fascist nacionalismo from which it had emerged to radical right- and left-wing forms of Peronism. Tacuara was characterized by extreme anti-Semitism (it was responsible for kidnapping, seriously injuring, and murdering young left-wing activists and/or Jews), by defense of the fascist legacy (including the Holocaust), and by the exclusive vision of a Catholic and militarized Argentina that was supposed to be the leading nation of Latin America.

Tacuara clearly appreciated the transatlantic fascist links with violence, politics, and spectacle. They also actively participated in the world of the early 1960s: a messy universe of dynamic interaction between political ideology, revolution, and at times sheer criminality. Tacuara had a clear impact on popular culture and Tacuara "characters" even appeared in popular films. [20] In real life, they robbed banks, hijacked planes, and bombed and killed. The Tacuaras attacked the Policlínico Bancario in 1963, stealing one hundred thousand dollars, in a criminal act that would end in the murder of two people. They also "invaded" the Malvinas/Falkland Islands in the South Atlantic when a few youths hijacked a plane and made it take them there, where they were later detained.[21]

At its peak Tacuara had between 2,500 and 7,000 members throughout the country. It was a group with a "fascist-nationalist" ideology according to an AP reporter who was allowed to witness a secret ceremony of initiation—"a ceremony which could have taken place in Hitler's Germany."

The youths pledged allegiance to the "nationalist cause" and promised to "fight against capitalism and Zionism with one hand, and with the other hand against communism." After the ceremony Tacuara leader Ezcurra, "whose headquarters is adorned with a crucifix," reiterated the traditional Argentine fascist position against capitalism and communism by emphasizing that Tacuara was "spiritually" influenced by the Catholic Church.[22] In another interview, Ezcurra told Argentine journalist Rogelio García Lupo: "Our movement aims to establish a new order; it is Christian insofar as it affirms the primacy of spiritual and permanent values in men and society. Our movement is nacionalista insofar as it thinks [of] the nation as supreme social unity. Our movement is socialist due to its conception which is socio-economic, anticapitalist, revolutionary and communitarian." This Christian nacionalista socialist view approach reiterated the nacionalista view of an all-or-nothing contest between God and its enemies. In their propaganda, Tacuaras made clear that they were standing against the "aims of the anti-Christ."[23]

The differences between Tacuara's right and left wings were evident in the early writings (from 1955 to 1959) when, forcefully bound by anti-Semitic hatred, Tacuaras still seemed like a youth group with a shared set of political and social views. Anti-imperialism was also present in the early Tacuara movement, as it had been in nacionalismo. But as opposed to the grand interwar notions of creating a new Argentine empire to counteract the more traditional ones, the Tacuaras often limited themselves to spectacular acts of irrepressible banality. They famously threw eggs and tomatoes at the Duke of Edinburgh during his visit to Argentina in 1962. They also attacked discos and stylish fashion stores and on one occasion blew up a prized bull (*toro campeón*) at Argentina's aristocratic Rural Society. Tacuaras saw these acts as emblematic of their radical rejection of aristocratic mores. They clearly identified the aristocracy with imperialism.[24]

In its view of anti-imperialism, Tacuara also reproduced the nacionalista view of history. Tacuaras believed that anti-imperialism could be conflated with an imperialist notion of Argentine supremacy in Latin America. They proudly graffitied walls with the words "sovereignty or death." For them defending Argentina was a heroic dangerous action which would result either in the killing of the "Other" or the sacrifice of the self.[25] Like nacionalistas before them, the Tacuaras used traditional Argentine cemeteries as places of memory.[26] Tacuaras regularly met at the Chacarita cemetery to commemorate their first "martyr," the nacionalista Darwin

Passaponti who had died for "God and the homeland."[27] These rites of initiation eventually led to violence. For example, in 1962 one thousand Tacuaras provoked a riot when they met in the Recoleta cemetery to pay homage to Facundo Quiroga, the nineteenth-century Argentine caudillo.[28] This mythical consideration of Argentina's history was not new. It was Tacuara's rehashing of the Argentine fascist revisionist tradition that once more was in vogue in the 1960s and also in early twenty-first-century Argentina.[29]

Last but not least, Tacuara youth were elated by the violent victimization of the enemy. They regarded violence as a source of political emancipation. Extreme violence would lead them to absolute power. They conflated aggressive preemptive physical actions with the affirmation of politics as desire. Like many other fascists, they regarded instinctual violence as a mythical source of political legitimacy. And in typical Argentine fascist fashion they conflated violence with the sacred. Their war was a "just war."[30]

To be sure, there was no difference between this reification of violence and the one that was presented by interwar nacionalistas. Both movements, for example, considered the Jewish body to be a site of sacrificial violence for the sake of God and the homeland. But Tacuara presented its actions in more spectacular terms. Jewish buildings with many Argentine Jews inside them were regularly machine-gunned and bombed, often on a weekly basis.[31] Nacionalistas had always treated acts of torture in rather opaque terms.[32] When Tacuara kidnapped Graciela Sirota, a 19-year-old argentine Jewish university student, and carved a swastika on her breast, it was anticipating an explicit ideological practice of biological inscription that would later be common in the Argentine concentration camps. During the same period, another youngster, Ricardo Heraldo D'Alessandro, was intercepted by five men who tattooed swastikas on both of his cheeks. Regarding the Sirota case and other events of violence, the position of the Argentine government of President Guido, as expressed by his interior minister Carlos Adrogue, was of a "deep preoccupation for the racial problem." Typically, the minister called for "all sectors" (that is, victims and perpetrators) to "collaborate" to solve the problem. Less ambiguously, the chief of police, retired Captain Enrique H. Green, actually accused the victim, Graciela Sirota, of lying and denied the reality of the anti-Semitic attacks. More formally, the federal police produced a communiqué that accused Sirota of being involved in an ideological and political game. For the Tacuaras themselves, the case was just an excuse for a Jewish campaign against nacionalismo that conflated "Freudian contents" with the accusation that nacionalistas wanted to revive in Argentina the conditions of Nazi Germany.[33]

This mixture of official apathy and implicit support for their actions emboldened the Tacuaras. In 1964, as Tacuara was looking for "revenge" against perceived threats, Jews and leftists were conflated in Tacuara's projective identification of the enemy. In this context, Tacuara assassinated a Jewish leftist student named Raúl Alterman. The killing was in cold blood, execution style. The idea was to fight Judaism and communism by killing a "Jewish communist dog."[34] Some weeks after the assassination of Alterman, Augusto Timoteo Vandor, the most important Peronist union leader in the country, wore an emblem of Tacuara during a rally in the city of Avellaneda. During those weeks, Tacuara acted as a sort of praetorian guard of the mainstream Peronist unions. Nobody in mainstream Peronism seemed to be bothered by Tacuara's terrorism and racist killings.[35] Tacuara's links with anti-Semitism were clearly part of a self-perceived transgenerational bond with previous anti-Jewish perpetrators, especially the Nazis.

A poem by Joe Baxter entitled "Nuremberg" highlights Tacuara's peculiar sense of victimhood in light of the legacy of the Holocaust. The defeat of global fascism provided a new myth of origins to the neofascist warriors of the Cold War. Whereas Catholicism had been a complicated filter through which to read the Holocaust and often demarcated a tenuous boundary between persecution and extermination, for the Tacuaras the need to uproot the Jews from Argentina was part of a global post-Holocaust constellation of perpetrators. They linked their post-Holocaust terrorist anti-Semitic activities with the extermination of the Jews in Europe. This transgenerational dimension that affected victims and perpetrators differently was similarly noted by Jewish victims. For example, a Jewish victim of Tacuara told a newspaper reporter that his mother had been exterminated in a European concentration camp.[36]

This legacy of the Nazi concentration camps shaped Tacuara's self-understanding. For Baxter, the fascist memory of the Holocaust was connected to present and future violence:

> He who defends his land, his city,
> He who kills the enemy, he who fights,
> That man...is a war criminal.[37]

For Baxter, Argentine nacionalismo, especially in the form of Tacuara, represented a new moment in the history of global fascism. Tacuara members maintained links with similar neofascist organizations in Europe and North Africa as well as with the American Ku Klux Klan.[38] For Baxter the role of Tacuara within a new fascist international was of the first order. The Argentines would promote a new ideological beginning:

> The youthful air of our idea,
> one born in the pampas and the hills
> of guerrilla America,
> will make the men of Europe rise up.
> This wind of hate will make them go after
> the tired idols of our
> dirty democracy
> and the great leaders
> who once opposed
> your perfidy
> will return.[39]

Baxter promises a new "dawn" in which "the star killed at Nuremberg will shine as never before." This was a return of the repressed and a negation of the legitimacy of international justice. Convicted war criminals were turned into formidable heroes. Baxter's poetic defense of Nazism and of the perpetrators of the Holocaust was reinforced by the actual connections between members of Tacuaras and Nazis hiding in Argentina, like the French member of the SS, Jacques Marie De Mahieu, and the former member of the Armed SS, Wilhelm Sassen, who became famous for his clandestine interview with Adolf Eichmann.[40] When the state of Israel captured Eichmann in 1960 and took him to Israel to be tried for his crimes, the members of Tacuara graffitied walls around the country with "Long Live Eichmann! Death to the Jews!" [41] Ezcurra argued that Tacuara was only defending "Catholic values" against "Marxist-Jewish-liberal-Masonic-capitalist imperialism." He stated, "We are not anti-Semites with racialist aims, but we are enemies of Jewry. In Argentina the Jews are the servants of Israeli imperialism [who violated] our national sovereignty when they arrested Adolf Eichmann."[42]

As famously noted by Hannah Arendt, Eichmann, when facing his imminent death, ceremoniously stated, "Long live Germany, long live *Argentina*, long live Austria. I *shall not forget them*."[43] Arendt identifies this moment as one of "grotesque silliness." According to Arendt, this was a moment of elation in which Eichmann sensed the relevance of his own death. But Arendt clearly stated that this realization implied a formulaic representation of the moment rather than its ideological understanding. She identified Eichmann's last words with "clichés" and the banality of evil. Other historians have preferred to emphasize how this elation, and more generally his Nazi past and crimes, was linked to Eichmann's deep ideological commitment to Nazism. [44] However, neither Arendt nor her critics have asked why Eichmann included Argentina among the nations deemed worthy of remembering in the afterlife. No one analyzed the relevance of the Argentine context of nationalism where Eichmann lived and interacted for many years. At his trial a telling exchange took place about his initial talks with Sassen in an Argentine pub. Eichmann's recollection of that dialogue with Sassen on the book project they were going to write on the extermination of the Jews shows how Eichmann consciously conceived of his memories of the Holocaust in light of Argentine nationalism, which he clearly differentiated from classic Peronism:

DR. Servatius [Eichmann's lawyer]: Was Perón still in power at the time when you dictated the book?

EICHMANN: Yes. I believe that at that time General Perón was still President of the Republic of Argentina.

Q. Was the book designed to suit this atmosphere, the Peronist atmosphere?

A. I do not think so, but as I have said, it would be better if it were somehow to follow nationalistic lines. I think that is perhaps a better way of putting it, although I am still not sure whether this is the right way to put it.[45]

Returning to his trinational dedication, Eichmann clearly saw it as a memory that linked a constellation of transatlantic right-wing movements. In his view, his own death would become part of the future ideological transcendence of his ideology and would represent a memory for the future generations of fascists. The hunted Nazi and then Argentine citizen wanted to link his death with an act of nationalistic remembrance of Germany, Argentina, and Austria. In turn, for the Tacuaras, Eichmann's last words constituted a belated endorsement of Argentina's nacionalismo. Feeling as if one of them had been victimized, Tacuaras demanded revenge for Eichmann's death. They promised a future reenactment of Nazi forms of genocidal victimization. During the trial, handwritten mural posters that

GRN-Tacuara glued to the walls of Argentina, stated: "Jews to the crematorium! Honor to Eichmann."[46]

In the eyes of Argentine fascists, Eichmann's last words created a transatlantic and transgenerational bond with the experience of Nazism and the Holocaust. But this was the Argentine fascist translation and appropriation of the Nazi experience. Most Tacuaras' anti-Semitism was formulated as a Catholic strain of Nazism.[47] One relatively new component of their thinking was the inclusion of "Zionism" as an element of their anti-Semitism. In this regard, the actions of the state of Israel were seen as part of a worldwide Jewish conspiracy that, in the view of Tacuara, spread even to Argentina. As a result, the members of Tacuara forged bonds with the Arab League in Argentina. Together, the two organizations linked anti-Semitism with criticism of the state of Israel and Argentine Jews, whom they did not consider Argentines but rather full-fledged agents of Zionism. Typically, both Ezcurra and Baxter preferred to highlight their anti-Zionism while denying any explicit anti-Semitism on Tacuara's behalf.

Following a rather traditional anti-Semitic mode of projection, the Tacuara leaders presented their acts as preemptive against supposed Jewish threats. Tacuaras regularly shouted "Jews out," stressing that the expulsion of Jews from Argentina was central to their program. Tacuara even wanted to force Argentine Jews to shout "Viva Hitler." In an exclusive interview with the *New York Times* Father Julio Meinvielle denied having any links with Tacuara but put forward the notion that the Tacuara actions were a response to a Jewish campaign against "Argentine nationalists." For Meinvielle the anti-Semitic attacks were not "a serious issue" because they were reactions to Jewish "provocation." In an interview with a nacionalista publication a year earlier, Meinvielle did not deny his links with Tacuara, praising them and comparing them positively with the American Ku Klux Klan and calling for the return of the Inquisition. Like Meinvielle, Tacuara saw denunciations of its terrorist methods as a "Jewish Anti-Tacuara campaign." [48]

The links between religion and the purity of Argentine blood were threatened by Jews, and these Jewish "provocations" presumably called for extreme repression. In an interview with the Argentine Jewish press, Baxter had stated in 1962 that Tacuara was anti-Jewish for political reasons, not racial ones. In turn, Ezcurra argued that Tacuara was not exclusively anti-Semitic and added: "[W]e have found anti-Semitism in all the political sectors of the country including radicals, communists and socialists."

But the fact that anti-Semitism was quite extensive in Argentina did not seem to be a deterrent for the Tacuara actions. In fact, they wanted to further radicalize more conventional forms of anti-Semitism. In this sense, Tacuara's intentions for the future were clear. They would not continue with more theological forms of racist segregation, nor with ghettoizing them. Argentina was going to get rid of the Jews. While its followers were singing "Jews to the gallows (*Judíos a la horca*)" the Tacuara leaders stated: " We want a homeland free of politicians and demagogues and Jews. We are willing to take steps to make them disappear."[49]

Tacuara's anti-Zionism seemed to acquire international dimensions when Tacuara was "saluted" by the Saudi delegate at the United Nations. The delegate criticized President John F. Kennedy and the state of Israel and "expressed hope" that Tacuara "would spread in Latin America and its ideas would be adopted by the United Nations." In turn, the Argentine envoy at the United Nations denied that Tacuara was a "national movement" and downplayed its size and importance.[50]

In Argentina, Tacuara developed strong links with the local representative of the Arab League, Hussein Triki. Triki established a tactical alliance between the League, Tacuara, and its breakaway group, *Guardia Restauradora Nacionalista Tacuara* (GRN-T), subsidizing them and even participating in joint anti-Semitic campaigns. Triki, who had been accused in an American Jewish publication of having been a collaborator of the Nazis in the Middle East during World War II, had a long list of nacionalista acquaintances in Argentina, including famous ones like Manuel Fresco and Alberto Baldrich. An anti-Semite who was well informed of the traditions of Argentine fascism, Triki quoted from the fake anti-Semitic tract *The Protocols of the Elders of Zion* and from the work of Hugo Wast. Like Wast and most Argentine fascists, Triki believed in the existence of a Jewish plan against Argentina.[51]

Tacuara and Triki were not alone in displaying this anti-Semitism camouflaged as anti-Zionism. Members of the Peronist right, such as the representative from Salta province, Juan Cornejo Linares, an acquaintance of Triki, wanted the Argentine congress to investigate Zionism, that "dangerous conspiracy that is going after the real essence of our nationality."[52]

In addition to anti-Semitism, Tacuara saw important links between their own set of nacionalista ascriptions to Peronism and Arab forms of populist nationalism such as Nasserism. Triki also reciprocated in signaling clear links between Tacuaras, the Arab League, and Perón. At the Buenos Aires Theatre on Corrientes Avenue in the capital, Tacuaras listened to Triki and sang odes to the transcontinental links of Peronism with the Arab world. The songs had a rhyme that mimicked a soccer chant from Argentine stadiums: "Nasser, Perón and the Third Position" [*Nasser, Perón y la Tercera Posición*] and "Here they are, these are the Tacuaras of Perón" [*Aquí están, éstas son, las tacuaras de Perón*].[53]

While Tacuara's theory and writings were not exactly original, this was offset by an extremely original set of trajectories that eventually led its members to join a number of different groups from the extreme right to the left. To be sure, Tacuara was no exception to the long-standing nacionalista tradition of splintering into many groups. However, most interwar nacionalistas never left the fascist fold. Tacuara was different. There were at least three clear groups of Tacuaras with far-reaching influence, as they were among the future leaders of the guerrilla movement, the Triple A, and the last dictatorship's paramilitary "task forces." Some former Tacuaras even held posts in the *peronista* Carlos Menem administration (1989–1999) and one former Tacuara became a justice on the supreme court in the 1990s.

Of the three main groups in Tacuara, two were on the right and one on the left. One right group, highly influenced by Father Meinvielle, split from the main group in 1960 and adopted the name *Guardia Restauradora Nacionalista Tacuara* (GRN), or Nationalist Revolutionary Guard of Tacuara. It differed little from the other group on the Catholic and nationalistic right led by the young Ezcurra. The group on the "left," founded in 1962, called itself *Movimiento Nacionalista Revolucionario Tacuara* (MNRT), or Nationalist Revolutionary Tacuara Movement. The MNRT was Peronist from its inception but retained some traits of Tacuara's anti-Semitism. Baxter, one of the leaders of MNRT, stated that to be an "antisemite now is only to create an artificial problem and to confuse those who want to fight the real enemies, the imperialists." However, Baxter also noted that Fidel Castro was a "nationalist" "who got rid of the exploiters" and then added that "the majority of Jews had to leave Cuba."[54]

MNRT's advocacy of expropriation and revolution would later lead some members to the Montoneros movement and even to the Marxist guerrillas of ERP. MNRT was led by Joe Baxter and José Luis Nell. Baxter claimed that the remaining members of the first group were "all retards."[55] Beyond this consideration of his former Tacuara friends and current enemies as mentally deficient, the main difference between Baxter's group and the other two Tacuara groups on the right was their degree of relation to Peronism.

A growing anticapitalism marked "left-wing" Tacuara. Rather than rejecting the legacy of nacionalista ideology, MNRT presented it as an earlier stage in the ongoing struggle against the enemies of the homeland. According to Baxter there was an "old" and a "new nacionalismo." He acknowledged that Argentina's nacionalismo had been born at the same time as European movements such as Nazism or fascism, but denied that Argentina's experiment had been successful. Quoting Father Castellani, the famous clerico-fascist intellectual, Baxter said that Argentina's nacionalismo was part of the nation's ongoing development and that it shared more contextual affinities with "India, Congo or Algeria." A Europeanist "false pride" had not allowed "old nacionalismo" to recognize the colonial reality of Argentina. Baxter argued that, in order for the "new nacionalismo" to succeed where the old nacionalismo had failed, it would need to consider Argentina as an "underdeveloped and colonized country that is not European. It belongs to what is today called the Third World." [56] This was for Baxter the meeting point between the Third World revolution and a refashioned Argentine neofascist form of nacionalismo. MNRT made clear to its Peronist friends that it was "neither right nor left." They were now a "Peronist and Revolutionary" organization. They still shared with other Tacuaras an apocalyptic belief in the upcoming final battle: "The homeland will be free or the flag will fly over its ruins. Perón or death!"[57]

Newly rooted in the Peronist national revolution, the revolutionary Tacuara desired the global liberation of Latin American nations. To be sure there were still links between the different groups of Tacuaras; all kept the Tacuara name and the general public and media regarded them as members of the same group.[58] However, MNRT's embrace of revolutionary Peronism and its presentation of the other Tacuaras as counterrevolutionaries separated the members of Baxter's faction from those who remained fixated on "old nacionalismo." There was "no middle ground" between them.[59] Members of MNRT believed that fascism only belonged to Europe and could not be "transplanted" to Latin America. As revolutionary followers of Perón they proposed that only Third World solutions could be applied in Argentina.[60]

The discussions within the bewildering ideological landscape of the Tacuaras often took place in the pages of the national and international press. The "new" nacionalista Joe Baxter accused his old comrade Ezcurra of having pedophile fantasies. Ezcurra said that he had expelled Baxter and his comrades from Tacuara after they had developed "Marxist ideas." Ezcurra accused the Baxter faction of using the name of Tacuara like a costume, while the Tacuara of Ezcurra remained what Tacuara had always been, a group of "nacionalistas" that conceived of themselves as soldiers of Catholic Argentina. Ezcurra left Tacuara in 1964 and became a Catholic priest in 1971, but he did not actually abandon nacionalista politics. As a Catholic priest he became private secretary of a bishop who was an active ideological supporter of the last military dictatorship's Dirty War.[61]

To be sure, as the Uruguayan writer Eduardo Galeano noted at the time, Tacuara was a "kingdom of paradoxes."[62] But these paradoxes can be explained by focusing on the dynamic nature of fascist ideas in Argentine history, and especially in the Cold War period in the country, with its unusual mix of Peronism, national socialist and transnational fascist tendencies, and the particular Argentine nacionalista conflation of fascism and the sacred. Despite the manifold insults tossed across the Tacuara spectrum, there was more ideological continuity and continued personal bonds among the different Tacuara factions than is generally recognized. The fascist language, the cult of violence, and the emphasis on the political dimensions of nacionalista Catholicism existed among all groups. To be sure, most Tacuaras, like previous nacionalistas, shared a concern about social issues, a revolutionary desire for change, and an opposition to the traditional right.[63] However, the question remains as to which real differences existed, aside from the question of Peronism. If only Peronism differentiated among the various groups of Tacuara, the Tacuara experience would not have been significantly different from that of the nacionalistas under Peronism in 1945–1946 as well as in 1954–1955. Most nacionalistas had been ambivalent toward Peronism, but they had never flatly rejected it. Some of them even agreed with the Tacuara journal *Mazorca* in advocating "the imposition of a new nacionalista order, which simply is the victory of the postulates of Christ and Perón."[64] And yet the Tacuara experience was different in this regard from previous Argentine fascist configurations.

The main difference between the previous nacionalista contexts and the Tacuara one was the latter's ideological dynamics of radicalization. Radicalization had been the main binding agent for Tacuaras, first uniting them against the old guard and then pulling them apart in many directions, moving them to the far right and to the far left. In this sense the implosion of Tacuara represented a true fascist dynamic of self-destruction. Many former Tacuaras still argue that it was less ideological than previous nacionalista formations. To be sure, they rightly stress the fact that Tacuaras were less focused on nacionalista theory than on the "logic of pistols."[65] But this "logic" is not a deterrent to the true development of fascism, rather a central element of fascist ideology. Violence is not a means but an end. For true fascism, violence as an expression of desire becomes a source of sublime ideological experience to the full-fledged believer. Violence represents the essence of power and is the ultimate mark of ideological achievement for fascists. In the context of Argentine cleric-fascist traditions Tacuaras believed in the "need" for a sacred form of political violence. They even argued that "violence of the people is sacred."[66] For the Baxter group, this was the violence of the oppressed against the oppressors. This idea of the violence of the weak legitimized actual violence against what Tacuaras saw as the structural violence of the imperialist system. They conceived of violence as an authentic form of revolutionary justice. Against imperialism and capitalism, "the exploited" used violence "when they become conscious of their rights and their strength."[67] Tacuara youngsters, like their transatlantic predecessors, wanted to forge "a fraternity of violence." They were warriors who would never "cry like a woman." However, unlike its nacionalista predecessors, Tacuara was very close to being an all-male organization, like the later Triple A. These male soldiers were engaged in a battle of "mystical" connotations.[68] As Eduardo Galeano noted in 1967, violence in the name of God was central to Tacuara self-identification.[69] As they put it on Argentine walls and in journals, "Forge the homeland. Kill a Jew."[70]

The Tacuara of the right, both as GRN-Tacuara (after 1960) and the remaining Tacuara of Ezcurra (after 1962), remained within the nacionalista fascist mainstream as exemplified by journals like *Combate*, *Azul y Blanco*, *Segunda República*, and *Cabildo* or the later versions of *Dinámica Social* and *Ahijuna*, and it belatedly joined the terrorist neofascist groups of the 1970s such as Triple A as well as the military dictatorship.[71]

GRN-Tacuara was the first significant group of Tacuara to leave the original organization. They were said to have been influenced in this defection by Father Julio Meinvielle who as "spiritual adviser of Tacuara" was horrified about the leftist leanings of some members of the group. Members of GRN would visit Father Meinvielle at his quarters in a convent, where they would kneel on one leg and kiss his hand in an apparent sign of ideological submission. Meinvielle often taught GRN the right nacionalista theory and often settled ideological scores and disputes. [72] Nonetheless, even in 1964, GRN conflated Peronist language with a "rabid nacionalismo."[73]

Tacuara, like the majority of the Argentine extreme right, opposed the succession of civilian and military dictatorships that rose and fell throughout the 1960s. Tellingly, Father Meinvielle, in an interview with his fellow nacionalistas, described the dictatorship of rightist General

Juan Carlos Onganía as participating in the global conspiracy of *sinar-quía*, a fictitious organization invented by anti-Semites, which he denounced as the expression of the "world government or the hidden world power." The nacionalistas of *Azul y Blanco*, directed by Marcelo Sánchez Sorondo and seconded by Juan Manuel Abal Medina (a member of GRN-Tacuara and the future general secretary of the Peronist movement), agreed with the idea of an "invisible government." Tacuaras also agreed with this view of General Juan Carlos Onganía's dictatorship as an inauthentic form of rightist politics.[74] It is clear that the type of military dictatorship known in the academy as the bureaucratic authoritarian model was not attractive to the majority of nacionalistas.[75] It probably brought them transgenerational memories of previous nacionalista entanglements with conservative Argentina. Only the neofascists of Tacuara could regard General Onganía's repressive rule as moderate. As Meinvielle saw it, the Onganía military dictatorship presented a "Catholic and rightist façade" that aimed, like the global *sinar-quía* as a whole, to reconcile capitalism and communism. As Meinvielle told the Tacuaras in an interview, the *sinarquía* even had infiltrated the Church, reaching cultural and ideological peaks of "subversion." The Jews, he argued, were central among the "natural enemies" of the Church. The "progressive" stances within Catholicism were inspired by "Freud and Marx."[76] Against this imaginary conspiracy of the *sinarquía*, Meinvielle called in retro-Argentine-fascist fashion for a nacionalista type of Catholic military power.[77]

Father Meinvielle wanted his Tacuaras to be a structural part of this cleric-fascist-military coalition. In fact, Tacuara had links with the state, but it was not a paramilitary organization. All in all, neither the civilian administrations, nor the military governments of the 1960s, seriously attempted to repress Tacuara's terrorist activities. Moreover, the security forces, and especially the army and the intelligence services, were initially sympathetic toward, and then turned a blind eye to, the racist and terrorist activities of Tacuara.

Even after Tacuara and GRN activities were officially banned in 1963, they continued to operate openly, like many other political organizations of the extreme right. The center-left publication *Primera Plana* observed at the time that the democratic administration of President Arturo Illia (1963–1966) was aware of the extensive links between Tacuara and certain segments of the security forces. Intelligence reports from the early 1960s also confirm the idea that both the federal secret service, SIDE, and

DIPBA (Security Directorate of the Province of Buenos Aires) were often sympathetic to Tacuara, which they saw as defending the nation against communist and "Jewish" activities. These reports often noted the links between Tacuaras, notorious members of the Church, and sectors of the military.[78]

The presidential executive order banning Tacuara in 1963 clearly stated that it undermined the tenets of Argentine democracy.[79] Tacuaras did not disagree with that statement. The two Tacuara movements of the right opposed the liberal constitution and waited for the right type of military dictatorship, which soon came to be fulfilled in the dictatorial Dirty War of the 1970s.

Time-tested political patience was not the tactic of the Tacuara of the left (the Baxter–Nell faction). This left-wing group of Tacuara recognized Perón as its unconditional leader and soon engaged in revolutionary violence in his name. Indeed, Baxter's long career would lead him to fight against the Americans in Vietnam where he fought "as an officer in the Vietcong" and was given a medal by Ho Chi Minh; to court and become the lover of the mother of Ché Guevara; to become one of the leaders of ERP (Argentina's most violent Marxist guerrilla group); to live and marry in Cuba; and, finally, to his own death when, in 1973, his plane mysteriously exploded upon arriving in Paris.[80]

The members of Tacuara were bound to both right- and left-wing Peronism, or they looked to an option that classic interwar nacionalismo had always offered: the armed forces and the security forces. Tacuara both used these arms of the state and was used by them. Later, this interaction of using and being used led some Tacuaras to an organization that would be a key agent of the extreme right in the early 1970s: the *Alianza Anticomunista Argentina* or Triple A.

The Triple A

The Triple A and Tacuara shared many members. The two groups also shared a close relationship with the security forces and the army, as well as connections to the "hard-core" sectors of Peronist trade unionism. As Tacuara had done before, the Triple A operated in a gray zone located somewhere between radical politics and mere criminality.[81]

The Triple A's secret nature makes its theory and intellectual history difficult to trace.[82] Like Tacuara, the Triple A understood its practice as an objectification of its theory. The Triple A outdid Tacuara, though, in terms of murdering "enemies."

Unlike Tacuara, the Triple A had the implicit blessing of Juan Perón and Isabel Perón and was directed by Perón's personal secretary, José López Rega. In this way, the Triple A was more like Uriburu's *Legión Cívica Argentina* of the 1930s and the ALN during Perón's first administration in the 1940s and 1950s. After Perón's return to power in 1973, the Triple A would become a para-state organization.

There was nothing new about General Perón having ties to a nacionalista organization; he never hesitated to use right-wing groups for his personal benefit, and the para-state work of the ALN from 1945 to 1955 was a reflection of that early Peronist trait. In his meeting with Joe Baxter at his house in Madrid in 1964, General Perón seemed to have been interested in forging with Baxter another bond of this type. Perón is said to have requested that Baxter, 23 years old at the time, assassinate the Peronist trade union leader Augusto Timoteo Vandor, who was interested in leading a Peronism without Perón. Baxter did not accept the assignment. When Vandor was murdered in 1969, the crime was never solved. In any case, in relation to the interview between Perón and Baxter, journalists Alejandra Dandan and Silvina Heguy have pointed out how important fascism was to the dialogue between the general and the young revolutionary. When Baxter walked into Perón's office, he was greeted by a portrait of Mussolini. Perón told Baxter that he had read Tacuara writings and was particularly impressed by an article that praised Mussolini and his fascist regime. He also related that he had visited Italy during the fascist period and been impressed by the fascist organization of the state as well as by Mussolini's writings.

"Baxter didn't respond to the comment and the conversation strayed towards Argentine politics. It is said that, after Baxter's first visit with Perón, Campos [Perón's aide at the time] was the one who remarked, 'Pardon me, General, but these kids read more Mao than Mussolini.' The next day, Baxter found something different on Perón's desk. Amidst his papers was a new portrait, one of the Chinese leader."[83]

Apocryphal or not, Baxter told everyone the anecdote when he returned to Buenos Aires.[84] It certainly reflects a feature of Perón's populist leadership, namely, covering his bases by betting on all political options. This strategy would grow increasingly dangerous, though, in the context of a Peronism that included armed organizations on the right and the left. The slaughter of more than one hundred people in Ezeiza in 1973 upon

Perón's return to the country demonstrated that the Triple A had become the principal enemy of the Peronist left. Police captain Alberto Villar—who had received American counterinsurgency training in Panama and later that year would become Buenos Aires police commissioner—was one of the minds behind the terrorist organization.[85] According to *Nunca Más* (The Argentine Truth Commission Report), Peregrino Fernández, a member of the Buenos Aires police department and collaborator with the ministry of interior during the dictatorship, had stated that Villar recommended reading, for example, "the works of Adolph Hitler and other Nazi and fascist writers."[86]

According to former general Jorge Rafael Videla, Perón was the real leader of the Triple A. The executioner and planner was José López Rega.[87] López Rega was the private secretary of Perón; after Perón became the Argentine president for the third time in 1973, López, or *El Brujo* (The Sorcerer), became the minister for social welfare and Perón's right hand in the national cabinet.[88] The paranoia about a synarchic communist and capitalist conspiracy that was fighting, according to López Rega, "the advance of National Socialism [*Socialismo nacional*]" was also present in fascist and neofascist circles during those years. For example, in 1973, Rosas and Perón were praised in "Peronist" Tacuara's speeches and debates. At the same time, participants conflated Judaism, Zionism, and "*sinarquía.*"[89] The elimination of perceived and actual opponents of the Peronist administration was the main task that Lopez Rega personally assigned to his Triple A warriors.[90]

Father Meinvielle's beliefs clearly influenced the ideological ruminations of "The Sorcerer," López Rega.[91] Perón himself also seemed to be attached to this ideology. General Perón said in 1972: "From 1946 to 1955, we liberated the country. No one stuck their nose in our business without getting what they deserved. This is a sovereign country. But the international synarchism run out of the United Nations, [a synarchism] that here has operated at the juncture of communism and capitalism, [worked] against this liberated country. Zionism also played a part. As did Freemasonry and, unfortunately, the Church."[92] The following year, a majority of Argentines elected him president of the country.

With Perón and "The Sorcerer" in power, the Triple A became a paramilitary organization of the populist Peronist administration. To be sure, the constant struggle between different segments of Peronism from right to left were reproduced in the national cabinet, in unionism, and in the growing tension between the leader and the Montonero organization. But it is also clear that the Triple A eventually got the upper hand. Especially after Perón's death in 1974 and the subsequent presidency (1974–1976) of his third wife, Isabel Perón, López seemed to be one of the most powerful figures in Argentine politics. Links between the Triple A and the security forces were often symbiotic, and after Lopez's ouster from government, they were not dissolved.[93] Here and elsewhere the trajectory of the fascist idea in Argentina is a central explanation of these links that transcended administrations and civilian and military leaders.

The ideology of the Triple A was clearly clerico-fascist, as had been the case of all other nacionalista formations in the past, from the uriburistas to the Tacuaras. For the Triple A, Argentina was essentially Catholic and thus any perceived opposition to Christ was clearly against the country. They stated, "Argentina is God."[94]

More than Tacuara, the Triple A differed from the nacionalismo that preceded it in its striking ability to murder; in ideological terms, the differences were less striking. Though the influence of American and French doctrines of national security and counterinsurgency as well as Perón's own "theories" about synarchism were relatively new, the long-standing Argentine fascist notion of the domestic enemy persisted. As the Triple A's mouthpiece openly stated, "Only the elimination of the enemy would grant us victory...the best enemy is the dead enemy." [95]

Anti-Semitism was a key component of the Triple A's ideological formation, connected to its anticommunism and the notion of the eternal enemies of nacionalismo. Members of the Triple A called for a pogrom of Argentine Jews.[96] They also advocated for the concentration and physical extermination of gays and lesbians. They considered homosexuality to be part of an imaginary Marxist plan against Argentina. They also regarded gays as agents of the CIA.[97] The Triple A's obsession with the sexuality of individuals, and its related anxieties vis-à-vis traditional forms of bourgeois respectability, was featured in its devaluation of psychoanalysis into a conflation of Freud, Judaism, and perversion. To put it simply, like their predecessors from the 1930s, they saw sexuality as a primary tool of the imagined Jewish-Marxist-capitalist conspiracy. In this context, Freudian psychoanalysis was "against the doctrine of God." It linked the revolution of the left with sexuality and occultism.[98] This conflation of fascism, magic, and the sacred clearly had a clerico-fascist genealogy.

The distinctive "esoteric" ideology of the Triple A represented in Tomás Eloy Martínez's fictional account, *The Perón Novel*, which traces López Rega's ideology and the travails of an ignorant foot soldier, presents an inaccurate image of the Triple A.[99] The Triple A featured a mixture of criminality and ideology typical of Tacuara. In addition, it also valued violent actions for their own sake. As was also the case with Tacuara, the Triple A had an ideology of its own that was clearly based in nacionalista ideological premises. It was a neofascist political organization embedded in the state and clearly belongs to the history of the fascist idea in Argentina.

Not only were members of the Triple A former nacionalistas but they were also, more specifically, former Tacuaras. Felipe Romeo, Triple A's main organic intellectual, had been a known Tacuara who even among Tacuaras was considered to be on the far right. Among the Tacuaras, Romeo was apparently nicknamed "Hitler's widow" because of his intense fixation on the Nazi legacy and his constant need to mourn the loss of Nazi Berlin.[100] Romeo was 28 years old when he became the director of the organization's "house organ," the magazine El Caudillo.

The other "intellectuals" of the Triple A's flagship journal were José Miguel Tarquini, another former Tacuara, and the nacionalista poet Gabriel Ruiz de los Llanos. Ruiz de los Llanos was the author of a dubious poem dedicated to his "unforgettable Fuhrer" in which he told a German Nazi acquaintance living in Argentina that their fight had been and was the fight of nacionalismo. The Triple A emphasized the notion of Peronism as clearly rooted in Argentina's fascist nacionalista traditions. With a nacionalista twist on Mussolini's famous dictum, they claimed "Perón is always right."[101]

For these nacionalistas, Argentina and nacionalismo were the ideological orphans left behind by the Nazis. The title of the Triple A's flagship journal was an obvious reference to caudillismo and to Perón, Rosas, and the revisionist historical legacies of nacionalismo.[102] Marking the continuity with the nacionalista tradition that preceded it, El Caudillo had a "Tacuara" symbol on its front page. The editorial offices of the magazine functioned as arsenal and meeting place for the terrorists of the Triple A. The journal regularly published a list of enemies, many of whom were subsequently assassinated by the organization. El Caudillo received extensive official advertising from the Peronist administration as well as from mainstream Peronist unions. In 2008, an Argentine federal court charged the Triple A and El Caudillo with carrying out "a generalized or systematic attack against the civilian population." This attack was "executed by an illegal organization that had been conceived within a sector of the state. This organization had the aim of clandestinely persecuting…political opponents."[103]

The Triple A was influenced by the French experience of repression in Algeria and by the US doctrine of national security. It also had conspicuous connections to Italian neofascists as well as members of the French OAS and Spanish Francoism.[104] Argentine nacionalismo was, nonetheless, the natural course of the river of blood opened up by the Triple A.[105] In cultural terms, Perón's administration and the administration of Isabel Perón, which succeeded it in 1974, encouraged the return of nacionalismo to the university and subsidized nacionalista publications like *El Caudillo*.

Unlike Tacuara or classic interwar nacionalismo, the Triple A was entirely Peronist. It also was deeply linked with right-wing Peronist unions and fascist Peronist intellectuals as well as with active members of the armed forces. And it was explicitly situated against left-wing Peronism, including the guerrilla Montoneros. The death of Perón in July 1974 eliminated once and for all the ambiguities of a Peronist government that had never fully embraced the right, although when Perón vociferously expelled the urban Peronist left guerrilla Montoneros from Plaza de Mayo on May 1, 1974, he seemed to identify violence exclusively with the left. At the time, Perón was still annoyed by the Montoneros' killing of his close political operative, union leader José Rucci, the previous year. Some days later, the Triple A killed Father Carlos Mugica, a recognized leftist priest. The symbolic connotations of this situation were clearly recognized by the Montoneros themselves. Facing Perón that day when he expelled them from the plaza, members of the Peronist left sang and asked Perón to fire Comisario Villar and other members of the Peronist right. They also sang that "if Evita were alive, she would be a Montonera." At one point in his speech, Perón referred to those singing as "those stupid [people] that are shouting." That same day Perón claimed that violence came from abroad, from "agents of chaos" who resented his fight against "colonialism."[106]

When she became president of Argentina Isabel Perón was the formal leader of the Triple A and, in that sense, became the world's first female leader of a fascist organization. As *The New York Times* put it, "The Spirit of Fascism Lives in Mrs. Perón's Regime."[107]

Isabel Perón stated that our "people are faithful to the doctrine that emanates from the clear and Christian thought of General Perón, the father of the Third World." She also warned about the "infiltration" of man himself through "the ideological contamination, of the imperialism of culture."[108] To fight this "contamination," she named the Peronist nationalist Oscar Ivanissevich, Minister of Education in 1974, and she made Alberto Ottalagano head of the Universidad de Buenos Aires.

Ivanissevich believed that the country was in a state of national emergency. This situation was used to promote strikes and general instability at the educational level. The "incitation to disorder" was promoted by those "psychopaths," "perturbed," and "drug addicts" who wanted "to replace our flag with the red rag." For this reason the minister thought that a teachers' strike was anathema. He believed that teachers were surrogate mothers for the students and rhetorically wondered whether mothers were allowed to go on strike.[109]

Ottalagano was a known nacionalista and anti-Semite, a former student of Jordán B. Genta, an admirer of Uriburu and Lugones, and a former member of the nacionalista movement in the 1930s and 1940s. He defined his group of nacionalistas as "Catholic fascists." Later on Ottalagano became a Peronist, insofar as he considered Peronism to be an authentic popular expression of nacionalista ideology.[110]

While other members of Ivanissevich's team branded the Education Minister's campaign towards the "depolitization" of universities a "crusade," Ottalagano compared his actions as university president with the "impetus of Hitler's Panzer Division."[111] He considered Argentina as "the only country in the world where the working class is vaccinated against Marxism." For him, Peronism was the substance of the inoculated vaccine. Perón, the university president argued, had based his power in three legitimate sources: the unions, the Catholic Church, and the armed forces. In typical Argentine fascist fashion, Ottalagano asserted in 1974, "this is the moment to be with Christ or against him." If there was any doubt about what this meant, Ottalagano—who had his personal guard of armed henchmen linked to the Triple A and Tacuara—clarified: "[W]e Christians possess the truth and we do not share it. The rest do not have it, and we shall treat them accordingly." These statements were inspired by traditional nacionalista ideology but they created a radically novel, murderous outcome.[112]

As the university president stated, the Triple A was not shy about its aims. In opposing the enemy, Triple A members even reconceived the Christian tradition. Rather that turning the other cheek to enemies, they threatened them with death and "disappearance."[113] The Triple A saw the university as a central battleground that had been taken by the "anti-patria."[114]

Ottalagano chose his collaborators in accordance with the tenets of Cold War nacionalismo, as shown by the case of Juan Martín Ciga Correa, Ottalagano's "security chief." Nicknamed "Christ," Ciga Correa, a former

Tacuara member, had collaborated with Augusto Pinochet's Chilean intelligence agency, the DINA, in its repression. In particular, DINA received information from Ciga Correa regarding the activities of Chilean students at the University of Buenos Aires.[115]

At the University of Buenos Aires Ottalagano designated Manuel Sánchez Abelenda, a priest and writer from the fascist journal *Cabildo*, as dean of the College of Philosophy and Letters. Sánchez Abelenda, a disciple of Father Julio Meinvielle, walked the classrooms with an olive branch and tried to exorcise from them the spirits of Freud, Marx, and Piaget. With his colleague and dean of the College of the Hard Sciences, Raúl Zardini, Abelenda aimed to "expel the demons" from the university. Like Ottalagano, Zardini was also an admirer of fascism, and their ideas were rooted in classic nacionalismo ideas. As Meinvielle had stated, the "mixing of Christianity with Freud and Marx" represented a "fight against the sacred."[116]

In addition to European critical theorists, for the Triple A, Argentine psychoanalysts were at the center of the "synarchical" conspiracy. They were "doctors of deceit" who wanted to "castrate individuals intellectually and morally." Against the textual universe of the left, and its putative strategy of anti-Argentine emasculation, the Triple A asserted that only violence was the "macho" thing to do.[117] Thus, the Triple A joined the designation of Ottalagano and the intellectual and religious campaign against critical theories with manifold terrorist actions inside and outside the university. Ottalagano was instrumental in expelling 1,350 professors. He bluntly told them to "go teach Freud in Paris and Marx in Moscow."[118]

Ottalagano had the full support of the Peronist right, from *El Caudillo* to the Peronist unions. For example workers of the construction union (UOCRA) regarded him as a "soldier of Perón" who was against "Marxists and Yankees." The secretary general of the union, Rogelio Papagno, praised Ottalagano's tenure as a way of "knocking Marxism really hard."[119] For Peronist Senator José E. Caro, Ottalagano's presence at the university represented the "triumph of social order over excess and subversion." In clear nacionalista neo-Hispanic fashion, for most supporters Ottalagano had achieved a "re-conquest of the University."[120]

On November 7, 1974 Isabel Perón's government instituted a state of siege for an indefinite period of time. Generally speaking, government denied the existence of the Triple A—although by 1974 almost every Argentine knew about it. As one member of the national cabinet, Carlos

Ruckauf, then minister of labor, stated, "In my opinion, the country is in a state of war and the whole society must become aware that the enemy is faced with all-out war."[121] The Triple A played an open role in this "war," although the government accepted and enhanced the role of the security forces in the repression of political alternatives as well as the left-wing guerrillas. The state's militarization of politics sought to counteract the specific and illegal violence of the guerrilla movements with a general, systematic, and unlimited violence that was sanctioned by the state apparatus.

In February of 1975, Isabel Perón brought in the army to repress the ERP guerilla movement in the province of Tucumán. As historian Luis Alberto Romero has stated, by then "the genocide was in the works."[122]

After the military coup in 1976, there was no longer a use for the Triple A. Many of its members, who were expert killers, joined paramilitary "task forces" or were given honorary positions in the military. López Rega already had established connections with Admiral Emilio Massera and General Carlos Suárez Mason, two key figures to the dictatorship, and many active members of the military, such as Colonel Mohamed Ali Seineldín, had been involved in the Triple A.[123]

Tallying up the actions of the Triple A presents a unique perspective on the genealogy of the military dictatorship's Dirty War. Between July and September of 1974 there were 220 attacks by the Triple A against its preconceived enemies (almost three per day), including bombings, rapes, 60 assassinations (one every 19 hours), 44 heavily injured and/or raped victims, and 20 kidnappings (one every two days). All in all, from 1973 to 1976, the Triple A executed more than 900 people it deemed enemies, including parliamentarians, journalists, human rights advocates and lawyers, Latin American exiles in Argentina, intellectuals, union representatives, and leftist militants and guerrillas.[124]

With the coup, the newly unemployed Triple A assassins found jobs with the state terrorism. Its intellectuals continued to be active as well. For the extreme right, supporting the dictatorship was almost the natural thing to do. This was how writer and radical Montonero militant Rodolfo Walsh described the relationship between the dictatorship and the extreme right in an open letter to the dictatorship written shortly before he was killed: "The Tres A are today the three wings of the Armed Forces, and the Junta that you preside over is neither the needle on the scale between 'different brands of violence' nor a fair referee between 'two terrorisms,' but rather the very source of terror that has lost its course and can only stammer the discourse of death."[125]

The Argentine fascist legacy was central to the dictatorship's ideology of the state, its "discourse of death." It represents a resounding objectivation of the nacionalista ideology that became tangible in the practice of extermination.

6

State Terrorism

THE IDEOLOGY OF THE ARGENTINE DICTATORSHIP

THE LAST MILITARY dictatorship in Argentina (1976–1983) was many things. Outside its concentration camps it presented the facade of a typical authoritarian state. Within them, however, it was fascist. The legacy of nacionalismo reigned in the camps. Inside of them, the long-standing Argentine tradition of fascist ideology of violence was fully put into practice.

The camps define the legacy of the dictatorial junta. They were not only a metaphor for the dictatorship as a whole, but also a representation of its ideal world, a place where there was no transaction with reality. Here ideology displaced other significant social, political, and cultural distinctions. Within them, there were only victims and perpetrators.

The military juntas systematically kidnapped, tortured, and killed between 10,000 and 30,000 Argentine citizens, as well as people of other European and Latin American nationalities. These killings were not random but carefully planned at the upper levels of the military government. Moreover, in several cases the Argentine military cooperated with other Latin American dictatorships in a transnational plot of kidnapping and murder called the Plan Cóndor, which operated throughout the Southern Cone, including Argentina, Brazil, Chile, Paraguay, and Uruguay.[1]

The words *"desaparecer"* and *"desaparecidos"* (to disappear and the disappeared) became euphemisms for state-sanctioned assassinations of actual and imaginary enemies of the dictatorship. These assassinations were not acknowledged by the state, hence the use of the category of the disappeared who were officially considered as such by the state. In many cases, the victims were confined in concentration camps, tortured, executed, and thrown into the Atlantic Ocean from military airplanes. The ideology that provoked this state violence had Argentine, European, North American, and Latin American roots, especially the theory of national security in its French and American incarnations.[2] Argentines had a long history of appropriating and reformulating theories from both sides of the Atlantic, but the influence of a particular strain of Argentine nacionalista Catholic fascist ideology must be regarded as central. Most of the generals and upper-level officers of the dictatorship had been trained as cadets during the late 1930s and early 1940s, that is, during the apogee of nacionalista ideology in the army which legitimized the "sacred" intervention of the armed forces in politics. As General Luciano Benjamín Menéndez, the leader of the Third Army Corps in the fight against "subversion" put it, "I belong to a military generation that felt at home in the revolution of 1930 and that from cadet to general suffered all the military interventions from 1943 to 1976."[3]

Anti-Semitism, anticommunism, and the idea of the internal enemy as a non-Argentine "Other" were key elements in the ideology of the junta. The perceived enemies were considered to be the personification of the *"anti-patria"* (the anti-homeland) and therefore opposed to the specific Argentine conflation of God and homeland that the military state represented.

This last dictatorship ended a historical cycle that began with General José Felix Uriburu's dictatorship in the early 1930s. Like Uriburu's government, the last dictatorship presented the combination of nacionalista ideology and the free-market economic tradition espoused by the Argentine upper classes. The junta banned political parties and political activities by ordinary citizens. It saw itself as situated beyond politics and reestablished the death penalty for some political crimes.[4] The dictatorship also joined the extreme right and a Catholic hierarchy that was almost totally identified with the ideological projects of that right. In the previous cycle of the extreme right (1932–1976), this ideology was at the service of a nacionalista discourse, and occasionally manifested itself in specific acts of violence, torture, and repression. But in the concentration camps of the dictatorship, ideology became reality itself.

This ideology excelled in the use of a symbolic vocabulary. The criminal actions of the junta were called the "Dirty War" by perpetrators, a term which was later used uncritically by its victims and bystanders alike. It is by no means ironic that the military junta called its regime Proceso de Reorganización Nacional (The Process of National Reorganization).[5] While the "process" was clearly nacionalista in terms of its ideology and the way it "waged" its war and its vision of the enemy, in other aspects it followed a bureaucratic and authoritarian logic like that of the military dictatorships of the sixties and their technocratic and authoritarian defense of the neo-classic form of free-market capitalism.[6]

In political terms, then, the dictatorship's ideology was nacionalista. The apparent disconnect between its economic and political policies created a hybrid model, leading supporters of a free-market economy to accept social repression at the political level, which they believed a necessary complement to a lack of market intervention. This combination of free-market economics and nacionalista politics in the fascist tradition led to unprecedented social repression. The extermination apparatus was often at the service of corporations. Ford and Citibank, for example, collaborated with the disappearance of workers who had been involved in the demands of left-wing trade unions. Guillermo Walter Klein, the right hand of Alfredo Martínez de Hoz, economic minister at the time, would put things in their proper place. He stated quite explicitly that the dictatorship's economic policy was "incompatible with any democratic system and only applicable if backed by a de facto government."[7] Large corporations and international credit institutions supported the dictatorship and its economic plan, as did "developed" countries. In 1976, at a meeting in Chile between Henry Kissinger and Admiral César Guzzetti, Kissinger was perfectly clear on the position of the US government. He told Guzzetti that it was necessary to find a quick "solution" to the problem of the "subversives" before Jimmy Carter took office in 1977.[8] Like the classic variations on fascism that preceded it, the dictatorship was not only a proxy of "big business" or foreign powers.[9]

A product of two strains (free-market economics and clerico-fascist nationalism), this dictatorial hybrid rejected all the populist "social" tendencies of nacionalista ideology and amplified the idea of the enemy through its fanatical and explicit practices. The supporters of the dictatorship only seemed to agree on the idea of the enemy. Mussolini himself had combined these two tendencies (the free-market economics of the establishment and the "social" economics of the proletariat) for almost two decades, after which he decided on social fascism for the Saló Republic from 1943 to 1945. Perón was greatly influenced by Italian fascism and by Argentine nacionalismo. But if Perón's first administration eschewed the more victimizing tendencies of fascism and embraced its social concerns, the dictatorship eschewed those concerns and fully identified with the ideology of free-market capitalism.

The dictatorship enjoyed widespread civilian support. In March of 1976 with the coup, in 1978 with the World Cup, and in 1982 with the Malvinas/

Falklands War, the dictatorship was as popular as Perón's regime had been in the 1940s and early 1950s. The Plaza de Mayo full of thousands of people cheering the war in 1982 was a widely supported ideological operation unique in the history of Argentina.

Fascist regimes advocate first domestic war and then foreign war. In fascist ideology, war is understood as a collective good, a shared source of national regeneration.[10] The fascist legacy is clear on this point and, given the particular Argentine interpretation of fascism in terms of the sacred, this legacy is necessarily conceived of as essentially "Christian." In the Argentine camps one can see a supreme instantiation of this fascist idea of regeneration through violence.

It was in the concentration camps that the dictatorship's nacionalista ideology changed reality and imposed a new reality. If the nacionalistas in the interwar period formulated that the enemy must be tortured with electric shocks, and hurled into the sea, with the dictatorship this discourse was finally made actual.

Enemies of God

The idea of the internal enemy is a key legacy of nacionalismo. The dictatorship appropriated that idea and considered it its logical tradition; it represented both its political culture and primary notion of ideological common sense. That ideology's version of an internal enemy that needed to be expunged from the nation was also carried on from the nacionalista past to the military present.

Like his nacionalista precursors, dictator Jorge Rafael Videla understood this enemy as a challenge to the very idea of the nation: "Because subversion is just that: subversion of the essential values of the national self" (May 25, 1976). Videla promised that the battle against subversion would finally "extirpate" it.[11] As early as 1976, the guerrilla movement had been militarily defeated, thanks to the illegal repression begun during the previous Peronist administration. The fact that its self-named rivals were no longer capable of seizing power was not seen by the military as a contradiction; after all, their nacionalista ideology had a much broader idea of the enemy. For them, the enemy was less a terrorist organization than an idea opposed to God and His Christian Argentina, the Argentina that the military intended to personify. As stated in the military proclamation of the junta that declared the coup: "The Armed Forces have taken control of

the Republic. The entire country must understand the deep and unequivo-
cal meaning of this fact so that collective responsibility and effort support
this endeavor that, in pursuit of the common good, will—with the help of
God—bring the full recuperation of the nation."[12]

In this context, the dictatorship represented the community and its
God. At the same time, the victims personified a general leftist attempt to
eliminate the ideology that sustained the nation. According to this view,
the victims wanted to provoke a "total modification of the Nation's political, social and economic structures according to their materialist, atheist
and totalitarian conception," as General Roberto Viola, the second leader
of the dictatorship, put it in 1977.[13]

Pseudoscientific and pathological ideas abounded in the ideology of
the junta. If the nation was conceived as a physical entity, the enemies,
"international subversives," were seen as a virus that had to be eliminated.
The idea of contamination was presented in television commercials. In
one such ad, Argentina is depicted as a fat cow attacked by a virus or
germs that the cow then kicks to death; later the cow is fattened up by a
gauchito who systematically gives it food. In essence, the cattle and corn-
fields are attacked, and the gaucho's war saves them. The ad ends with the
word "unanimous." The pastoral landscape where this battle takes place
is essentially nacionalista; it has nothing to do with modern Argentina, its
cosmopolitan cities, and its ideas about an ethnic melting pot.

In these types of ads, the idea of the domestic war announced in
the 1930s by fascist clerics was put into practice. The junta was fighting what Videla defined as a "conspiracy against Civilization." It was an
all-or-nothing fight against the subversion that worked against "national
destiny...our faith and lifestyle."[14] In the indoctrination of repressors,
Videla's words on war, extermination, and the Argentine being were constantly repeated.[15]

The idea of an enemy whose only possible fate was death was justified
by the impossibility of restoring the enemy's humanity, especially once
the enemy had to be ideologically consecrated for the nation. As General
Cristino Nicolaides, future commander of the army, said in 1976, "The
enemy who is committed to subversion, who has fought [against us], is, in
my view, a hopeless criminal with no hope of reform." Similarly, Admiral
Massera stated there was no middle ground or the possibility for compromise in the fight against subversion: "there will be winners and there will
be losers."[16] General Antonio Domingo Bussi concurred: "[W]e will not
stop until we kill the last of these cowards"[17] One year later, in May 1977,

General Ibérico Saint Jean, the future governor of Buenos Aires province, explained this expansive conception of the enemies as well as their ultimate fate: "First we will kill all subversives, then we will kill all of their collaborators, then those who sympathize with subversives, then we will kill those that remain indifferent and finally we will kill the timid."[18]

In a typical totalitarian projection, the attack against the enemy was presented as a lethal act of self-defense. Vice-Admiral Armando Lambruschini presented this action as a reassertion of transcendental trans-historical forces. In this context, he dubiously argued that international terrorism had a formidable apparatus of propaganda and "the culprits are presenting themselves as victims."[19] Subversion could not be a truly Argentine enterprise. Its agents were controlled by the external forces of "atheism," as Archbishop of San Juan Monsignor Ildefonso Sansierra put it. This "dirty and infamous war has been imposed on us from abroad," he stated.[20] Brigadier General Orlando Agosti explained the forgetting of "God and the sense of transcendence" was thriving in the international scene. In this context, Videla posed the existence of a conspiracy of "international scale."[21]

To the members of the junta biblical metaphors seemed to be appropriate for the situation. General Viola argued that Argentina had walked a "via crucis." Those "without God and without Patria" had challenged the nation.[22] The choice was clear. Brigadier Agosti opposed "our faith in God, our love for the Patria" against the enemy's "totalitarianism and slavery."[23] General Luciano Benjamín Menéndez concurred. The first reason they were fighting the enemy was "in order to keep on believing in God."[24] Videla claimed that the "guns" had to be used because Argentine "virile traditions" and "our sacred values" had been attacked by "an enemy without faith, without patria and without God." The attacker had to be "annihilated in all its manifestations."[25]

There were no limits to the Dirty War of the military. For Lieutenant Colonel Hugo Ildebrandro Pascarelli, "[T]he history of our land never witnessed a fight similar to the one we are fighting today. This fight does not have ethical or natural limits. It is being fought beyond good and evil."[26] The explanation lay in the sacred nature of the contest. The enemy had committed "the greatest offense against God and against the patria."[27] Pascarelli's boss, General Santiago Omar Riveros, argued that there was no possible redemption for the enemies because they were "traitors without return." In confronting "barbarism," Riveros asked God to protect Argentina's soldiers and its people in "their triumphal march along the paths of Argentineness."[28] All in all, for military repressors like Pascarelli and Riveros it was not only the enemy that had to be sacrificed but also the self. Riveros thought that violent acts were going to justify his own condition as an Argentine soldier. In his thinking, Dirty War fighters were participating in the ultimate form of sacrifice: "[T]he fight will have one limit: the limit of our life in death. This is a sublime paradox where the greatest physical pain which is death is fused with the most precious good of the spirit, which is achieving the ethical aim of meeting with the Supreme good which is God, in his infinite perfection and the eternity of his time."[29]

In the logic of the junta, extreme violent actions of repression became somehow ethical when confronted with the military will to face death. In death the ethical imperatives that were put aside in the fight would apparently re-emerge. This was an outcome that justified the men with guns as the prime makers of a redemptive future. When Massera said that Argentines needed to "take the future by assault," he also told them "we will not fight until death, we will fight until we achieve victory, either beyond or before death."[30]

Death opened the way for a new Argentina of peace, one where, as Videla claimed, "human rights" were being defended with Argentine "blood."[31] The blood of Argentine soldiers was sacrificed for God. As General Leopoldo Fortunato Galtieri explained: "[W]hen terrorist criminals attacked the soil of the homeland, it was the blood of heroes and martyrs, civilians and military that redeemed the Argentine people before God."[32]

In a sense the self and the enemy became sacrificial objects. They were distinct sources of national redemption. The enemy's death especially was both justifiable and served to justify ideology.[33] This is what Hugo Vezzetti understands to be the criminalization of the state which, in the name of Christian faith and civilization, "consecrated the redemptive power of violence." Many would have to die, Videla prophesied in 1975, for the nation to be at peace.[34] The notion that the criminal acts of repression and murder were in fact a "holy war" was tightly bound to the idea of purifying sacrifice. Priests like the Archbishop of Paraná, Victorio Bonamín, justified the repression, calling it "a blood bath" and maintaining that the function of the Army was to "atone for our country's impurity."[35]

The idea of the army as a political instrument of the will of God was repeated by the director of the *Escuela Superior de Guerra* (Army War College), General Juan Manuel Bayón, in his 1978 essay, "*Lo nacional. El*

Nacionalismo." As chief of the Operations Department of the Army 5th Cuerpo in 1976, General Bayón oversaw the "unit of combat against subversion" and was one of the key planners of clandestine repression and disappearances in Patagonia. According to Bayón, God did not believe in democracy. Nor did he approve of populism. What he wanted was government by those who were, supposedly, best fit: "Populism is radically subversive: it violates the natural and Christian order of society and the State; it turns all social hierarchies upside down, elevating the lowest levels....As the Church teaches...power or political sovereignty comes from God, but does not descend to those who cannot exercise it. Hence, the people, materially considered a mass of individuals, are not, due to their ineptitude, the first, nor the second, holder of power." Bayón concluded, "There is a theological reason for the convergence of Plutocracy and Communism, and that is their agreement on atheism, their negation of Christ and of his divine redemption." The struggle against atheism was only as genuine as nacionalismo, since "when that nacionalismo or reaction is pure, it leads to a politics of Truth, Sacrifice and Hierarchy."[36]

Widely shared by his colleagues, the root of General Bayón's thinking lies in nacionalismo and in the great Argentina "promised" by God to Argentine fascists in the 1930s and 1940s. As early as 1976, Bonamín thought he was shedding light on that promise, bluntly adding that, "It was written, it was in God's plans, that Argentina not lose its grandeur, which was protected by its natural guardian, the Army." Figures like Bonamín were the theoretical and spiritual leaders of the military's repression, as Father Meinvielle and company had been in earlier decades.

In 1976, dictatorship intellectuals like Mariano Grondona presented this alliance between God and the army as a possible response to the abyss: "What would become of Argentina without the Sword and the Cross? Who would want to go down in history as the one who deprived Argentina of either one of these two? Argentina is Catholic and military. There is, in these times, no greater responsibility than safeguarding that connection between the Church and the Army."[37]

Grondona's thinking reflected the sense of imminent catastrophe that nationalism saw in secularism and democracy. This logic is based on an ideological dichotomy between the secular and the sacred. It is equally symptomatic of an apocalyptic ideology that merged religion and politics, and promised redemption through the destruction of anyone who thought otherwise. For Bonamín, the struggle in Argentina was between "atheistic materialism and Christian humanism." It was a struggle for a politically nationalistic Argentina as well as for "its altars." It was "a struggle in defense of God. That's why I ask for divine protection in this dirty war in which we are embroiled."[38]

The defense of legal short cuts and violations of human rights is not surprising considering the history of Argentina. In 1996, Nobel Laureate Adolfo Pérez Ezquivel would recall, "The Archbishop of Paraná province, Monsignor Adolfo Tortolo...justified torture, except the use of electric shocks," which he deemed a waste of electricity. The archbishop worked in tandem with famous nacionalistas. Father Ezcurra, who had been the leader of the fascist anti-Semitic organization Tacuara, was the monsignor's private secretary.[39]

Clerical fascism was an active part of the dictatorial repression. Admirers of Meinvielle, like the priest Christian Von Wernich, actively took part in torture sessions. In his testimony, the prisoner Luis Velasco recalls that, "I once heard Christian Von Wernich tell a detainee who begged for his life that the life of men depends on God and your collaboration...." On another occasion, Von Wernich told a repressor that disappearing the enemy "was a patriotic act that God knew was for the good of the country."[40]

Like Von Wernich, many other members of the Church were actively involved in the repression. Monsignor Emilio Grasselli, secretary of the military vicariate, kept files with information on the disappeared. He presented victims' relatives with fictionalized versions of the concentration camps as well as with an ideological defense of the dictatorship that justified the death of those who could not be reformed or saved.[41]

The bishop of Jujuy province, Monsignor Medina, also visited the camps: "I remember that during my stay at the Penitentiary [*Penal de Villa Gorriti—Jujuy*], the Bishop of Jujuy, Monsignor Medina, gave mass. In his sermon, he said that he knew what was going on, but that it was all for the good of the Homeland. He said that the military was doing the right thing, and that we should tell everything we knew, to which end he would receive confessions."[42]

What that bishop did for perpetrators in Jujuy was not exceptional. In almost all cases, the Church hierarchy supported the "holy war" that the dictatorship took to its final consequences. Only four prelates of the 84 members of the Episcopal Conference publicly condemned the illegal repression; generally speaking, the Church actively and publicly supported it.[43] As human rights advocate Emilio Mignone maintains, this support was based on the intellectual background of most Argentine bishops and on the belief that the military dictatorship constituted a last line of defense against global communism. For Mignone, "there were two tightly bound tendencies in the thinking of most of the Church hierarchy: traditionalism and the ideology of national Catholicism." Mignone maintains that, though the difference between the two blurred in practice, they were distinct. Mignone describes "national Catholicism" as the "notion that Christianity should encompass State structures, and Catholicism becomes a sort of national religion. Like Religion and the King in earlier times, Religion and the Homeland—both in capital letters—merge. Not accepting Catholicism and its prayers…means being a bad Argentine." [44]

The idea of the bad Argentine lasted for decades. The bad Argentine that did not conform to the mores of nationalism and religion was potentially an internal enemy. In 1977, the archbishop of La Plata, Monsignor Antonio Plaza, stated that the victims of the dictatorship were "bad Argentines who leave the country, work against the homeland from abroad with the support of dark forces…in concert with others who work secretly within our territory." The archbishop was unambiguously identified with the dictatorship and its politics of victimization. "We pray for a favorable outcome to the arduous task of those who spiritually and temporally govern us. May we be the children of a Nation in which the Church enjoys a respect unknown in all condemnable Marxist countries." [45] Later, in 1983, Plaza would justify the dictatorship's actions and defend the need for a law of military self-amnesty which he called "evangelical." Plaza supported "reconciliation," understood as a free pass for the perpetrators. "Throughout the world and its tradition, amnesty laws have never been a bad thing. They quiet the spirits. This should not become our version of Nuremberg, where we look for and kill people and commit so many irregularities, even taking away poor Eichmann." [46]

Plaza called the trial of the Argentine perpetrators "Nuremberg inside out," a "bunch of junk," "where the criminals are judging those who defeated terrorism." [47] According to many witnesses, Monsignor Plaza visited several concentration camps during the dictatorship, which was common for many Argentine priests in those years.

The Church in Argentina had an almost organic relationship with disappearing individuals. Indeed, in many cases the Catholic hierarchy knew about these disappearances and could have stopped them from occurring—though it usually did not—especially when those kidnapped were priests. As journalist Horacio Verbitsky states, "Adolfo Servando Tortolo, then president of the Episcopal Conference and the military Vicar, requested that, before arresting a priest, the Armed Forces inform the appropriate Bishop." Verbitsky cites the work of Mignone: "[S]ometimes the green light was given by the Bishops themselves. On May 23, 1976 the Marine Infantry detained priest Orlando Yorio in the Bajo Flores section of Buenos Aires and 'disappeared' him for five months. One week before his arrest, Archbishop Aramburu had withdrawn Yorio's license for no apparent reason. Several things that Yorio heard during his captivity make it clear that the Armed Forces interpreted that decision and, perhaps, some criticism from his superior in the Jesuit Society, Jorge Bergoglio, as authorization to take action against him. Most certainly, the military had warned both Aramburu and Bergoglio of the supposed danger that Yorio posed."[48]

The basis for this "danger," which was apparently accepted by Bergoglio, who would become the senior cardinal of Argentina and later Pope Francis I, rested on a notion accepted by most bishops: any condemnation of human rights violations was a threat to the homeland and God. That is, most Argentine bishops either actively or passively, and in public, accepted the actions of the dictatorship. The dictatorship understood these actions as part of a common Christian undertaking against the "atheistic subversion," whose justification was ecclesiastical and whose actions were military. In March of 1977, Admiral Massera clearly summed up this connection between the secular and the sacred: "When we act as a political power, we do not cease to be Catholics; when Catholic priests act as a spiritual power, they do not cease to be citizens. Pretending that both are infallible, as well as their judgment and decisions, would be sinfully arrogant. We all act on the basis of love, which is the sustenance of our religion. We don't have any problems and our relationship is optimal, as it should be among Christians."[49]

Like in the previous instantiations of "Christianized fascism," the intimacy between God and its military nation was highly emphasized.[50] The foot soldiers of the repression shared this sort of sacred sentiment, which was at the root of the Argentine reformulation of fascist ideology conceived in the 1930s and 1940s. It seems that the torturers proved their loyalty to the Cross and the Sword by shouting, while performing kidnappings, "For God and the Homeland!" During one of the kidnappings, the perpetrators wrote on the walls of the victim's home, "Long Live Christ The King" and "Christ Saves." The nacionalistas' idea that they were God's envoys on earth was constantly repeated in the camps. They forced prisoner Nora Iadarola, for example, to repeat "five hundred times" the following phrase from the nacionalista liturgy, "Long live Videla, Massera and Agosti! God, the Homeland and the Home!" The mandatory repetition of this nacionalista principle by the victim did not represent clerico-fascist ideology but rather its actualization. It was the ultimate realization of the legacy of the fascist idea in Argentina.

Death and Ideology

The dictatorship's nacionalista theories were by no means original. Long-standing arguments were constantly repeated. The Cross and the Sword continued to articulate the idea of the nation. However, the exterminatory practice took on new meanings, broadening its ideology and turning itself into an ideological postulation. The means became an end. In short, practice became a central element of the theory of the dictatorship. Massive torture, violence, and death were sources of national ideological regeneration.

If the Nazi practices of total extermination are compared with those of the dictatorship, the quantitative and even "qualitative" differences are more significant than the similarities. Nonetheless, unlike other totalitarian regimes, the Argentine military and the Nazis were both fascinated by secrecy and used a language of extermination that was rich in euphemisms. This was not a chance occurrence but rather the product of a chosen affinity.

Among the most unique of the Argentine extermination practices was the stealing of children, which apparently did not take place in European fascist regimes. Nunca Más (the truth commission report) describes it like this: "The repressors who seized the children of the disappeared from their homes and from mothers during delivery determined the fate of those creatures as coldly as if they were dispensing with war booty."[51]

The idea of war booty enabled the military to take "disappearance" one step further. If the victim loses his or her identity through degrading and dehumanizing torture, that situation culminates in the ultimate sacrifice of identity as represented in death via disappearing. For Videla, the unreality of the disappeared ensured that the military would own the prisoners' fate even in death: "The disappeared are just that, disappeared. They are neither alive nor dead; they are disappeared."[52]

Children born in captivity are also, in a certain way, disappeared insofar as they do not know and hence continue to embody the theft of the biological identity of their dead parents. The theft of the identity of the children of the disappeared ensures a distorted memory of the military camps, a memory in keeping with how the military would like them to be represented. Children as war booty represent the military's attempt to ignore a past bound to the lost identity of parents; they ensure the perpetrators an ideological victory in the realm of memory for generations. In this sense, the memory policies of the extreme right, which after 1983 were continued under democracy, started in the camps themselves. This is not an Argentine particularity. If the Nazis, for example, destroyed any trace of their victims by destroying the memory of the family unit, the Argentine dictatorship was satisfied with the physical sacrifice of parents and the appropriation of their children's identity.

The Argentine camps, then, were factories of invented identities fueled by torture. As indicated in testimonies on the concentration camp at the *Escuela Superior de Mecánica de la Armada* (ESMA): "...when we arrived at ESMA, we saw many women on the ground, on mats, awaiting the birth of children. Some were from [camps in] other branches of the Armed Forces (the Air Force, the Federal Police, the Córdoba Army, the Mar del Plata Navy). Others were 'from' ESMA." Taking away children, which ensured that those with "no hope of reform" would receive the ultimate punishment—mainly, knowing that their children would not know that they had been their parents—was organized according to very clear and systematic guidelines. The efficacy of these operations was cause for pride among the perpetrators, who perhaps, through the deformation of Christian values accomplished by the ideology of Catholic nacionalismo, considered them acts of Christian charity: "The then director of ESMA, Captain Rubén Jacinto Chamorro, personally accompanied visitors, generally high-ranking members of the Navy, showing them where pregnant prisoners were housed. He bragged of the 'Sardá' (which is the most important maternity hospital in Buenos Aires) set up in the camp."[53]

Generally, the new "parents" were chosen from among the groups that supported the dictatorship. As so effectively depicted in the films *The Official Story* (1985) and *Captive* (2003), these were people with ideological, religious, and/or financial ties to the military. Victims' testimonies indicate that "at the Naval Hospital there was a list of Navy couples that could not have children who would be willing to adopt children of the disappeared."[54] The sacrifice of the victims was the ideological reward for those parents willing to receive children coming out of the disaster and offer them a deformed version of family love.

The connection between the nacionalista myth and reality was often tenuous. In the case of the children appropriated by the dictatorship, the secret ideological mark was to be imposed for generations. Since they did not know their true identities, these children were the true products of the camps.

While justifying disappearances and the stealing of children, nacionalismo glorified fascist ideas that often determined who lived and who died. Outside the camps this ideology of death took on another form, attempting to adapt to a society that could engage in racism in daily practice but did not tolerate an explicit articulation of racist ideas. Society at large preferred silence. For those who wanted to see it, what was going on inside the camps was clear. If nacionalista ideology was the xenophobic product of a country undergoing radical transformations, largely due to the arrival of European immigrants, the words of General Albano Harguindeguy, minister of the interior under the dictatorship, on the need to continue immigration out of racial concerns can only be understood from this historical perspective. In 1978, Harguindeguy spoke of the need to encourage European immigration. For the general, this was an urgent concern in order "to continue to be one of the three whitest nations in the world."[55] This explicit racism took the form of an open recognition of the need to eradicate other "non-European" expressions of the nation. The depth and scope of this desire was, once again, manifested in the camps.

Anti-Semitism and the Radical Other

Racism was a critical component of the camps. Prisoner Sergio Starik recalls that one detainee "was beaten more, and they told him it was because he was dark skinned...and they shouted 'negro de mierda' at him."[56] Racism was also linked to a sexualized image of the enemy; the enemy was generally defined as sexually heterodox, whether as heterodox women and/or prostitutes or homosexual men. On occasion, male prisoners were forced to dress like women. Insults were common as their bodies served as ideological metaphors. In 1984, the Dyszel family published a condemnation of the disappearance of their son in the newspapers, and the response they received from one perpetrator was symptomatic of this ideology as a whole:

Jewish bastard: I am one of the people who killed your WORTHLESS PIECE OF SHIT of a son and your whore of a DAUGHTER-IN-LAW.

There are now 2 FEWER JEWISH ZIONISTS IN THE WORLD. If
you only knew where we had BURIED them!! You would drop dead,
Judío puto.[57]

The crudeness of this communication represents an ideology that
emphasizes the supposed machismo of perpetrators but in no way
allows them to speak openly. The secret must be kept. It would seem
that the perpetrators seek to relive the continuous disappearance of the
victim and the ongoing nature of the resulting trauma. Through the
compulsive repetition of trauma, the perpetrators feel more powerful,
though in some cases they were no longer active. The perpetrator wants
the parents of the victim to suffer the loss as a transcendental absence.[58]
The argument that if the parents knew the truth they would metaphorically die disguises the fact that if the parents actually die the immediacy
of the trauma vanishes, which the perpetrator wants to prevent from
happening. Whereas, for the victim's family, finding out where their
disappeared relative was buried was an important step toward working
through the trauma, for the perpetrator the disappearance of the victim
had to mean constant trauma, and hence the repressor identified the
parent's finding the child's grave with the death of the parent. The message really entails a projection of the killer's desire. It is not the parent
of the victim but rather the perpetrator who would be degraded if the
site of the child's grave was revealed. In the ideological formation of the
perpetrators, the mystery of a disappearance must be a legacy that keeps
the memory of extermination alive, and the perpetrators must project
the disappearance onto the victims' relatives. What for the killers is a
victory over death that must be repeated time and again is for the relatives an open wound that the killers do not want to heal.

In 1981, Jacobo Timerman wrote about his experience in the Argentine
concentration camp system. Timerman had been illegally kidnapped by
Argentine military personnel in 1977 and was subsequently tortured in
three clandestine camps and held in two prisons. After intense international pressure, in 1979 the Argentine dictatorship stripped Timerman of
his Argentine citizenship and deported him to Israel.[59] Timerman emphasizes the centrality of anti-Semitism to the Argentine dictatorship.[60]
Argentina did not experience genocide in the classical sense but the concentration camp experiences of Argentine Jews had genocidal dimensions.
Outside the camps, Argentine Jews were not targeted for being Jewish, but
once inside the camps the situation changed. The main reason behind

this state antisemitism inside the camps was rooted in the Argentine traditions of fascist ideology. Timerman was the first to make explicit this central dimension of dictatorial anti-Semitism. [61] His writing on his experiences first appeared in *The New Yorker* and American liberal intellectuals and newspapers broadly supported him. For pundits on the American right, Timerman was "irresponsible and dishonest." For American conservative pundit Irving Kristol, "though Anti-Semitism may be rife in certain segments of Argentinean society the government has been doing—and is doing—its best to render it ineffectual." Kristol concluded, "Jews in Argentina today lead lives that are not very much more nervous or fearful than those of non-Jews." He claimed that "Mr. Timerman and his left-wing associates" were criticizing a Republican administration that was trying to move the Argentine dictatorship "towards greater liberalization."[62]

Former Secretary of State Henry Kissinger believed, "There is no doubt that there are many anti-Semitic trends in Argentina, but not in the Nazi sense." For Kissinger the lack of a Nazi dimension to Argentine anti-Semitism somehow downplayed Timerman's point about the centrality of anti-Semitism in Argentina. Argentine human rights advocate, progressive Catholic thinker Emilio Mignone was visiting New York during the affair and he simply stated that "Timerman has told the total truth." Mignone explained that, "All political prisoners or dissidents have a hard time of it when they are arrested, but the Jews suffer more than the others. They get the worst beatings, the crudest torture, the vilest insults. The important thing about Timerman is that he spoke up; that is the best policy in facing a repressive regime."[63]

In Argentina, Mignone represented a notable exception. While mainstream conservative commentators in the United States sought to downplay Timerman's book as an "exaggeration," in Argentina the book's contention that the military dictatorship put forward an anti-Semitic program was met with either silence or anti-Semitic attacks.[64]

Most testimonies concur with Timerman's account. While she was being tortured, the Argentine Jewish citizen Nora Strejilevich could hear the perpetrators "assuring her that 'the problem of subversion' was their primary concern, but 'the Jewish problem' was followed in importance, and they were archiving information." Miriam Lewin, who was held in a concentration camp of the Argentine air force, remembers that inside the camp, "The general attitude was of deep-rooted anti-Semitism. On one occasion they asked me if I understood Yiddish. I replied that I did not, that I only knew a few words. They nevertheless made me listen to a cassette they had obtained by tapping telephones. The speakers were apparently Argentine business-men of Jewish origin, talking in Yiddish. My captors were most interested in finding out what the conversation was about.... They collected the informa-tion obtained in files, including in them the names and addresses of people of Jewish origin, plans of synagogues, sports clubs, businesses, etc....The only good Jew is a dead Jew, the guards would say." [65]

The military concern over Jewish activities in Argentina had its ori-gins in long-standing conspiracy theories of Argentina's fascist ideology. Timerman recalled later that he was accused of being a leading member of the Argentine section of the Jewish conspiracy.[66]

The zigzagging, and often opaque, connections between anti-Semitism, authoritarianism, and the Argentine state ran through an array of dis-courses and practices in twentieth-century Argentina, from what is called the Tragic Week of 1919 to fascists and Catholic nacionalistas, and from Uriburu's dictatorship to the concentration camps of the 1970s.

Timerman argues that from the point of view of the perpetrators, torturing Jews was complemented by a sense of elation. With prisoners in general the perpetrators made clear that they wanted to destroy them mentally and physically, but "with Jews, however, there was a desire to eradicate. Interrogating enemies was a job; but interrogating Jews was a pleasure or a curse. Torturing a Jewish prisoners always yielded a moment of entertainment to the Argentine security forces, a certain pleasurable, leisurely moment."[67]

Timerman signals the central role of jokes and physical degradation in the Argentine concentrations camps. The two were intrinsically linked. As several testimonies show, the dictatorship literally inscribed anti-Semitic discourse in the bodies of the victims. Different forms of torture were used in order to establish in physical terms the ideologically proposed ani-mality of Jewish corporality.

Former inmate Pedro Miguel Vanrell remembers that there was a Jewish prisoner at the camp of Club Atlético, "[a perpetrator] would make him wag his tail, bark like a dog, lick his boots. It was impressive how well he did it, he imitated a dog as if he really were one, because if he did not satisfy the guard, he would carry on beating him.... Later he would change and make him be a cat....There Julían, the Turk, always carried a key ring with a swastika and wore a crucifix round his neck. This character would take money from the relatives of Jewish prisoners."[68]

Daniel Eduardo Fernández, who was a prisoner at the same camp, recalls that while he was being tortured, "They continually went on at me as to whether I knew any Jewish people, friends, shopkeepers, anybody, as long as they were of Jewish origin....There was a torturer there they called Kung-Fu, who would practice martial arts on three or four people at a time—they would always be prisoners of Jewish origin—who were kicked and punched."[69]

Fernandez continues, "Jews were punished simply because they were Jewish. They would be told that the DAIA (the Argentine Jewish umbrella organization) and international Zionism subsidized subversion, and that the organization of the *pozos* [holes/camps] was financed by ODESSA [an international group which supports Nazism]....All kinds of torture would be applied to Jews, especially one which was extremely sadistic and cruel: the rectoscope, which consisted of inserting a tube into the victim's anus, or into a woman's vagina, then letting a rat into the tube. The rodent would try to get out by gnawing at the victim's internal organs."[70]

This torture reinforced the supposed dirtiness and animality of the Jewish victims. It is not surprising that most testimonies regarding these practices are from non-Jewish witnesses who survived the camps. Most Jewish prisoners did not.

The Nazi example was a source of inspiration for the perpetrators. Delia María Barreda y Ferrando remembers, "One of the military personnel who called himself the Great Führer made the prisoners shout Heil Hitler!, and at night they could frequently hear recordings of Hitler's speeches." [71] In addition, the perpetrators painted the faces of Jewish prisoners with "Hitler moustaches." In several camps Jewish prisoners had to sit down on their knees when facing portraits of Hitler and Mussolini. They also were obliged to insult themselves as Jews. In other camps, they were ordered to say "I love Hitler."[72] Prisoners also had swastikas sprayed on their backs in order to be identified and punished as Jewish.

These acts represented the callous humor prevalent in the Argentine concentration camps. The "joke," of course, was only funny to perpetrators insofar as it presented the bodies of Jewish victims as physical fulfillments of the ideological wish to exterminate them. Inscribing Jewish self-hatred on the bodies of the victims became an example of their total submission.

Timerman points out that when non-Jewish prisoners were tortured, the torturers mockingly spoke of whether they "sang" a "tango" or an "opera": if the torturers did not get much information, they said that the victim had sung a tango. Timerman argues that other "jokes" used the

Nazi gas chambers as the place the Jewish victims were being sent to. The Argentine perpetrators established a transhistorical fascist dialogue of sorts. They normally would tell their Jewish victims, "We'll show the Nazis how to do things."[73]

This sort of humor was connected to favorite nacionalista topics. Due to its supposed lack of heroism and overly emotional nature, the nacionalistas did not value tango as a form of national expression. Similarly, they believed that Argentine nacionalismo was in fact much better than European fascisms due to its direct ties to God, as pointed out by, for example, nacionalista Enrique Osés in his 1941 book *Means and Aims of Nacionalismo*.[74] But what in 1941 had been ideological rhetoric became daily practice in the Argentine concentration camps of the dictatorship.

The perpetrators' identification with the victims was part of a broader sacrificial notion that had been developed by nacionalista ideology in particular, and fascism and Nazism in general. The number of victims is a source of pride and their torture an opportunity for feelings of redemption and regeneration. For the perpetrators the method is justified by the fact that just a select group can "take it" without breaking down. That is, few can accept the logical consequences of the ideological mandate.[75]

In 1943, Heinrich Himmler, the leader of the SS, made reference to this ideological situation before a select group of SS officers in his famous secret speech in Posen: "I am referring here to the evacuation of the Jews, the extermination of the Jewish people. This is one of the things that are easily said: 'The Jewish people are going to be exterminated.'"[76] Himmler highlighted the difference between the discourses of victimization and the actual experience of radically victimizing others. For him the latter was only the privilege of a select few. Referring to the first group of ideological perpetrators, he said, "Of all those who talk like that, not one has seen it happen, not one has had to go through with it. Most of you men know what it is like to see 100 corpses side by side, or 500 or 1,000. To have stood fast through this and except for cases of human weakness to have stayed decent, that has made us hard."[77]

"Decency" was a key element to the Nazi vision of a genocide that was deemed ethical insofar as it obeyed the norms established by the ideology itself. Himmler concluded that, "This is an unwritten and never-to-be-written page of glory in our history, for we know how difficult it would be for us if today under bombing raids and the hardships and deprivations of war we were still to have the Jews in every city as secret saboteurs, agitators, and inciters. If the Jews were still lodged in the body of the German nation, we would probably by now have reached the stage of 1916–17."[78]

In this radical version of fascism, the idea of generating genocide was conceived as a way to preempt national disaster and was justified by the defense of the homeland against its secret enemy. In Argentina, the certainty about the magnitude of the enemy-generated disaster was felt throughout the chain of command. The killers shared the idea that their slaughtering was a milestone in the history of the homeland. General Cristino Nicolaides stated, "We are witnessing the most important chapter in the history of Argentina."[79] Similarly, Brigadier Agosti related the military version of history as being in need of constant reclamation: "the peoples without memory are condemned to constantly suffer the same mistakes."[80] For Nicolaides and Agosti and many others, their own historical significance as actors in the recent events seemed to be evident.

From the perspective of nacionalista ideology, Argentina was the scene of a millenarian struggle between communism and Christianity. A privileged group was not witness to the global struggle against "international subversion" but rather the architect of its practice. A few years later, in an interview granted to María Seoane and Vicente Muleiro, General Videla himself would recall that only a few chosen ones could grasp and accept what society at large could not. Videla explained the existence of a systematic plan for extermination. The truth of the disappearances was the sole property of a group that could neither explain it nor answer questions about what was happening. All they could do was "take it": "No, [open] killings were impossible. Let's take a number, let's say five thousand. Argentine society would not have stood for so many shootings: yesterday two in Buenos Aires, today six in Córdoba, tomorrow four in Rosario, and so on up to 5,000. There was no other way to do it. We all agreed on that."[81]

Trauma, Death, and the Memory of the Holocaust in the Argentine Camps

With the dictatorship, the machinery of death became a symbol of ideological consecration through the degradation of its victims. As in Nazi concentration camps, the need to take ideology to its final consequences explained the drive to humiliate victims. Humiliation was a means to ensure that the logic of the ideology and the dynamic of its practice would be accepted by those who suffered them. The figure of the one who "cracked" became a sign of ideological power. The idea that a person could crack demonstrated that, for the perpetrators, the desired destruction was not only physical, but also part of a need to prevail ideologically.

The majority of the few surviving Jewish prisoners stresses the substantial link between the Holocaust and the Argentine genocidal campaign. To be sure, survivors of other genocides also refer to the Holocaust as a frame of reference. But rather than emphasizing structural issues (namely, historical similarities between the two regimes and their campaigns of extermination), Argentine survivors stress that the perpetrators explicitly made reference to the Holocaust as both something to be emulated and as frame of reference that should be surpassed. The victims, in turn, experienced these events as a displacement of Holocaust memory, which they inevitably conflated with their own traumas.

Alicia Portnoy remembers that, while she was tortured, the military torturers threatened her "with converting me into soap (for I was Jewish)."[82] The Argentine Jewish citizen Pedro Krepplak recalls, "When they were putting pressure on me they would call me 'damned Jew,' swine, and they would also say 'we are taking you to the gas chambers.'" His perpetrators also told Krepplak that "they were going to take me to unknown place and they were going to make soap out of me, in the same way it was done to my brethren in Germany."[83] Nora Strejilevich was told the same: "They threatened me for having uttered Jewish words in the street (my surname) and for being a piece of shit Jew, whom they would make soap out of." Timerman was also told that he was going to be sent to the "gas chambers." [84]

References to the Holocaust (by victims and perpetrators) were symptoms of what could be defined as a transgenerational presence of trauma.[85] The perpetrators exacerbated this trauma insofar as they submitted the victims to a mandatory reenactment of the suffering and losses of their forebears. At the same time, perpetrators repeated the "actions" of their ideological siblings. Their ideological will to present themselves as "continuing" the Holocaust presents a unique type of transhistorical situation where trauma and ideology mutually complement each other. The victims cannot tell whether they are in the concentration camps of the Nazis or the Argentines. They cannot tell the difference between past and present.

Herein lies one of the most singular aspects of the Argentine camps, namely that they were thought to produce the context of the Holocaust in a post-Holocaust world. Although several genocides repeat certain elements of the Holocaust, only in Argentina did perpetrators present their actions of abduction and extermination as a reenactment of the Holocaust.

Reproducing Auschwitz was, of course, an impossible aim, but it nevertheless led perpetrators to historical hyperbole and messianic notions of redemption thought violence and torture. It was their memory of Auschwitz (which they saw as fully positive) that led them to justify their anti-Semitic killings. Timerman was told by one of his captors: "Hitler lost the war. We will win."[86]

From his cell, a victim of the Argentine dictatorship, Adolfo Pérez Esquivel, recalled the transhistorical connections with the Nazi genocide as an ideological particularity of the Argentine camps: "One of the things that really shocked me was [the thought], 'Am I in Argentina or in Nazi Germany?' There was a swastika painted on—almost covering—a large wall, and under it was the word Nationalism written with a Z." Another prisoner, Jorge Reyes, recalls that "When they beat us, they would say 'We are the Gestapo!'" During the torture sessions, the perpetrators would shout, "We are fascists."[87] The figure of Mussolini was in the camps along with that of Hitler, as was the idea of synarchism introduced by Father Meinvielle in the 1960s and later appropriated by the Triple A and Juan Domingo Perón in the 1970s.[88]

In the Argentine concentration camps, the Auschwitz universe was presented as the consecration of a patriotic ideal. If, under the Nazis, Jews could simply not exist for their alleged actions against the Aryan race, in Argentina the killings were justified by the long-standing tradition of Argentine fascism, which combined the Nazi type of anti-Semitism with a more traditional brand of religious anti-Semitism.[89] This combination was not so much the result of a systematic theory of the enemy. It was, above all, an ideological feeling, a circular vision of the world. Argentine perpetrators acted it out with the anti-Semitic practice of the camps. This was, in short, the legacy of Argentine fascist ideology, actualized in the camps.

Culture, Violence, and Ideology

Timerman asked: "What was the ideology of the armed forces? It could only be discerned through its activity, its repression, the world that it hated."[90] Rather than presenting practice as opposed to ideology, Timerman suggests that ideology is condensed in its victimizing practices. Timerman's point stands out for it is through the victimizing practices inside the camps that one actually observes a sort of compulsive repetition of ideology and how it is linked to practice. The *Nunca Más* highlighted, "Antisemitism was presented as a deformed version of Christianity in particular and of religion in general. This was nothing other than a cover for political and ideological persecution. The defense of God and of Christian values was a simple ideological motivation which could be understood by the agents of repression, even at their lowest organizational and cultural levels."[91]

This Argentine tradition blended Catholicism with a particular anti-Semitic idea of the enemy. This fusion was extreme insofar as it informed a long-standing type of Argentine fascism. But without being fascist, Argentine society at large still shares a significant pattern of this political culture, namely the idea that Argentina is essentially Christian and its enemies are not.

The "bodies" of a large number of future victims began to be constructed in the writings of nacionalista and Catholic intellectuals during the 1930s. The notion of the "domestic enemy" had been defined in terms that partook of the Catholic anti-Semitic traditions in Argentina, the fatal ideological combination of victimization and pathology. Through the construction of the stereotype of the Jew, this symbolic connection laid the ideological groundwork for disaster early on.

Though for different reasons, the military dictatorship was, like Uriburu's administration, not wholly fascistic. It did, however, inherit from fascism, and put into practice, the ideological imaginary of fascist nationalism defined as an alliance between the Cross and the Sword. The Lugonian sword was once again exemplified by military dictatorship.[92]

Though the objectivation of nacionalista ideology in the concentration camps points to a critical aspect of the ideology of the military, in terms of socioeconomic ideology the dictatorship entailed a return to a Uriburist type of nationalism that conceived of the economy in antipopulist neoconservative terms. If, after the death of Uriburu, nacionalistas were inclined to anticommunist populist social reform, with the last military dictatorship they reformulated the idea of society in neoconservative economic terms. As during Uriburu's administration, the dictatorship repressed labor, though its repression was far harsher than anything that came before. Of course, the situation was more complicated than in Uriburu's time; the traditional elite was working with the new upper class which consisted of business sectors that had benefited from the dictatorship's "free market" economic reformulation. Nonetheless, the continuities with nationalism's earlier course of action are striking. Education, particularly at the university level, again became the sole terrain of the nacionalistas. Argentine public universities and colleges became the places where they hunted down alternative ideologies and positions. Outside the camps, the dictatorship's ideology was fairly successful, though it failed to impose the total vertical universe it did within them.

Outside the camps, the symbolic torturers were media figures, the talking heads of military ideology. From a supposedly moderate position, journalists like Mariano Grondona broadcast nacionalista ideological motifs that, in the most nacionalista media like *Cabildo*, became more explicit.[93] In his magazine, *Carta Política,* Grondona formulated the "Jewish problem" and condemned the influence of Marx and of Freud; his arguments differed little from those of Filippo, Lugones, Castellani, and their followers. In the 1930s, Father Filippo had maintained that the Jewish plot to take over Argentina was based on the theories of Freud, Marx, and Einstein. Lugones said the same thing, although he excluded Einstein, a personal friend, from the list of enemies of God and the homeland.[94] Like nacionalista ideology in general, the nacionalista idea of the enemy was marked by the belief that Argentina was Catholic above all else, especially above Freud, Marx, and Einstein.

In keeping with a nacionalista ideology that imagined an enemy like Freud, whose strategy entailed conquering Argentines at night while they were dreaming, Admiral Massera himself said at a university lecture in 1977: "In the late 19th century, Marx published three volumes of *Capital* and, in so doing, cast doubt on the sanctity of private property; in the early 20th century, the sacred intimate sphere of the human being was attacked by Freud, in his *Interpretation of Dreams*. And as if that weren't enough to question society's positive values, Einstein, in 1905, published his theory of relativity, which puts into crisis the static nature of matter." [95] Massera made the speech in an academic ceremony after he received an honorary doctorate from the Jesuit University of Salvador in Buenos Aires.

For Massera, the enemy wanted to spread the "fragmentation" of the self that was in sharp contrast with the "totality" sought by the dictatorship.[96] Massera proposed to use a "natural resistance, smart antibodies" against "subjective criteria" and "nihilist" philosophical formations. He saw a short distance between the "terrorist faith" and these ideologies of "dissociation and melancholy, of death, promiscuous sex" and drugs.[97]

Similarly, Monsignor Guillermo Bolatti, the bishop of Rosario, stated that engaging in "unrestrained sexual pleasure" favored subversion either "consciously or unconsciously." He added that guerrillas, those "without God," put a special emphasis on recruiting people with "drug problems or sexual aberrations." He asked the Virgin Mary to "liberate" Argentines from this "ideological penetration," from the "homicidal weapons" of the enemy. Only then would Argentina achieve a future with the "Peace the Lord has given to us."[98]

The armed forces and their allies were fighting an ideological crusade against the unbridled forces of sex, drugs, and radical political desires. Massera finished his university "lecture" stressing the need for a future where the right balance between "affect and reason" would finally "restore life, the life that God, our Lord has given us, as a supreme value for us all." [99] For Massera and Bolatti, and many others, this future would arrive as a moment of "peaceful" ideological realization. Peace was only possible when the enemy was exterminated. Peace meant the death of the Other. This was going to be a moment of Argentine purification. It would signal the reemergence of an absolute national authenticity where culture would be restored as a central element of the "Christian" and "Western spirit."[100]

For the ideology of the dictatorship this spirit was not dead but just inactive and manipulated by the enemy plan of Freud, Marx, and Einstein. A majority of military ideologues believed that psychoanalysis, as *Cabildo* claimed, intended, "to destroy the Christian concept of the family."[101] The attack was part of a larger conspiratorial projection against Argentine Jews. The esoteric anti-Semitic view of an Argentine Jewish plan to dominate bodies and minds through these authors, and especially Freud, played an important role in the anti-Semitism put forward by the dictatorship.[102]

The constant references to the mental abnormality of the enemy and, more specifically, to the mothers of Plaza de Mayo as those "crazy old women," should be understood in the context of an ideology that posed them as agents of the foreign master plan against Argentine mental normality.[103] In short, in projecting the idea of mental domination onto the putative plans of the enemy, the military dictatorship saw the Dirty War as a contest for the minds and souls of Argentines. But this was not all. There were not one but two essential enemies. Massera argued that although "we are defeating the external enemy that manipulates cruelty and death" there was another enemy, the "interior one," which was immersed in the self, "in each of us." This enemy needed to be defeated by refusing to engage in apathy, in the "habits of thinking" of the past, as well as by enforcing the self-sacrificial practices of the present.[104]

Though Massera, Grondona, and *Cabildo* might not have agreed on the economy, all the "conservatives" who supported the dictatorship were, like their predecessors from the 1930s, anti-Semitic.[105] In terms of the relationship between violence and politics, in terms of racism, and even in terms of the condemnation of the fictional Jewish Marxist Freudian conspiracy, they differed little from the fascists of the past. For all of them, if Marx provided the theoretical basis for subversion, psychoanalysis constituted its cultural strategy. The difference between the nacionalistas of the past and the dictatorship lies in their practices. During the dictatorship, many psychoanalysts and Marxists were persecuted and killed.

The influence of nacionalismo and its concerns on all intellectuals who supported the dictatorship, whether fascist or not, is striking. The message—which combined racism with the idea of eliminating a domestic enemy—was the same. The idea of Marxist ideological "infiltration" was central. During the dictatorship, guides to help recognize the enemy in schools on the basis of their lexicon were published: "Marxist lexicon for use with students:... The first visible sign is the use of a determined vocabulary which, though apparently harmless, is very important in effecting the 'ideological switchover' that concerns us. And so the words dialogue, bourgeois, proletariat, Latin America, exploitation, structural change and capitalism are heard frequently."[106]

The fight against the enemy had no limits. In 1976, General Videla stressed the global nature of the contest: "[T]he fight against subversion is not exhausted by a purely military dimension. It is a global phenomenon. It has political, economic, social, cultural and psychological dimensions."[107] Outside the camps the family was a center stage of this fight.

General Albano Harguindeguy, the interior minister, ordered fathers, mothers, and sons to "guard the security of the home."[108] In the popular magazines *Gente* and *Para Ti*, Argentine parents were warned that their children might have become "subversives," that is, enemies of God and the homeland.[109]

In the world of high culture, as in all social spheres, the dictatorship had the support of important figures. For example, in 1976 Videla enjoyed a lunch with writers Ernesto Sábato, Jorge Luis Borges, and the clerico-fascist priest, Leonardo Castellani. Later, Borges said to the press, "I personally thanked [Videla] for the coup on March 24th, which saved the country from ignominy, and I expressed my support for his having taken over responsibility for the government." Sábato, who would later be one of the architects of *Nunca Más*, stated, "General Videla made an excellent impression on me. He is a cultivated, modest and intelligent man. I was struck by the sound judgment and cultural level of the President." Castellani remembers that Borges, Sábato, and Videla had spoken of "war" as a purifying undertaking.[110] If there are any doubts about the Lugonian origin of this thinking, one look at Borges's speech in Chile in 1976 will suffice. Upon receiving a medal from General Augusto Pinochet, Borges maintained, "In these times of anarchy, I know that here, between the mountain and the sea, lies a strong country. Lugones preached of a strong country when he spoke of the time of the Sword. I say that I prefer the Sword, the clear Sword, to furtive dynamite, and I say it knowing very clearly what I mean. I do believe that my country is now joyfully emerging from the swamp. I believe that we deserve to leave the swamp we have been in. And we are leaving it thanks to the work of the Sword. Here, you have already emerged from the swamp. And so Chile, this region, this country, is both a long country and an honorable Sword."[111]

For both Borges and Lugones, the Sword must be upheld by culture. In the aforementioned encounter, Videla spoke little, but he did tell the writers that cultural development was essential to the nation. What did the military mean by "culture"? The dictatorship "disappeared" writers and thinkers, closed publishing houses, newspapers, and magazines, and waged a true campaign against books and more generally against Argentine liberal culture as a whole.[112] To this liberal secular culture, the military opposed their belief in a sacred homogenous culture, that, as Videla claimed, "belongs to all of us and is not only the privilege of the few."[113] This was a symbolic reversal of sorts. The military reemphasized the popular importance of a traditionally elitist rightist canon. However, repression and censorship were also important aspects of the dictatorship's cultural self-understanding. In short, its culture was equally defined by what it opposed as by what it stood for.

The burning of books and banning of suspicious authors was just another instance of nacionalista ideology going beyond the concentration camps to be received without many reservations by a population that, at times, did not seem to have any trouble adjusting to new situations or readings. Mignone cites the following case, which is indicative of a general tendency: "On April 29, 1976 the late General Jorge Eduardo Gorleri used these words to order, in Córdoba, a spectacular book burning: . . . 'this measure has been taken so that this material ceases to deceive our youth about the true good of our national symbols, our family, our Church, our most deeply rooted tradition as epitomized in God, Homeland and Home.' "[114]

Typically, the Secretariat for State Intelligence (SIDE), which reported directly to the president's office, would argue in secret reports that certain books undermined the "principles of our national constitution." In their elaborated reports, which often can be read as detailed reviews, the censors identified these principles with "democracy," the Argentine way of life, and "the traditional values of our Christian culture." The authors considered dangerous were foreign or quickly accused of so being. Works by Marx, Pablo Neruda, Antoine de Saint-Exupéry's *The Little Prince*, and even Stendhal's highly suspicious text *The Red and the Black* were on the list of banned books. Other banned authors included Perry Anderson, Armand Mattelart, Talcott Parsons, David Viñas, Herbert Marcuse, and Ariel Dorfman, as well as a variety of Marxist and/or psychoanalytic theorists.[115] In an extensive secret review of Jürgen Habermas, for example, the military reader–censor argued that although Habermas "holds relevant positions in cultural centers of Germany and New York," he articulated a "materialist philosophy that denies the sense of the human person and its transcendental aims and thereby [Habermas] undermines our lifestyle and the legal and moral principles that guide us."[116] Anti-Semitic texts were generally allowed with the argument that "they lacked Marxist references which tend to undermine the principles of our national constitution." However, this was not the case with other texts read through the prism of the Catholic understanding of Nazi paganism and therefore were censored.[117]

Whereas the censored books were obviously not acceptable for ideological reasons, in 1979, the *Ministerio de Educación y Cultura* declared by decree that Catholic confessionary studies be mandatory material in courses on civic and moral instruction. The curriculum's bibliography recommended Catholic and nacionalista writers like Father Meinvielle and Jordán Bruno Genta. Against the liberal tradition of Argentina, the juntas presented a nacionalista tradition which was thought to be another weapon in the search for the desired destruction of the enemy and the defense of the "West." In fact, they thought that the West itself (in Europe) had left behind this authoritarian Catholic tradition and for this reason they presented Argentina as a last bastion, the last defense of the "Western spirit" in the Cold War.[118]

Generally speaking, the dictatorship considered the enemy a foreign element. Given that most of the people persecuted and disappeared were

Argentine citizens, it is hard to grasp this categorization as an effective form of propaganda for the general public. Regardless, it was very successful in specific contexts of national euphoria, especially during the 1978 soccer World Cup. Its effectiveness lay in the widely accepted fantasy that the enemy was not really Argentine or was only Argentine "by circumstance."

Thus this nacionalista ideology that saw the enemy as opposed to the homeland was taken to the soccer field in 1978. During the World Cup, the coach of the Argentine team, César Luis Menotti, thanked Admiral Massera for the "invaluable moral support" he gave the team. The idea that soccer was somehow connected to the brand of nacionalismo promoted by the dictatorship was widely shared during the event. In 1978, Ernesto Sábato stated that in the World Cup Argentina proved to both itself and the rest of the world its true character, its willpower and, furthermore, "that thrilled me...I was moved by the national passion that our people have shown." But Borges touched on a sore spot when he said that he doubted that 11 players truly represented a national character or nationalism: "It is not possible for a country to feel represented by its soccer players. It's as if we were represented by our dentists. Argentina has two things that no other country in the world has, and they are *milonga* music and *dulce de leche* [Argentine caramel]. What other identity do they want?"[119] Borges's criticism of official propaganda was circumstantial; he had no trouble when it came to the Sword, though he did not like the idea of soccer representing a key component of the war against its enemies.

Borges was an exception in the chorus of nationalism, and the World Cup was presented by official propaganda as a defense of the true Argentina against its enemies. If those enemies represented the foreign and anti-Argentine element, the dictatorship was identified with the sacred, with peace that, as Videla said, could only be reached through death. In his message at the opening of the World Cup, Videla claimed that it was a day of jubilation for the nation as a whole and, hence "I ask God, our Lord, that this event contribute to affirming peace, that peace that we all want for the whole world."[120]

The World Cup was one of the occasions on which the dictatorship and its "peace process" gained popular support on a mass scale. When Argentina won, people took to the streets, filling them with a message of joy about the achievement. This message was soon appropriated by propaganda, which linked the accomplishment to the dictatorship. This strategy was not only top-down; many sectors identified Argentina's victory in the

World Cup, as well as hosting the event itself, with the victory of the military over the "subversives."

It is no surprise that the Lugonian nationalist symbol par excellence, the gaucho, was the World Cup's mascot. The victory at the World Cup, that "celebration of all Argentines," presented in the propaganda film by director Sergio Renán, was equated with what journalist Roberto Maidana had called the Argentine people's "will to be." For Maidana the dictatorship had initiated a new historical process, a refounding of the country. This ontological notion of national existence coincided with a sexualized idea of the Argentine male, a being with "his trousers on straight," a "mature people no longer in knickers." Renán's film is an example of nacionalista cinema and, as film critic Santiago García has pointed out in quoting Captain Jorge Bittleston, the military-appointed director of the Instituto Nacional de Cinematografía (National Institute of Cinema), nacionalista cinema meant "all films that extol the spiritual, Christian, moral and historical or contemporary values of the nation or films that affirm the concepts of family, order, respect, work, fruitful effort and social responsibility in order to ferment an optimistic attitude for the future."[121] Another film of the dictatorship, "*Brigada en acción*" (1977), directed by Ramón "Palito" Ortega, contains the following song:

> Woe is the people who don't know where to go
> Those who have lost the light of truth
> Those who no longer believe in God
> Those who have given up on the word love.
> Woe is the people who have forgotten their religion
> Those who do not value life
> Those who have mistaken the word freedom
> Those who are forever alone.

The relationship between religion and truth, on the one hand, and the state of being "forever alone"—a clear reference to the disappeared—on the other, are symptomatic of what the dictatorship understood as a war between those who, in "forgetting" their religion, also forgot their innate Argentineness, and the true Argentines, those whom the dictatorship defended.

As García points out, Ortega's films even make implicit reference to the dictatorship's most extreme acts. In *Qué linda es mi familia!* (1980) Ortega "plays an adoptive son whose adoptive father...rejects the biological father when he comes for his son."[122] In the dictatorship's cinema, there are no transactions with reality and the ideological reality of the concentration camps is reproduced in cinematic narration. In that 1980 film Ortega, playing an Argentine sailor, sings: "I like the sea / I guard my borders / where my land begins / the others' end." It's not a question of Ortega's film forecasting the Malvinas/Falklands War of 1982, but rather reproducing the nacionalista ideology that would later serve as the ideological basis for that war. Ortega, who after the return of democracy would become a Peronist governor of Tucumán province, was one of the dictatorship's greatest propagandists. In television commercials, he supported the dictatorship because "together we grasp the need to defend our sovereignty and protect our rights."

The idea of a war on the issue of sovereignty and the "internal war" is related to the fascist idea of permanent war so often invoked by Hitler and Mussolini. War has its costs and is never really over. As General Viola said in 1979: "Like in all wars, in this one life has a different value. Lines are crossed; life and death mingle for the sake of victory. The worst thing is not to lose one's life. The worst thing is to lose the war....This war, like all wars, has consequences, terrible wounds that time and only time can mend. These wounds are the dead, the injured, the detained, and those forever missing."[123] According to Viola, the dead are to blame for their deaths, and their families must blame them accordingly: "Terrorist crime so arrogantly maintained that by killing it could break the will to victory of armed men and of the immense majority of the population. But [those terrorists] were man and woman born on this bountiful land just *by circumstance.* They fooled themselves, and they fooled and saddened the land of their cradle." If here the enemy was Argentine just by chance, after the domestic war would come the war against a foreign enemy. As Brigadier Agosti explained with traditional nacionalista metaphor, "We have won a non-conventional war and not just a mere war game. We have won it within the national territory but the aggressor is only a tentacle of a monster whose head and whose body are beyond the reach of our swords." In fact, military Argentina was in a state of permanent global war: "the armed combat is finished but the global confrontation continues."[124]

Cold War politics was waged by means of the Plan Cóndor, by which Argentina, Chile, Uruguay, Bolivia, Paraguay, Peru, and Brazil coordinated their state terrorism plans by "capturing" domestic enemies. In support of the US Cold War strategies, Argentina, once again secretly, also waged war against the Central American left by offering its expert torturers in illegal counterinsurgency actions in Guatemala, Honduras, and El Salvador.[125]

According to the dictatorship's ideology, war was a value in and of itself; the rhetoric of war and its expansion culminated in the preparation for the never-waged war against Chile in late 1978. That war was avoided thanks to pressure exerted by the Catholic Church, which proves that had it wanted it could have effectively worked against the violation of human rights in Argentina.[126] But if for the Church the "domestic war" was holy, for the military that war had to be taken elsewhere after the domestic war was over.

In fact, nacionalista ideological imperatives finally led the military to engage in an external war in which the dictatorship, once again, mobilized the population which had been prepared by years of nacionalista preaching. According to the nacionalista argument, the Malvinas/Falklands War was an anticolonial struggle for God and for the homeland. Dying for the sake of some islands that are part of the British Empire became meaningful for most of the population, which enthusiastically supported the dictatorship in this new adventure. But this time the enemy were armed soldiers who fought back and refused to disappear despite the ideological insistence that "we are winning" heard over and over again in the Argentine mass media. This time the dictatorship was not attempting to eliminate civilians it considered enemies of the nation but rather a conventional army.

The dictatorship's military inefficiency was demonstrated by its defeat in the armed forces' only true area of competence. But, in terms of nacionalista ideology, the Malvinas/Falklands War of 1982 was clearly an ideological battle.[127] If in the concentration camps nacionalista ideology rested on those persecuted, or more precisely on their tortured bodies, in the Malvinas/Falklands War that ideology proved insufficient when it came to affirming the nacionalista idea of a Great Argentina in the face of a British army that easily defeated its troops. The justification for the war was not original; the nacionalistas had already wielded it in the 1930s,. The originality lay in the practice of a war that could not be won, as opposed to the Dirty War against defenseless citizens and a guerrilla movement that had been defeated before the coup.

Epilogue

THE PAST AND THE PRESENT

THE ARGENTINE CONCENTRATION camps were sites of ideological ful-fillment. In terms of the legacy of fascist ideology, they represented the inner sanctum of the nation and the ultimate outcome of the Dirty War. Perpetrators believed that the camps would help realize the promise of a new national foundation. Torture and death were key elements of these laboratories of Christianized fascism.

In the camps, quotes from Rosas were written on the walls, as if the cur-rent struggle against the internal enemy was a continuation of the work of that nineteenth-century caudillo. Unlike historical revisionists, many mili-tary intellectuals also defended the figures of Sarmiento and Alberdi. Their admiration for these writers was based on their authoritarian rendering of the liberal project and entailed a return to an Uriburist, pre-populist conception through the incorporation of revisionist elements. Nonetheless, San Martín, the premier independence warrior, was still the hero of choice. As General Ramón Camps said, "I just admire San Martín (I don't admire Hitler); I do agree with Hitler on some points, for example, my humanist interest in sav-ing man from the ongoing and lie-ridden Communist campaign."[1]

In the context of "Hitler's humanism" Rosas's authoritarian legacy was integrated with the military nationalism of the future. For General Ramón Díaz Bessone, if Rosas was a "tyrant," he had also defended national sover-eignty. A reader of nacionalistas such as Gustavo Franceschi and Ernesto Palacio, Díaz Bessone was the dictatorship's *Ministro de Planificación* and proposed founding a "New Republic" under military influence until the year 2000.[2]

The preference for the word "republic" over the word "democracy" was first articulated by Uriburu in 1932 and used much later by Videla in inter-views in 1998, 1999, 2012, and 2013.[3] The nacionalista genealogy of the military document prepared by Díaz Bessone was not just etymological but an ideological source for the junta's future. Díaz Bessone's document affirmed the irrefutable existence of God as well as the existence of an Argentine racial type. It was no accident that the title of the first major nacionalista publication, *The New Republic*, was announced as the ultimate aim of his dictatorial "National Project." In this new republic, the present would be a mere return to the repressed past of Argentine fascism. History, however, played out differently than dictatorial nacionalista expectations. In great part, due to the sound defeat of the dictatorship in the Malvinas/Falklands War against the United Kingdom in 1982, the military eventually surrendered power in 1983.

A new democracy emerged in Argentina after 1983 and has had its longest uninterrupted rule since 1930. Most Argentines agree that this has been a highly significant collective and institutional achievement. The creation of the Argentine Truth Commission or Conadep (*Comisión Nacional sobre la Desaparición de Personas*) and the Trial of the Juntas in the 1980s represented milestones in the political undoing of dictatorial rule in Argentina. Argentina set a precedent for the national judgment of mass atrocities. Conadep was formed by the democratically elected government of President Raúl Ricardo Alfonsín in 1984 with the goal of investigating and reporting the violations of human rights by the junta military dictatorship and its findings were used as evidence at the trials. The commission included members from many segments of Argentine society and was chaired by the writer Ernesto Sábato who, notwithstanding the fact that he had previously supported the military dictatorship, became an icon of the punishment of the worst military offenders.[4] The commissions and the trials left a lasting impact. Thus, after an infamous impasse with the passing of exculpatory laws for the military in 1986 and 1987 during the Alfonsín administration, and the presidential amnesties given by Peronist President Carlos Menem in 1989 and 1990, the reemergence of investigations and indictments of the perpetrators in the 2000s have been complemented by new laws for gender and sexual equality in the 2000s and early 2010s under the Peronist Kirchner administrations with majority support from most political sectors. Some parties of the right, including some sectors of Peronism, and the Catholic Church opposed the law's expansion in the 2010s of civil rights for marriages of same-sex couples. Pope Francis, then Argentina's most important priest, presented the equal marriage law as "motivated by the devil." The passing of the law was an unusual instance of wide political agreements. Generally, political polarization prevailed. A relatively more independent supreme court has also been complemented by a reinvigorated civil society that, as in previous moments of Argentine history, was at odds (politically, culturally, and economically) with an increasingly autonomous political class. As in the past, the liberal, secular Argentina increasingly turned its back to the official world of the state. This escape from politics, as Argentines experienced it, has had enormous consequences in the past century. This retreat enhanced state authoritarianism. This continues to be the case in the new century. At the critical moments when civil society confronted the political world (as for example in the multi-class protests of the 2001 crisis), the former was often absorbed, and metaphorically neutralized by newly configured partisan arguments. New configurations of populist leadership reemerged along with the classic Peronist idea that nothing mediates between the mind of the leader and the desires of the people. In this view, the leaders are not only elected mediators between the people and governmental institutions but the personification of both. Thus the leader personifies the nation as a whole and embodies the ideal interaction between the people and the state. This praxis downplays actual citizen participation in decision-making and minimizes pluralism. It also tends to distance the leader and the represented.[5] After 1989, and especially at the beginning of the new century, the state was increasingly conflated with the needs and aims of different political administrations at the national and municipal levels. State or municipal publicity from different political sectors was increasingly turned into party propaganda. Vertical forms of increasingly directed mass mobilizations led to new forms of political polarization. From the perspective of the populist state, the population was divided between those who ascribed to the leader and the official order of things and those who questioned both for a variety of social and political reasons. Intense political discussion at the bottom tended not to affect policy making at the top. Thus the perennial contradiction of modern Argentine politics was continued during the first two decades of the century. Highly partisan discussions among the citizenry had no significant institutional correlation with a system of checks and balances. Civic engagement and official disengagement from civic debate were intrinsically linked. The majority of citizens were entitled to argue and vote but had almost no input in the running of the country. In this sense, civil society and official society continued their mutual disregard for each other, what sat at the center of Argentine tensions between politization and depolitization. Notwithstanding its recurrent clientelistic forms of mobilization, social paternalism, authoritarian practices, sectarian understandings of political antagonists as foes, and an ever-increasing notion that the political leader is a quasi-sacred representative of the nation, this new democracy stands still. Despite the downplaying of consensual politics and deliberation across the political spectrum, Argentina at the beginning of the new century had left dictatorship behind.

But does this mean that the fascist idea in Argentina is gone for good?

To be sure, nacionalista groups in the military attempted to overthrow democracy and failed in the 1980s. And small nacionalista and neo-Nazi groups have remained active, sporadically attacking their enemies and collaborating with nacionalista elements in the security forces in acts of anti-Semitic vandalism, but the legacy of past fascist actions or ideas is less important than the hegemony of nacionalista ideas in daily life in Argentina, such as in soccer stadiums, the racism and xenophobia faced by immigrants, the jingoistic populist defense of the Falklands/Malvinas War, and the idea that one political movement or administration is truly representative of the nation. Nacionalista egocentricity, a feeling of superiority over the rest of Latin America, is still a component of right-wing thinking in Argentina and, indeed, much of the society as a whole. Many Argentines discriminate against immigrants from Bolivia, Paraguay, and other South American countries, believing themselves to be "whiter" than them. Anti-Semitism has diminished after the dictatorship but it is still concentrated in various security forces, in the extreme right, and in the mentality of a population that often legitimizes it by ignorance or omission. The anti-Semitic bombings of 1992 and 1994 were possible due to the domestic collaboration of those left unemployed after the closing of the concentration camps.[6] All of these "nacionalista" attitudes underlie a way of thinking and acting that is widespread in Argentine political culture. The origin of that political culture partially lies in the nacionalismo of the extreme right, that is, Argentine-style fascism. In this specific sense the nacionalista legacy embodied in the dictatorship is still alive.

The dictatorship was part and parcel of the society from which it emerged and which accepted it. As historian Luis Alberto Romero states, "After 1983, a unanimous choir condemned the 'demon' that had usurped the rights of 'society,' its innocent victim. But that demon emerged from the same society."[7] Argentine society prefers not to remember its role in the Dirty War, whether it was a passive or an active justification. The classic nacionalista tendency to rewrite history to achieve political aims ends up ignoring history. Thus, according to nacionalista ideology, professional historiography becomes a part of the conspiracy against the eternal Christian Argentina, and the only tenable stance is a combination of denial and "reconciliation," a shutting down of the past.

According to information published in Argentine newspapers, in 2003 General Bendini, the chief of staff of the army, announced, and then denied having announced, the existence of a Jewish plan to occupy Patagonia. Thus Bendini repeated an old anti-Semitic trope very close to the history of Argentine fascism: the "Plan Andinia," in the eyes of clerico-fascists, had been a perennial Jewish plan to take Patagonia from Argentina.[8] In 2007, Bendini, who kept his post during the early years of the Cristina Fernández de Kirchner administration, spoke of the need to heal the wounds of the past. For him, all that meant was not examining the most tragic parts of that past. He was apparently inspired by similar statements made by Jorge Bergoglio, the Argentine cardinal and archbishop of Buenos Aires at the time. In the context of a political campaign, in which some candidates were accused of having had links with the previous Peronist administration, Bergoglio stated that to examine the past is to curse "into the past."[9]

One key aspect of the nacionalista legacy is the notion that the Church and its political representatives should play a central role in Argentine politics. If, through the army, the Church and nacionalismo managed to position themselves at the heart of the ideology of the military in the last century, it is, in times of democracy, believed that the Church should play a critical role in politics. The idea that politicians should consult organized religion on political matters breaks with the Enlightenment tradition of strict separation of religious beliefs and the state. For Argentine nacionalistas and for their Church, this break was problematic as, for them, God took precedence over the political system and the will of the majority. Indeed, those who did not agree with the ecclesiastical stance that nacionalismo, and then the army, represented in the political order were categorized as non-Argentines or simply as "traitors." At the beginning of the twenty-first century, this idea was still upheld by politicians who, on the basis of religion, tried to articulate either neoclassic or neopopulist projects for the nation. This should not be surprising in the cyclical history of Argentina that, at other decisive moments, operated in the same terms: for or against Perón, political coalitions turned to the Church to build opposition fronts. For example, if the last military dictatorship legitimized its crimes by drawing on the support of the Church and nacionalista ideals, Argentine democracy at times might be walking a similar path. The idea of Argentina as an ideal embodiment of the Christian West is widely shared. Having the Church officiate politics was a central component of the ideology that the fascists from the 1930s bequeathed to the country. Though in political terms the last dictatorship ended up discrediting the military, it did not discredit the Church, one of its main bases of support. The Church never expelled highly compromised figures such as Bonamín, Medina, and Von Wernich.

In the minds of perpetrators, their actions were legitimized by the fact that key leaders of the Argentine church actively defended the military. One year before his death, Videla said that the bishops and the papal nuncio "gave us advice" regarding how to best handle the topic of "the disappearances of people." In another interview, the dictator concluded, "[M]y relationship with the Church was excellent. We had a cordial, sincere and open relationship."[10] Support was combined with silence. In most cases, the Church's silence about military crimes was connected to the Cold War notion that the victims were "internal enemies" of the Cross and the Sword.

By sins of commission or omission, was the entire Church guilty? In his important study, Hugo Vezzetti points out that it is necessary to bear in mind that not all the bishops "shared the fascist exaltations of Bonamín or Medina, and some even confronted the dictatorship despite the consequences." He goes on, "If the dictatorship not only put society and its leaders to the test but also revealed and enacted their worst sides, the Church...was at the head of the society's moral degradation."[11] Similarly, human rights advocate Emilio Mignone states that the doors of the cathedral were always shut to the *Madres de Plaza de Mayo* and, more than once, when they finally did get in, "They threatened to call the police." In his book, Mignone states, "It would seem that the officials tightly connected to the most traditional Catholicism encouraged by chaplains and bishops were the ones with the most striking homicidal fervor and opposition to democracy. That is the result, in the end, of the attitude and teaching of most parish priests." [12]

The Church, whose hierarchies so actively supported and justified the dictatorship's worst crimes, has not suffered the same decline in prestige and influence as its ally, the military. In 2005, while criticizing the then minister of health's position on abortion and the distribution of condoms to prevent HIV/AIDS, Bishop Antonio Baseotto maintained that the Minister deserved "to have a millstone hung from his neck and be thrown into the sea."[13] Though certain sectors of the population condemned the statement of this well-known nationalistic and anti-Semitic bishop as a clear reference to the dictatorship's "flights of death," Baseotto was not expelled from the Church. On the contrary, presumably due to pressure from his Argentine peers, he was recognized by Pope Benedict XVI in 2007 for his "correct interpretation of the Church's doctrine...his special human and Christian gifts, and his prudence."[14]

This lack of self-policing, despite three episcopal requests to be "forgiven" for its inactions but without addressing actual collaboration, does not seem to have affected the collective memory or the Church's stance. The persistence of the clerico-fascist ideology that gave rise to Argentine-style fascism is part of the historical response to this question. Unlike other Latin American countries, the Church hierarchy in Argentina actively worked to silence dissident voices within and often even disappeared them. In times of democracy, the Sword seems to have been replaced by a new union between politics and the Cross. The Argentine state would continue to pay the salaries of Catholic priests, a glaring symptom of the continued resistance to the separation of Church and state. Pope Francis I has participated in this tradition of silence, from remaining silent at the time of the abuses to never trying to fully acknowledge the significant responsibility of the Argentine Church that he led for many years. The Church's reluctance to open its archives of the repression might be rooted in the specifics of mass atrocities and how and why the military repression in Argentina was ideologically legitimized by the hierarchy of the Church. The combination of ideological and practical support for the repression was matched by the widespread passive acceptance of the crimes. This combination of support and indifference was a key factor in making the systematic killing of thousands of Argentine citizens a historical reality.

Since then, many things have changed in Argentina, but Argentina remains above all a Catholic nation. Constant references to the politics of the sacred and the exaltation of the Argentine conflation of anti-imperialism, *caudillismo*, nationalism, and territorial reclamation crisscross the political spectrum.

According to its ideology, had the dictatorship continued and won the Malvinas/Falklands War and the peace, the country would have become a globalized concentration camp, a country of victims kept in check by the military. The explanatory myth of the "two demons" is a manifestation of this internalized ideology. By limiting the state's responsibility, this myth blames and, indeed, constructs as an enemy those who performed criminal acts, including acts of urban terrorism and kidnapping, and, hence, should have been legally tried, rather than conflated with the history of persecution and extermination addressed in this book. This myth minimizes the extreme victimization of everyone who was illegally placed in concentration camps and then disappeared. Finally, as Vezzetti points out, for the society that has produced it, this myth serves to "confirm its innocence and otherness in the face of the barbarism that unfolded before its eyes."[15]

Shared by many, the political culture of nacionalismo is a better explanation for the ideology of the dictatorship and its political and cultural hegemony in those years. The nacionalista idea of civil war posits the existence of two gangs, dramatically distancing society from a spectacle with which it deems itself hardly involved. Ironically, the society that bought the nacionalista package of the dictatorship and its brief economic boom ended up supporting this notion of "two evils" for reasons partly nationalistic. A South Atlantic war for a nacionalista cause still seems justifiable to much of Argentine society. Discrimination, anti-Semitism, and criticism of difference are still something of a national pastime. The efforts at "reconciliation" with the past have become, for the perpetrators, a denial of the tragic legacy of the fascist idea in Argentina.

The shift in the perception of the legacy of the dictatorship poses new challenges to Argentina's efforts to come to terms with its violent past. In the first decades of this century, Argentine politicians accused opponents of having been fascists, associated with the dictatorship, or, if they were too young to have participated, wishing for its return. The dictatorship had thus become an ultimate political insult, a populist means of political polarization. Equally problematic were the efforts by the Kirchner administrations to present the victims as heroes. In effect, this marked a shift from a legal perception of perpetrators and victims under the junta, to a moral one of a real "war" between heroes and villains. This is exactly how Videla and the other leaders of the junta wanted to be remembered—as warriors in a violent political contest. President Cristina Fernández de Kirchner and her husband and predecessor, Néstor Kirchner, saw themselves on the other side of this war, as warriors against absolute evil, though neither had played any visible role in the resistance to the dictatorship. Thus history as populist melodrama presented a vision of past victims as proto-supporters of current politics. The idea of redeeming the victims from their past served the purpose of legitimizing very different strands of Peronist populism. There are serious historical inadequacies with these images of the past. The crimes of the state only made sense to perpetrators. From the perspective of the victims their victimization had no meaning at all. No victim would find in the concentration camps the political con-notation that many populist political interpreters later ascribed to their experience. And yet Peronist officials in the 2000s constantly claimed that the victims represented a true form of nacionalismo; theirs was a proverbial *just war* insofar as they were defending the true nation of the people from its oppressors.[16] The history of radical victimization (espe-cially the Holocaust and comparative genocide and massive killings of citizens by the state) avoids analyzing the victims as the main source of perpetrator motivations. The ethnic and/or political subjectivities of the victims (either Jewish, Mayan, or communist) were not the main ratio-nale of perpetrators. Actually, the main driving force behind their kill-ings was the absolute ideology of the killers. In that sense, in Argentina there was no real war, but instead the state-sanctioned mass killings of citizens, as in Cambodia, Chile, fascist Spain, and Guatemala.

In addition, recent efforts to view the political identities of the victims at the root of their victimization anachronistically place the crimes of the state within the political sphere. And yet these crimes were in a judicial sense well outside politics. This populist redemptive take on the victims implies an uncanny return to issues of ideological legitimacy and the theory of two sides at war. In contrast with this official history, this book has argued that the conflation of ideology and violence in the tradition of nacionalismo remains the most formidable cause for the Dirty War and the concentration camps.

This investigation set out to study the powerful influence of the nacio-nalista and fascist prism on twentieth-century Argentine history. The fact that many aspects of this ideology are still felt in the country, mostly by its past and present victims, shows that the nacionalista fiction about the country's reality was ultimately accepted by many. The long and tragic course of that ideology is both historic and ongoing. Nacionalista ideol-ogy rewrites history and, repeating past ideas, it has aspired to deny the most tragic sides of that history. The intellectual origins of the dictatorship are those of "Christianized fascism," an Argentine-style fascism that has enduring powers.

Notes

INTRODUCTION

1. See Raanan Rein, "Argentina, World War II and the Entry of Nazi War Criminals," in his *Argentine Jews or Jewish Argentines? Essays on History, Ethnicity and Diaspora* (Boston: Brill, 2010). See also Ronald Newton, *The "Nazi Menace" in Argentina, 1931–1947* (Stanford: Stanford University Press, 1992).

2. On Argentina as a landmark of liberalism see Tulio Halperín Donghi, "Argentina: Liberalism in a Country Born Liberal," in Joseph Love and Nils Jacobsen (eds.), *Guiding the Invisible Hand* (New York: Praeger Publishers, 1988), 99–116.

3. See United States Department of State, *Consultation among the American Republics with Respect to the Argentine Situation* (Washington, DC, 1946), 44; *Archivo del Ministerio de Relaciones Exteriores y Culto. Argentina*, Guerra Europea. Mueble 7. Casilla 43. Exp. 549. Año 1943.

4. See Federico Finchelstein, "The Holocaust, Fascism and the Sacred," in Dan Stone (ed.), *The Holocaust and Historical Methodology* (Oxford: Berghahn Books, 2012).

5. See Enzo Traverso, *El totalitarismo: Historia de un debate* (Buenos Aires: Eudeba, 2001).

6. Stanley G. Payne, "Historical Fascism and the Radical Right," *Journal of Contemporary History* 35(1), 2000, 111; Emilio Gentile, *Fascismo: Storia e interpretazione* (Roma-Bari: Laterza 2002); Geoff Eley, *Nazism as Fascism. Violence, Ideology, and the Ground of Consent in Germany 1930-1945* (London: Routledge, 2013); Zeev Sternhell, "How to Think about Fascism and Its Ideology," *Constellations* 15(3), 2008, and the essays in the same issue by Emilio Gentile, Marla Stone, S. Falasca Zamponi, Federico Finchelstein, and Enzo Traverso.

7. See Sandra McGee Deutsch, *Las Derechas: The Extreme Right in Argentina, Brazil, and Chile 1890–1939* (Stanford: Stanford University Press, 1999), and Sandra McGee Deutsch (ed.), *La derecha argentina* (Buenos Aires: Vergara,

2001); Alberto Spektorowski, *Argentina's Revolution of the Right* (Notre Dame: University of Notre Dame Press, 2003); Loris Zanatta, *Del estado liberal a la nación católica* (Bernal: Universidad Nacional de Quilmes, 1996), and his *Perón y el mito de la nación católica* (Buenos Aires: Sudamericana, 1999). For a historiographical study see Federico Finchelstein, *Fascismo, Liturgia e Imaginario: El mito del general Uriburu y la Argentina nacionalista* (Buenos Aires: Fondo de Cultura Económica, 2002), 10–27; Olivier Compagnon, "Le XXe siècle argentin: Historiographie récente sur la nation et le nationalisme," *Le mouvement social* 230, 2010, 3–6.

8. See, for example, Greg Grandin and Gilbert M. Joseph (eds.), *A Century of Revolution: Insurgent and Counterinsurgent Violence during Latin America's Long Cold War* (Durham and London: Duke University Press, 2010); Pablo Piccato, *The Tyranny of Opinion: Honor in the Construction of the Public Sphere* (Durham and London: Duke University Press, 2010); Virginia Garrard Burnett, *Terror in the Land of the Holy Spirit: Guatemala under General Efraín Ríos Montt 1982–1983* (New York: Oxford University Press, 2010); Hugo Vezzetti, *Sobre la violencia revolucionaria: Memorias y olvidos* (Buenos Aires, Siglo XXI Editores, 2009).

9. For an earlier approach that emphasized the transnational Latin American dimensions of right-wing ideology, see José Luis Romero, *El pensamiento político de la derecha latinoamericana* (Buenos Aires: Paidos, 1970).

10. "La Missione militare argentina esalta l'organizzazione delle Forze Armate Italiana," *Il Giornale d'Italia*, September 12, 1940. See also *Archivo del Ministerio de Relaciones Exteriores y Culto. Argentina*, División Política. Mueble 7. Casilla 1. Guerra Europea. Exp. 14. Año 1939. Telegrama. Roma, Julio 4 de 1940.

11. Federico Finchelstein, *Transatlantic Fascism: Ideology, Violence and the Sacred in Argentina and Italy, 1919–1945* (Durham and London: Duke University Press, 2010)

12. See Emilio Mignone, *Iglesia y Dictadura* (Buenos Aires: Ediciones del Pensamiento Nacional, 1986), 17.

13. Ibid. 27.

14. Fernando Almirón, *Campo santo* (Buenos Aires: Editorial 21, 1999), 122–23.

15. Marcos Novaro and Vicente Palermo, *La dictadura militar (1976–1983)* (Buenos Aires: Paidós, 2003).

16. "Desaparecidos: Intervista con mons. Juan Carlos Aramburu arcivescovo di Buenos Aires e Primate d'Argentina," *Il Messagero* (Rome), November 11 (1982), 20.

17. See my critique in Federico Finchelstein, *Transatlantic Fascism*, 8–9.

18. For some fine examples of this historiography, see Marysa Navarro Gerassi, *Los Nacionalistas* (Buenos Aires: Jorge Álvarez, 1968); Enrique Zuleta Álvarez, *El nacionalismo argentino* (Buenos Aires: La Bastilla, 1975); Fernando Devoto, *Nacionalismo, fascismo y tradicionalismo en la Argentina moderna: una historia* (Buenos Aires: Siglo XXI Editores, 2002); Marie-Monique Robin,

Escadrons de la mort, l'École française (Paris: La Découverte, 2004). David Rock also represents this trend. He provides a traditional intellectual history of the nacionalistas. Rock tends to ignore the practical implications of fascist ideology and disengages theory from practice. His analysis of the second half of the century, and especially the 1970s, is based primarily on secondary sources and does not investigate extensive archival materials and/or central neofascist publications of the time. Rock's stress on the imitative nature of Argentine fascism blocks any possible interpretation of the interactions between the transnational and local contextual dimensions of the ideological origins of the military junta. See David Rock, *Authoritarian Argentina: The Nationalist Movement, Its History and Its Impact* (Berkeley: University of California Press, 1993).

19. On the notion of habitus see Norbert Elias, *The Civilizing Process* (Oxford: Blackwell, 2000) and his *The Germans: Power Struggles and the Development of Habitus in the Nineteenth and Twentieth Centuries* (New York: Columbia University Press, 1996). On Elias see Roger Chartier, "Elias, proceso de la civilización y barbarie," in Federico Finchelstein (ed.), *Los alemanes, el Holocausto y la culpa colectiva: El debate Goldhagen* (Buenos Aires: Eudeba, 1999), 197–204. See also by Chartier: *Escribir las prácticas: Foucault, De Certeau, Marin* (Buenos Aires: Manantial, 1996); "Pour un usage libre et respectueux de Norbert Elias," *Vingtième Siècle. Revue d'histoire* 2(106), 2010.

20. In this sense, I agree with the important works of Feitlowitz and Novaro and Palermo. Marguerite Feitlowitz, *A Lexicon of Terror: Argentina and the Legacies of Torture* (New York: Oxford University Press, 1999), and Marcos Novaro and Vicente Palermo, *La dictadura militar.*

21. On the Cold War, see Gilbert Joseph, "What We Now Know and Should Know: Bringing Latin America More Meaningfully into Cold War Studies," in Gilbert Joseph and Daniela Spenser (eds.), *In From the Cold: Latin America's New Encounter With the Cold War* (Durham and London: Duke University Press, 2008).

22. See, for example, the important work of Tanya Harmer, "Fractious Allies: Chile, the United States, and the Cold War, 1973–76" *Diplomatic History* 37(1), 2013, 109–43 and her book *Allende's Chile and the Inter-American Cold War* (Chapel Hill: University of Carolina Press, 2011).

CHAPTER 1

1. On Mitre and history see Tulio Halperín Donghi, "Mitre y la formulación de una historia nacional para la Argentina," *Anuario del IEHS* 11, 1996. See also Tulio Halperín Donghi, *Una nación para el desierto argentino* (Buenos Aires: Prometeo, 2005); Jeremy Adelman, *Republic of Capital: Buenos Aires and the Legal Transformation of the Atlantic World* (Stanford: Stanford University Press, 1999); Elías Palti, *La nación como problema: Los historiadores y la "cuestión nacional"* (Buenos Aires: Fondo de Cultura Económica, 2002).

2. See José Luis Romero, "La conformación de la Argentina aluvial," *La Vanguardia*, April 29, 1947, 12.

3. *AGN*. Archivo Agustín P. Justo. Caja 49. Doc. 166.

4. For my criticism of this historiography see my *Fascismo, Liturgia e Imaginario*, 10–27.

5. Domingo F. Sarmiento, *El Progreso*, September 27, 1844. See also Manuel Gálvez, *Vida de Samiernto* (Buenos Aires: Emecé, 1945), 147–48.

6. See Curruhuinca-Roux, *Las matanzas del Neuquén: Crónicas mapuches* (Buenos Aires: Plus Ultra, 1990), 150–57, 160–61; Jorge Páez, *La conquista del desierto* (Buenos Aires: Centro Editor de América Latina, 1970), 105–10. See also Walter Delrio, *Memorias de expropiación: sometimiento e incorporación indígena en la Patagonia, 1872–1943* (Bernal: Universidad Nacional de Quilmes, 2005).

7. Rodolfo and Julio Irazusta, *La Argentina y el imperialismo británico* (Buenos Aires: Condor/Tor, 1934), 199. For the Uriburu dictatorship and the "Campaign of the Desert" see *AGN*. Ministerio del Interior Año 1931 Legajo 8 and 1931 Legajo 11.

8. *AGN*. Archivo Roca Hijo. Legajo 6 Sala VII 3107. Doc. 97.

9. Ernesto Palacio, *La historia falsificada* (Buenos Aires: Difusión, 1939), 63.

10. See "Inmigración israelita," *La Nación*, August 26, 1881; Julián Martel, *La bolsa* (Buenos Aires: Imprenta Artística Buenos Aires, 1891).

11. See Sandra McGee Deutsch, *Las Derechas*, 26–37; Federico Finchelstein, *Transatlantic Fascism*, 145. See Gálvez's fascist writings in Manuel Gálvez, *Este pueblo necesita* (Buenos Aires: A. García Santos, 1934); *AGN*. Archivo Agustín P. Justo. Caja 45. Doc.146; *AGN*. Fondo Manuel Gálvez. Legajo 1. Sala VII 3365.

12. See Sandra McGee Deutsch, *Counter Revolution in Argentina, 1900–1932: The Argentine Patriotic League* (Lincoln: University of Nebraska Press, 1986), and "The Visible and Invisible Liga Patriótica Argentina, 1919–1928: Gender Roles and the Right Wing," *Hispanic American Historical Review*, 64(2), 1984.

13. Hannah Arendt, "Ideology and Terror: A Novel Form of Government," *The Review of Politics* 15(3), 1953, 303–37.

14. See Zeev Sternhell, with Mario Sznajder and Maia Asheri, *The Birth of Fascist Ideology: From Cultural Rebellion to Political Revolution* (Princeton, NJ: Princeton University Press, 1994); Zeev Sternhell, *Les anti-Lumières: du XVIIIe siècle à la guerre froide* (Paris: Fayard, 2006).

15. Leopoldo Lugones, *Odas seculares* (Buenos Aires: Arnoldo Moen y hermano editores, 1910), 33.

16. Idem, *La voz contra la roca* (San José, Costa Rica: Colección Ariel, 1912), 12, 18.

17. Leopoldo Lugones (Hijo), *Mi Padre: Biografía de Leopoldo Lugones* (Buenos Aires: Centurión, 1949), 327.

18. Leopoldo Lugones, *Acción: Las cuatro conferencias patrióticas del Coliseo* (Buenos Aires: Círculo Tradición Argentina, 1923), 14, 17

19. Idem, "La hora de la espada," in Leopoldo Lugones, *La patria fuerte* (Buenos Aires: Círculo Militar-Biblioteca del Oficial, 1930), 13–19.

20. Julio Irazusta, "Demagogia socialista," *La Nueva República*, October 28, 1931 and "Los radicales gritan hoy contra el fraude igual que lo hacían ayer los conservadores," *La Nueva República*, November 9, 1931. For a similar warning, see also Manuel Gálvez, "El deber de las clases dirigentes," *Criterio*, October 1, 1931. See also Julio Irazusta (ed.), *El Pensamiento político nacionalista*, vol. 3 (Buenos Aires: Obligado, 1975), 143, 222.

21. Julio Irazusta "El despotismo de la libertad," *La Nueva República*, October 26, 1931; Julio Irazusta (ed.), *El Pensamiento político nacionalista*, 141.

22. See Juan Donoso Cortés, *Ensayo sobre el Catolicismo, el liberalismo y el socialismo* (Madrid: Imprenta de La Publicidad, 1851), 202. On Donoso Cortés see Alberto Spektorowski, "Maistre, Donoso Cortes, and the Legacy of Catholic Authoritarianism," *Journal of the History of Ideas* 63(2), 2002.

23. Federico Ibarguren, *Rosas y la tradición hispanoamericana* (Buenos Aires: 1942), 3.

24. Leopoldo Lugones, *La Grande Argentina* (Buenos Aires: Babel, 1930), 202.

25. See Rodolfo Irazusta, "Aclaración sobre la democracia," *Criterio*, September 21, 1933; Rodolfo Irazusta, "La política," *La Nueva República*, April 28, 1928; "Dictaduras efímeras y dictaduras permanentes," *Bandera Argentina*, April 5th, 1933, 1; "Fascismo verdadera democracia," *Clarinada*, July 31, 1940.

26. Rodolfo Irazusta, "El aniversario de la Constitución," *La Nueva República*, May 5, 1928. See also Federico Ibarguren, *La aristocracia y la cultura* (Buenos Aires: Ediciones de la Liga Republicana, n.d.), 11.

27. See Jorge Luis Borges, *El idioma de los argentinos* (Buenos Aires: Gleizer, 1928); Raúl Scalabrini Ortiz, *El Hombre que está solo y espera* (Buenos Aires: Gleizer, 1931); Ezequiel Martínez Estrada, *Radiografía de la pampa* (Buenos Aires: Babel, 1933).

28. See César Pico, "Hacia la hispanidad," *Sol y Luna* 9, 1942. On the critique of indigenismo, see also Lizardo Zia, "Vida literaria," *Criterio*, December 15, 1932, 257; "La crisis intelectual," *Bandera Argentina*, July 6, 1939.

29. On this topic, see Paulo Cavaleri, *La restauración del Virreinato* (Bernal: Universidad Nacional de Quilmes, 2004); Federico Finchelstein, *Transatlantic Fascism*, 144–51.

30. Hector Saenz y Quesada, "¿Un continente con contenido?" *El Restaurador*, June 12, 1941, 1. See also Benjamín Villafañe, *El destino de Sudamérica* (Buenos Aires: Talleres Gráficos Perú, 1944), 113, 116–17.

31. "Hay que dar al alma nacional un sentido heroico de la vida," *Bandera Argentina*, December 24, 1936.

32. Julio Irazusta, "El oficio de gobernar," *La Nueva República*, May 12, 1928, 1. See also Julio Irazusta, "El Estado y sus funciones," *La Nueva República*, June 2, 1928, 1; Ernesto Palacio, "Incultura democrática," *La Nueva República*, May 26, 1928, 1.

33. Leopoldo Lugones, *La Grande Argentina* (Buenos Aires: Babel, 1930), 191, 202.

34. "Reflector nacionalista," *Choque*, January 3, 1941.

35. Rodolfo Irazusta, "Las falsas adaptaciones," *Criterio*, October 5, 1933, 104–5.

36. For an extensive analysis of this topic, see my book *Fascismo, Liturgia e Imaginario*.

37. See the proclamation in *La Fronda*, September 7, 1930. See also Leopoldo Lugones (Hijo), *Mi Padre*, 347.

38. Leopoldo Lugones, *Política revolucionaria* (Buenos Aires: Anaconda, 1931), 52, 53, 65–66.

39. On LCA propaganda and ideals, see *AGN*. Archivo Agustín P. Justo. Caja 49. Documents 166, 167, 168, 169, 170, 172, 173, 174.

40. *AGN*. Archivo Uriburu. Legajo 20. Sala VII 2596. Carpeta recortes s/n.

41. Ibid. See also J.M. Espigares Moreno, *Lo que me dijo el Gral. Uriburu* (Buenos Aires: Durruty y Kaplan, 1933), 138; and Pablo Calatayud's recollection, "El Pensamiento político del General," *Aduna*, September 6, 1934, 3; *AGN*. Archivo Uriburu. Legajo 20. Sala VII 2596.

42. *AGN*. Archivo Uriburu. Legajo 20. Sala VII 2596. Carpeta recortes s/n.

43. Ibid.

44. Ibid.

45. AGN. Archivo Agustín P. Justo. Caja 49. Doc. 232. See also Doc. 382; "La Legión Cívica Argentina," *Aduna*, November 15, 1933, 1.

46. See *AGN*. Archivo Agustín P. Justo. Caja 49. Doc. 233 and ibid., Caja 45. Doc. 67.

47. "El Ejercito y la política," *Aduna*, July 15, 1936.

48. "Teoría y práctica," *Aduna*, September 6, 1935.

49. *AGN*. Archivo Agustín P. Justo. Caja 45. Doc.146; "Discurso que podría ser programa," *Bandera Argentina*, May 3, 1933, 1. See also Juan P. Ramos, "Significación del adunismo," *Crisol*, February 1, 1934, 9. See also Hildebrando, "La marcha sobre Buenos Aires," *Bandera Argentina*, September 6, 1933, 2.

50. *Archivo Privado de Leopoldo Lugones*. Papeles y carpetas de Leopoldo Lugones. *Guardia Argentina. Propósitos*, 6–8.

51. "Soldados de la Patria con el fascismo," "Viva el fascismo y el ejército," *AGN*. Archivo Agustín P. Justo. Caja 54. Doc. 12.

52. On AJN, see Sandra McGee Deutsch, *Las Derechas*, 232–34. On PFA see also Federico Finchelstein, *Transatlantic Fascism*, 112–13.

53. *AGN*. Archivo Agustín P. Justo. Caja 104. Doc.149.

54. "A propósito de la orientación política de la Revolución," *Alianza*, Segunda Quincena, November 1943, 2.

55. "Alianza: Justicia, sindicalismo y revolución," *Alianza*, December 6, 1945.

56. Sandra McGee Deutsch, *Las Derechas*, 203–47. See also Mariela Rubinzal, "La disputa en las plazas: Estrategias, símbolos y rituales del primero de mayo nacionalista. Buenos Aires, 1930–1943," *Historia y Política* 19, 2008.

57. See Federico Finchelstein, *Fascismo, Liturgia e Imaginario*, 113–30.

58. "Las fuerzas armadas están para defender a la Nación," *Crisol*, October 7, 1936. See also "Respeto al Ejército," *Choque*, January 3, 1941, 1; "El gran Ejército para

la realidad de la Grande Argentina," *El Federal,* November 18, 1944; Carlos
M. Silveyra, "¡Viva la Patria salvada por el Ejército!" *Clarinada,* July 1943.

59. "A propósito de la orientación política de la Revolución," *Alianza,* Segunda
Quincena, November 1943, 1; "En brillante acto tomó posesión de su cargo el
Dr. Jordán B. Genta," *Cabildo,* June 7, 1941, 12.

60. For some examples, see "Origen y significado de la doctrina del corporativismo,"
Aduna, October 15, 1933, 1; Guido Glave, *Economía dirigida de la democracia cor-
porativa argentina* (Buenos Aires, Imprenta L.L. Gotelli, 1936), 7, 30; Hector
Bernardo, *El régimen corporativo y el mundo actual* (Buenos Aires: Adsum, 1943);
El Pampero, February 28, 1942; *Abrojos* 1(1), November, 1933; *AGN.* Archivo
Agustín P. Justo. Caja 104. Doc. 51; Homo, "Régimen Corporativo," *Abrojos,*
November 1933; *AGN.* Archivo Agustín P. Justo. Caja 49. Doc. 29.

61. See Hector Bernardo, "Reflector nacionalista," *Choque,* January 3, 1941.

62. "Carta del General Juan Bautista Molina a la Alianza de la Juventud Nacionalista.
25 de Mayo de 1941." Biblioteca Nacional de la República Argentina. Folleto
273855. See also *AGN.* Archivo Agustín P. Justo. Caja 104. Doc. 111. Folleto "La
palabra del Gral. Juan Bautista Molina al Nacionalismo Argentino," 1° de mayo
1942. On Molina and nacionalismo, see also *AGN.* Archivo Agustín P. Justo.
Caja 104. Doc. 459.

63. "Dictaduras efímeras y dictaduras permanentes" *Bandera Argentina,* April 5,
1933, 1.

64. Bonifacio Lastra, *Bajo el signo nacionalista: escritos y discursos* (Buenos
Aires: Alianza, 1944), 51.

CHAPTER 2

1. "... Y sigue el confusionismo," *Clarinada,* June 30, 1941.

2. "Alianza. Ubicación del nacionalismo," *Alianza,* October 2, 1945.

3. Enrique Osés, *Medios y fines del nacionalismo* (Buenos Aires: La Mazorca, 1941),
57, 60.

4. See *Archivo del Ministerio de Relaciones Exteriores y Culto.* Argentina, División
Política, Caja 22. Italia. "Entrevista concedida por el señor Mussolini al señor
Juan Carlos Goyeneche." Exp. 7. Año 1943. Folios 1–4. See also *Archivio Centrale
dello Stato.* Italia. Ministero della Cultura Popolare. D.G Serv. Propaganda.
B. 8 Argentina 1938 I/4/1 T. 487; Federico Finchelstein, *Transatlantic Fascism,*
163–64.

5. *Archivio Centrale dello Stato.* Italia. Ministero della Cultura Popolare. D.G
Serv. Propaganda. B. 9 Argentina 5/1/8 and *Archivo del Ministerio de Relaciones
Exteriores y Culto.* Buenos Aires. Argentina, División Política, Caja 22. Italia.
Telegrama cifrado. N 511. N 34. Estrictamente reservado y muy confidencial.
Folio 1. Junio 4/4 1943.

6. Federico Finchelstein, *Transatlantic Fascism,* and Ronald Newton, *The "Nazi"
Menace in Argentina.*

7. Felipe Yofre, *El fascismo y nosotros* (Buenos Aires: Liga Republicana, 1933), 18, 40.

8. Carlos Ibarguren, *La inquietud de esta hora: liberalismo, corporativismo, nacionalismo* (Buenos Aires: Librería y Editorial La Facultad, 1934).

9. Folleto Luis F. Gallardo, *La Mística del Adunismo* (Buenos Aires, 1933), 15 in *AGN*. Archivo Uriburu. Legajo 26.

10. Felipe Yofre, *El fascismo y nosotros*, 18, 21, 28, 36, 42, 43.

11. See Speech by Ramos in *AGN*. Archivo Agustín P. Justo. Caja 45. Doc. 146.

12. *AGN*. Archivo Agustín P. Justo. Caja 49. Doc. 29. Boletín Oficial del Partido Nacional Fascista. Roberto A. Rolón (hijo), "La Voz de Abrojos," *Abrojos*, November, 1933.

13. Federico Finchelstein, *Transatlantic Fascism*, 115–17.

14. Alberto Daniel Faleroni, "Imperialismo, nacionalismo, revolución," *Clarinada*, September, 1943, 6.

15. E.M., "Universalidad del fascismo," *Nueva Idea*, January 19, 1935; *AGN*. Archivo Agustín P. Justo. Caja 36. Doc. 271.

16. Idem, *AGN*. Archivo Agustín P. Justo. Caja 36. Doc. 271.

17. On this topic, see Federico Finchelstein, *El Canon del Holocausto* (Buenos Aires: Prometeo, 2010), Chapter 4.

18. Juan E. Carulla, *Al filo del Medio Siglo* (Buenos Aires: Huemul, 1964), 241.

19. Julio Irazusta, "La personalidad de Hitler," *Nuevo Orden*, May 14, 1941. See also "El miedo al adunismo," *Aduna*, March 31, 1935, 1.

20. Nimio de Anquín, "Liberalismo subrepticio y libertad cristiana," *Nueva Política* 12, June, 1941, 7.

21. *AGN*. Archivo Agustín P. Justo. Caja 104. Doc.149; Doc.148 and Caja 104 bis, Doc. 318.

22. "Un lenguaraz extranjero," *Nuevo Orden*, September 5, 1940.

23. Alberto Ezcurra Medrano, "La obra del liberalismo y sus pretensiones actuales," *Nueva Política* 18, December, 1941, 22.

24. See *Archivio Centrale dello Stato*. Italia. Ministero della Cultura Popolare. D.G. Serv. Propaganda. B. 9 Argentina 5/1/8; *Archivo del Ministerio de Relaciones Exteriores y Culto. Argentina*, División Política, Caja 22. Italia. Telegrama cifrado. N 511. N 34. Estrictamente reservado y muy confidencial. Folio 1. Junio 4/4 1943. See also División Política. Mueble 7. Casilla 40. Guerra Europea. Ex, 448. Año 1942. Telegrama cifrado 460; División Política. Mueble 7. Casilla 37. Guerra Europea. Ex, 365. Año 1941.

25. César Pico, "Inteligencia y revolución," *La Nueva República*, January 1, 1928; Julio Irazusta (ed.), *El Pensamiento político nacionalista*, 29.

26. Alberto Ezcurra Medrano, *Catolicismo y nacionalismo* (Buenos Aires: Adsum, 1939), 49.

27. "Lo que queremos y lo que no queremos," *Crisol*, October 18, 1936.

28. See T.P. y T., "Adunismo," *Criterio*, June 1, 1933, 204; "El congreso Eucarístico," *Aduna*, July 31, 1934, 1. See also "La injuria a Dios," *Aduna*, September 30, 1934, 1.; "¡Christus Regnat!" *Aduna*, October 15, 1934, 1.

29. See Loris Zanatta, *Del estado liberal a la nación católica*. On the church see also Roberto Di Stefano and Loris Zanatta, *Historia de la Iglesia argentina. Desde la conquista hasta fines del siglo XX* (Buenos Aires: Grijalvo, 2000), and Luis Alberto Romero, "Una nación católica 1880–1946," in Carlos Altamirano (ed.), *La Argentina en el siglo XX* (Buenos Aires: Ariel, 1999).

30. César Pico, *Doctrina y finalidades del comunismo* (Santiago: Editorial Difusión Chilena, 1942), 51.

31. Idem, *Carta a Jacques Maritain sobre la colaboración de los católicos con los movimientos de tipo fascista* (Buenos Aires: Francisco A. Colombo, 1937), 7–8, 13–14, 20, 21, 36, 40–41, 43.

32. Luis Barrantes Molina, "Fascismo y totalitarismo," *El Pueblo*, February 22–23, 1937, 4.

33. Julio Meinvielle, *Concepción católica de la política* (Buenos Aires: Cursos de Cultura Católica, 1941), 252.

34. On Schmitt and his influence in Argentina see Jorge Dotti, *Carl Schmitt en la Argentina* (Rosario: Homo Sapiens, 2000).

35. See Enrique Harriague Coronado, "Sigue el reajuste del estatuto colonial," *La Voz del Plata*, September 30, 1942, 4; Federico Ibarguren, *Rosas y la tradición hispanoamericana* (Buenos Aires: [s.n.], 1942); "Como se ha venido achicando la Patria," *Choque*, January 3, 1941, 6; "Ylex Paraguayensis," *Nueva Política* 13, July, 1941, 6; H. Sáenz y Quesada, "¿Qué sería una política imperial argentina?" *Nueva Política* 9, February, 1940; Armando Cascella, "Hay que retomar la ruta del virreynato," *Nuevo Orden*, August 8, 1940.

36. *Archivo Privado de Leopoldo Lugones*. Papeles y carpetas de Leopoldo Lugones. *Guardia Argentina. Propósitos.* 1933. P. 10.

37. Ramón Doll, "Un pleito protocolar: la Suprema Corte y el cardenal," *La Voz del Plata*, July 29, 1942, 5.

38. Idem, *Acerca de una política nacional* (Buenos Aires: Difusión, 1939), 165, 169, 175, 189. See also Ricardo Font Ezcurra, *La Unidad Nacional* (Buenos Aires: Editorial La Mazorca, 1941), XI, XII, 200.

39. José Ingenieros, *La evolución sociológica argentina: de la barbarie al imperialismo* (Buenos Aires: Libr. J. Menéndez, 1910), 86, 90. See also "El día de la raza," *Nueva Política* 28, October, 1942.

40. Rodolfo Irazusta, "Los ingleses y el progreso argentino," *Reconquista*, November 30, 1939.

41. Marcelo Sánchez Sorondo, "Dialéctica del imperio," *Sol y Luna* 1, 1938, 107, 109–10.

42. Juan P. Ramos, "La cultura española y la conquista de América," *Sol y Luna* 9, 1942, 47.

43. Alberto Ezcurra Medrano, "Libertad y totalitarismo," *Nueva Política* 28, May, 1943, 13.

44. César Pico, "Totalitarismo," *Sol y Luna* 3, 1939, 79.

45. Ernesto Palacio, *La historia falsificada* (Buenos Aires: Difusión, 1939), 151.

46. "El Dr. Nimio de Anquín pide sea reconsiderada su exoneración," *Crisol*, September 9, 1939.

47. "La Unión Nacional Fascista de Córdoba," *Crisol*, October 4, 1936.

48. *AGN*. Archivo Agustín P. Justo. Caja 36. Doc. 271.

49. Leopoldo Marechal, "Carta a Eduardo Mallea," *Sol y Luna* 1, 1938.

50. "Incomprensión," *Clarinada* 1(8), December, 1937.

51. See Carlos M. Silveyra, *El Comunismo en la Argentina. Origen, desarrollo, organización actual.* Segunda Edición revisada y corregida. (Buenos Aires: Editorial Patria, 1937). Prologue by Virgilio Filippo, 7.

52. Eugenia Silveyra de Oyuela, "El gobierno totalitario no está contra el dogma católico," *Clarinada* 5(54–55), October–November, 1941, 2–4. See also Federico Finchelstein, *Transatlantic Fascism*, 131–32 and 284, and Sandra McGee Deutsch, *Crossing Borders, Claiming a Nation: A History of Argentine Jewish Women, 1880–1955* (Durham: Duke University Press, 2010), 303.

53. Luis G. Martínez Villada, *Una lección magistral de nacionalismo* (Rosario: Unión Nacionalista Santafesina, 1939), 24.

54. Felipe Yofre, *El fascismo y nosotros*, 40–41.

55. César Pico, *Carta a Jacques Maritain sobre la colaboración de los católicos con los movimientos de tipo fascista*, 33.

56. "La hora que viene," *Clarinada*, 2 (23) March 31, 1939.

57. Julio Meinvielle, *Un juicio católico sobre los problemas nuevos de la política* (Buenos Aires: Gladium, 1937), 52–57; "De la guerra santa," *Criterio*, August 19, 1937, 378–83.

58. See all by Gustavo J. Franceschi, *Criterio*, September 21, 1933, 56; "El despertar nacionalista," *Criterio*, October 20, 1932, 55; "La inquietud de esta hora," *Criterio*, August 2, 1934, 318; "Argentina," *Criterio*, January 27, 1938, 78.

59. See Gustavo J. Franceschi, "El eclipse de la moral," *Criterio*, May 27, 1937, 77, and his *En el humo del incendio* (Buenos Aires: Difusión, 1938); *Archivio Centrale dello Stato*. Italia. Ministero della Cultura Popolare. D.G Serv. B. 7 Argentina 1937 I/4/18.T. 105; Federico Finchelstein, *Transatlantic Fascism*, 126–29, 145.

60. Antonio Hilario Varela, *Profetas, apóstoles y redentores (episodios de la gesta emancipadora, consciente y organizada)* (Buenos Aires, [s.n.], 1934). On nacionalista propaganda for children see also, for example, "Pequeña Historia para el uso de los niños," *Nueva Política*, February, 1942, 28.

61. Leonardo Castellani, *Camperas. Cuentos de la pampa y el monte* (Buenos Aires, Editorial La Mazorca, 1941), 9.

62. Idem, *Camperas*, 26, 48.

63. Idem, *Camperas*, 61–64.

64. Leonardo Castellani, *Las Canciones de Militis. Seis ensayos y tres cartas* (Buenos Aires: Ediciones Dictio, 1973), 207.

65. Leonardo Castellani, *Camperas*, 61–64.

66. Idem, *Camperas*, 64.

67. Federico Ibarguren, *Orígenes del nacionalismo argentino 1927–1937* (Buenos Aires: Celcius, 1969), 275.

68. Idem, *Orígenes del nacionalismo*, 214.

69. Juan Sepich, "El problema fundamental de la cultura," *Sol y Luna* 5, 1940. See also Ernesto Palacio, *La historia falsificada* (Buenos Aires: Difusión, 1939), 61.

70. See Federico Ibarguren, *Orígenes del nacionalismo*, 303–4.

71. Leonardo Castellani, *Esencia del liberalismo* (Buenos Aires: Huemul, 1971), 14.

72. "Nacionalismo y catolicismo," *Clarinada* 1, December, 1937.

73. Julio Meinvielle, *Un juicio católico sobre los problemas nuevos de la política*, 44.

74. Héctor Llambías, "Review of Tristán de Athayde, *El problema de la burguesía*", *Sol y Luna* 3, 1939, 176.

75. Julio Meinvielle, *Un juicio católico sobre los problemas nuevos de la política*, 45.

76. Juan Carulla, "Carta a un nacionalista de San Martín," *Bandera Argentina*, December 27, 1936.

77. Carlos M. Laprida, "Rodeo de cipayos," *Clarinada*, June 30, 1941.

78. See Virgilio Filippo, *Música de ideas* (Buenos Aires: Tor, 1936), 183–84.

79. See *Combate*, June–July, 1943.

CHAPTER 3

1. See the document in *Espacios* 26, 2000. For an analysis of the document see Federico Finchelstein and Esteban Speyer, "El hilo pardo: una mirada nazi sobre Argentina," in the same issue. The original version, "Die Judenfrage in Argentinien," is anonymous, AA/PA, Inland II A/B, Akten betr. Judenfrage in Argentinien, 1940 ca.

2. On Nazis and Nazism in Argentina and their support for the Argentine fascists see Ronald Newton, *The "Nazi Menace" in Argentina*; Leonardo Senkman and Saul Sosnowski, *Fascismo y Nazismo en las letras argentinas* (Buenos Aires: Lumiere, 2009). On Italian fascist support see Federico Finchelstein, *Transatlantic Fascism*. On Wast's links with the Nazis, see also *Archivo IWO*. CAJA Organización Popular contra el Antisemitismo. Correspondencia Panfletos. Publicaciones C. 1936–1937. C. 1939. informe Org. Pop contra el Ant, 1937.

3. Luis Barrantes Molina, "Judaísmo y comunismo," *El Pueblo*, September 12, 1936.

4. Gustavo Franceschi, "El problema judío VI," *Criterio*, July 13, 1939, 245–50.

5. On this topic see Daniel Lvovich and Federico Finchelstein, "L'Holocauste et l'Eglise argentine. Perceptions et Réactions," *Bulletin trimestriel de la Fondation Auschwitz* 76–77, 2002.

6. See Leonardo Castellani, *Deciamos ayer* (Buenos Aires: Editorial Sudestada, 1968) 332.

7. Gustavo Franceschi, "Antisemitismo," *Criterio*, December 7, 1933, 321.

8. Idem, "Como se prepara una revolución," *Criterio*, September 14, 1933, 30. See also "Antisemitismo," *Criterio*, December 7, 1933, 321.

9. Idem, "Como se prepara una revolución", *Criterio*, September 14, 1933, 30; "Una Europa sin judíos," *Bandera Argentina*, February 1, 1941, 1.

10. Julio Meinvielle, "Catolicismo y Nacionalismo," *El Pueblo*, October 18, 1936, 3.

11. Idem, *Entre la Iglesia y el Reich* (Buenos Aires: Adsum, 1937), 68.

12. Idem, *Los tres pueblos bíblicos en su lucha por la dominación del mundo* (Buenos Aires: Adsum, 1937), 7, 27, 49, 55, and 62.

13. See ibid. 55, and Julio Meinvielle, *Concepción católica de la economía* (Buenos Aires: Cursos de Cultura Católica, 1936), 158.

14. Julio Meinvielle, *El judío* (Buenos Aires: Antídoto, 1936), 11.

15. Virgilio Filippo, *Los Judíos. Juicio histórico científico que el autor no pudo transmitir por L.R.S. Radio París* (Buenos Aires: Tor, 1939), 111. See also idem, "El grupo israelita," *Clarinada*, March 31, 1939.

16. Idem, *Conferencias radiotelefónicas* (Buenos Aires: Tor, 1936), 215. See also "Democracia enferma," *Bandera Argentina*, August 20, 1933, 3; "Comerciantes, profesionales y ex miembros de la Zwi Migdal son en Entre Rios propagandistas rojos," *Crisol*, February 18, 1937.

17. Idem, *Conferencias radiotelefónicas*, 215.

18. Idem, *Los Judíos*, 216. See also pages 185, 212–13. On this topic see also Federico Finchelstein, "The Anti-Freudian Politics of Argentine Fascism. Antisemitism, Catholicism and the Internal Enemy, 1932–1945," *Hispanic American Historical Review* 87(1), 2007.

19. "El problema judío en Argentina," *Bandera Argentina*, August 27, 1932, 2.

20. "Nosotros y los judíos," *Bandera Argentina*, April 5, 1933, 1. For the idea of cleansing Argentina of Jews and other "enemies of God" see also *AGN*. Archivo Agustín P. Justo. Caja 36. Doc. 277. Reacción. 1 quincena junio 1935 n° 1.

21. Victoria Campos, "Oda al Loro," *La Maroma* 2 (Segunda Quincena, 1939) 13.

22. Virgilio Filippo, *Los Judíos*, 48, 86. *Clarinada*, January 31, 1941, 1, and *Clarinada*, March 31, 1941, 1; Virgilio Filippo, *Música de Ideas*, 43.

23. *Clarinada*, December 31, 1941, 1; Daniel Lvovich, "Un vocero antisemita en Buenos Aires: la revista Clarinada (1937–1945)," *Nuestra Memoria* 7(16), 2000. See also Norman Cohn, *El mito de la conspiración judía mundial* (Buenos Aires, Milá: 1988), 266.

24. "Judas, siempre es Judas!" *Clarinada*, July 31, 1941.

25. "Judíos corruptores de menores," *Bandera Argentina*, August 2, 1933, 3. The context for this reference was the antifascist activities of students from the University of Buenos Aires's high school, *Escuela Superior de Comercio Carlos Pellegrini*.

26. See *Clarinada*, September 30, 1941. For a converging motif see "El rapto de América Latina," *Clarinada*, October–November, 1941.

27. See Sandra McGee Deutsch, "Contra 'el gran desorden sexual': Los nacionalistas y la sexualidad, 1919–1940," *Cuadernos del CISH* 17–18, 2005, 127–50;

McGee Deutsch, *Las Derechas*, 234–38 and Federico Finchelstein, *Fascismo, Liturgia e Imaginario*, 113–30. See also "La mujer argentina y el nacionalismo," *Nuevo Orden*, December 11, 1940, 5. See also, "Una católica argentina," *Crisol*, July 24, 1934, 2; Hildebrando, "La mujer y el nacionalismo," *Bandera Argentina*, May 17, 1935, 1, 3.

28. See Santiago Diaz Vieyra, "La mujer y el nacionalismo," *Bandera Argentina*, September 6, 1933. See also Juan Carulla, "El voto femenino," *La Nueva República*, April 28, 1928; "Encuesta de Los Principios. Sra ¿Quiere Ud. Votar?" *Los Principios*, September 6, 1932, 3; Tomás D. Casares, *Catolicismo y Acción Católica* (Buenos Aires: Junta Parroquial del Santísimo Redentor, 1932) 44; *AGN*. Archivo Agustín P. Justo. Caja 49. Doc. 29. Una Mujer Argentina, "La palabra de una mujer argentina," *Abrojos*, November 1933, 12.

29. See "El mitin feminista," *Bandera Argentina*, September 25, 1932, 1; "Ha muerto una marimacho famosa," *Bandera Argentina*, June 22, 1932, 1; "Oscarwildeanos de 'amigos del arte,'" *Crisol*, October 8, 1936; "Regreso de la U.R.S.S. por Andre Gide," *Bandera Argentina*, December 22, 1936; Enrique Osés, "La Patria ante todo," *El Federal*, February 8, 1944, 1.

30. "Proclamas del Partido Fascista Argentino," *Bandera Argentina*, August 20, 1932, 3.

31. Gabriel Riesco, *Nuestra misión histórica* (Buenos Aires: Imprenta Guadalupe, 1941), 82–85.

32. Julio Meinvielle, *Entre la Iglesia y el Reich* (Buenos Aires: Adsum, 1937), 66, 68.

33. "Proclamas del Partido Fascista Argentino," *Bandera Argentina*, August 20, 1932, 3.

34. Juan Carulla, "Capítulo de historia. El año 1932," *La Nueva República*, May 26, 1928.

35. "La estrella de Sión contra la Cruz del Sur," *Clarinada*, September 30, 1941.

36. See Leopoldo Lugones (hijo), "El que se creyó fusilado: Leopoldo Bard," *Bandera Argentina*, March 7, 1933, 1; idem, "El doctor Bard, el abogado de 'Crítica' y el sujeto Melilla," *Bandera Argentina*, August 12, 1933, 2. See also *AGN*. Archivo Agustín P. Justo. Caja 46. Doc. 107.

37. See George L. Mosse, *Nationalism and Sexuality: Respectability and Abnormal Sexuality in Modern Europe* (New York: Howard Fertig, 1985), and *The Image of Man: The Creation of Modern Masculinity* (New York: Oxford University Press, 1996).

38. Daniel Lvovich, *Nacionalismo y antisemitismo* (Buenos Aires: Vergara, 2003), 489–507.

39. Hugo Wast, *Oro* (Buenos Aires: Editores de Hugo Wast, 1935), 216.

40. Ibid. 216.

41. Ibid. 283.

42. Ibid. 307.

43. See Dominick LaCapra, Preface to Federico Finchelstein (ed.), *Los Alemanes, el Holocausto y la culpa colectiva*, 9–28.

44. Hugo Wast, "¿Es lícito en la Argentina hablar de los judíos?" *Bandera Argentina*, September 5, 1935, 5.

45. See Daniel Lvovich, *Nacionalismo y antisemitismo*, 502–3.

46. Ventura Chumillas, *Crónicas y críticas literarias* (Buenos Aires: El Pueblo, 1936), 270.

47. See Luis Barrantes Molina, "La última novela de Hugo Wast," *El Pueblo*, June 20, 1935; *Archivo IWO*. CAJA Organización Popular contra el Antisemitismo.

48. *Archivo IWO*. CAJA Organización Popular contra el Antisemitismo 5. See also Ramón Doll, *Acerca de una política nacional* (Buenos Aires: Difusión, 1939), 65.

49. Lázaro Schallman, *Hugo Wast, Anticristiano. Disparates, contradicciones y paralogismos acumulados por el fantaseador de 'El Kahal'* (Rosarios: Talleres Gráficos Musumarra Hnos., 1936), and César Tiempo, *La Campaña antisemita y el director de la Biblioteca Nacional* (Buenos Aires: Ediciones Mundo Israelita, 1935). For other antifascist criticisms of Wast see, for example, Archivo IWO. CAJA Organización Popular contra el Antisemitismo. Correspondencia Panfletos. Publicaciones C. 1936–1937 C. 1939.

50. "Paulatinamente los judíos se infiltran en nuestra patria," *Acción Antijudía Argentina*, n° 14, 1939. On accusations of infiltration see also "Como forman la cadena para burlar los decretos sobre restricción de la inmigración," *Bandera Argentina*, December 17, 1936.

51. For some examples, *Bandera Argentina*, December 29, 1936; Rodolfo Irazusta, "Entre gallos y medianoche," en *La Voz del Plata* 1(1), 1942, 1.

52. "Los enemigos del nacionalismo," *Clarinada*, August, 1938.

53. *Clarinada*, August, 1938, 1.

54. *Clarinada*, August, 1938. The protocols were also published in the Catholic newspaper *El Pueblo*. See also "Gracias colegas," *Bandera Argentina*, October 30, 1932, 2; *AGN*. Archivo Agustín Justo. Caja 49. Doc. 247; Walter Degreff, "El quinto sanhedrin cabalístico de 1851," *Crisol*, October 20, 1936. For an influential version of the protocols in Argentina see *El Judío sin careta. Los protocolos de los sabios de Sión: el libro más importante de la historia* (Buenos Aires: s.n., 1936). See also Lvovich's excellent account of the history of the Protocols in Argentina in Daniel Lvovich, *Nacionalismo y antisemitismo*, 467–507.

55. Gustavo J. Franceschi, *Criterio*, September 21, 1933, 56.

56. See Virgilio Filippo, *El plan quinquenal de Perón y los comunistas* (Buenos Aires: Lista Blanca, 1948).

57. Bruno Jacovella, "El judío es el enemigo del pueblo cristiano," *Crisol*, October 13, 1936.

58. *Clarinada*, June, 1942, 31.

59. See *Clarinada*, March 31, 1939, 25. See also "Admonición," *Bandera Argentina*, August 5, 1933, 3.

CHAPTER 4

1. On Peronism and fascism, see Paul H. Lewis, "Was Perón a Fascist? An Inquiry into the Nature of Fascism," *Journal of Politics* 42(1), 1980, 242–56; Cristián Buchrucker, *Nacionalismo y Peronismo* (Buenos Aires: Sudamericana, 1987); Alberto Spektorowski, *Argentina's Revolution of the Right*.

2. I deal more extensively with the Argentine fascist view of Perón in the next chapter.

3. On Argentine antifascism and anti-Peronism see Andrés Bisso, *El antifascismo argentino* (Buenos Aires: CeDInCI Editores, 2007); Marcela García Sebastiani, *Los antiperonistas en la Argentina peronista* (Buenos Aires: Prometeo, 2005); Jorge Nállim, *Transformations and Crisis of Liberalism in Argentina, 1930–1955* (Pittsburgh: University of Pittsburgh Press, 2012). On the general context of European antifascism see Enzo Traverso, *A feu et à sang. De la guerre civile euro-péenne 1914–1945* (Paris: Stock, 2007).

4. See *L'Antidiario*, July 9–16, 1950, and *L'Antidiario*, July 16–23, 1950, 342–43. I want to thank Italian historian Claudio Pavone for his reference to the Italian partisan civil war knowledge of Perón and the Argentine military dictatorship.

5. Hannah Arendt, "The Seeds of a Fascist International," in Jerome Kohn (ed.), *Essays in Understanding 1930–1954* (New York: Harcourt Brace, 1994), 149.

6. Tulio Halperín Donghi, *Argentina en el callejón* (Buenos Aires: Ariel, 1995), 30.

7. Ibid. 35.

8. See "Desde los balcones de la Casa de gobierno despidiéndose de los traba-jadores concentrados en la Plaza de Mayo. Octubre 17 de 1945," Coronel Juan Perón, *El pueblo ya sabe de qué se trata. Discursos* (Buenos Aires: 1946), 186.

9. For some important works on classic Peronism see Juan Carlos Torre, "Interpretando (una vez más) los orígenes del peronismo," *Desarrollo Económico* 28(112), 1989; Juan Carlos Torre (ed.), *Los años peronistas, 1943–1955* (Buenos Aires, Sudamericana, 2002); Miguel Murmis and Juan Carlos Portantiero, *Estudios sobre los orígenes del peronismo* (Buenos Aires, Siglo Veintiuno Editores, 1971); Tulio Halperín Donghi, *La larga agonía de la Argentina peronista* (Buenos Aires: Ariel, 1994); Raanan Rein, *In the Shadow of Perón* (Stanford: Stanford University Press, 2008); Mathew Karush and Oscar Chamosa (eds.), *The New Cultural History of Peronism* (Durham and London: Duke University Press, 2010); Loris Zanatta, *Breve historia del peronismo clásico* (Buenos Aires: Sudamericana, 2009.)

10. On Wast see David Rock, *Authoritarian Argentina*, 137; Loris Zanatta, *Perón y el mito de la nación católica*, 104–15.

11. See James W. McGuire, *Peronism Without Perón. Unions, Parties, and Democracy in Argentina* (Stanford: Stanford University Press, 1997), 52.

12. Robert Potash, "Las fuerzas armadas y la era de Perón," in Juan CarlosTorre (ed.), *Los años peronistas, 1943–1955*, 92–94. On this topic, see also Leonardo

Senkman, "Etnicidad e inmigración durante el primer peronismo," *E.I.A.L.* 3(2), 1992.

13. On the coup, Perón and the Catholic Church, see Loris Zanatta, *Perón y el mito de la nación católica*; Lila Caimari, *Perón y la Iglesia Católica. Religión, Estado y Sociedad en la Argentina (1943–1955)* (Buenos Aires: Ariel, 1995); Susana Bianchi, *Catolicismo y peronismo: Religión y política en la Argentina, 1943–1955* (Tandil: Instituto de Estudios Histórico Sociales, 2001).

14. "Discurso del Pbro. Dr. Juan R. Sepich," Universidad de Buenos Aires, *De la soberanía argentina y la fortaleza nacional* (Buenos Aires: Imprenta de la Universidad, 1944), 33. See also Luis Barrantes Molina, "Tácticas del liberalismo ante el nuevo gobierno," *El Pueblo*, June 17, 1943. See also by Molina, "El derecho a la justa rebelión," *El Pueblo*, June 26, 1943.

15. "Carta al editor," *Criterio*, July 1, 1943, and Gustavo Franceschi, "Un grave problema Argentino imaginario," *Criterio*, January 27, 1944. See also Alberto Ciria, *Partidos y poder en la Argentina moderna* (Buenos Aires: Hyspamerica, 1986), 121.

16. See Juan Carlos Torre, "Introducción a los años peronistas," in Juan Carlos Torre (ed.) *Los años peronistas* 22–23.

17. Tulio Halperín Donghi, *La República imposible (1930–1945)* (Buenos Aires: Emecé, 2007) 301–2.

18. See *Archivo Cedinci*, Documentos del Gou. On Perón and the GOU see Robert Potash, *El ejercito y la política en la Argentina I 1928–1945* (Buenos Aires: Hyspamerica, 1985), 263–340; Tulio Halperín Donghi, *La República imposible (1930–1945)*, 300–15; Alberto Spektorowski, *Argentina's Revolution of the Right*, 176–200.

19. See *Archivo Cedinci*, Documentos del GOU.

20. See *Archivo Cedinci*, Documentos del GOU, and Robert A. Potash, *Perón y el GOU.* (Buenos Aires: Sudamericana, 1984), 104–5.

21. See Juan Domingo Perón, "En la Bolsa de Comercio. 25 de agosto de 1944," in Coronel Juan Perón, *El pueblo quiere saber de qué se trata* (Buenos Aires: 1944), 154, 168–69. See also "El Coronel Perón expuso las obligaciones de los patronos y de los obreros en la Bolsa de Comercio," *El Federal*, September 4, 1944.

22. See *Archivo Cedinci* Documentos del GOU.

23. See Sandra McGee Deutsch, *Las Derechas*, 331.

24. "El Mussolini Argentino: General Fasola Castaño" *El Momento Argentino*, March 16, 1936, 1.

25. See Juan Carlos Torre, "Introducción a los años peronistas." On Perón and the Uriburu dictatorship, see also "El General Perón acusa al Capitán Perón" *La Vanguardia*, September 21, 1948, 2. On Fasola and the myth of Uriburu see my book *Fascismo, Liturgia e Imaginario*, 90–91. On Fasola see also *AGN*. Archivo Agustin P. Justo. Caja 49. Doc. 203.

26. Alberto Spektorowski, *Argentina's Revolution of the Right*, 190.

27. *AGN.* Fondo Documental Secretaría Técnica. Legajo 484. Presidencia de la Nación. Ministerio de Asuntos Técnicos. Organización del pueblo-Población, 1.

28. Juan Perón, *Perón expone su doctrina* (Buenos Aires: Presidencia de la Nación, Subsecretaría de Informaciones, 1951), 10.

29. On Perón and the group of FORJA see Alberto Spektorowski, *Argentina's Revolution of the Right*, 197–98. For some examples of early contacts between Scalabrini and Perón, see his letters to Major Fernando Estrada (July 28, 1944) and to General Orlando Peluffo (August 9, 1944) in *Archivo RSO.* Carpeta Correspondencia RSO 1930–1958.

30. See Letter to Coronel Francisco Bosch. Buenos Aires, November 19, 1940. In *Archivo RSO.* Carpeta Correspondencia Linio Marchetti, Macedonio Fernández y otros. 1934–1948. See also Scalabrini's letters to Carlos Ibarguren (March 31, 1943); Alberto Baldrich (May 4, 1944), ibid. For his support and connections with the military men of the dictatorship of 1943 see his letters to Admiral Leon Sasso (November 26, 1943); General Arturo Rawson (July 19, 1943), and General Orlando Peluffo (June 7, 1944).

31. On this topic, see Gino Germani, *Authoritarianism, Fascism and National Populism* (New Brunswick, NJ: Transaction Books, 1978); Federico Finchelstein, "Fascismo y Peronismo: Una lectura de Gino Germani," *Storiografia. Rivista Annuale di Storia (Pisa–Roma)* 7, 2003–2004, 171–76.

32. Tulio Halperín Donghi, *Argentina en el callejón*, 54.

33. On populism, see Raanan Rein, "From Juan Perón to Hugo Chávez and Back: Populism Reconsidered," in Mario Sznajder, Luis Roniger, and Carlos Forment (eds.), *Shifting Frontiers of Citizenship* (Boston: Brill, 2012). See also Kurt Weyland, "Clarifying a Contested Concept: Populism in the Study of Latin American Politics," *Comparative Politics* 34(1), October, 2001, 1–22; Nadia Urbinati, "Democracy and Populism," *Constellations* 5(1), 1998, 110–124; Carlos de la Torre, *Populist Seduction in Latin America* (Athens Ohio University Press, 2010); Andrew Arato, "Political Theology and Populism" *Social Research* (80)1, Spring 2013, 143–172.; Nadia Urbinati, *Democracy Disfigured. Opinion, Truth, and the People* (Cambridge, Mass: Harvard University Press, 2014).

34. Juan Perón, *Perón expone su doctrina*, 351.

35. On the March, see Jorge Llistosella, *La Marcha peronista* (Buenos Aires: Sudamericana, 2008). On the concept of *la Grande Argentina* see Leopoldo Lugones, *La grande Argentina* (Buenos Aires: Babel, 1930).

36. *Archivo Privado de Leopoldo Lugones.* Papeles y carpetas de Leopoldo Lugones. *Guardia Argentina. Propósitos.*

37. Juan Perón, *Perón expone su doctrina*, 155.

38. See Tomás Eloy Martínez, *Las vidas del General* (Buenos Aires: Aguilar, 2004), 42.

39. Juan Domingo Perón, "En la Bolsa de Comercio. 25 de agosto de 1944."

40. Juan Carlos Torre, "Introducción a los años peronistas," 27, and Juan Perón, *Perón expone su doctrina*, 372. See also Juan Carlos Torre, *La vieja guardia sindical y Perón: Sobre los orígenes del peronismo* (Buenos Aires: Sudamericana, 1990).

41. José Luis Romero, *Las ideas políticas en la Argentina* (Buenos Aires: Fondo de Cultura Económica, 1996), 254–55.

42. Juan Perón, "Política peronista: El sentido de lo orgánico," *Mundo Peronista*, October 10, 1951, 3.

43. See Matthew Karush, *Culture of Class: Radio and Cinema in the Making of a Divided Argentina, 1920-1946* (Durham and London: Duke University Press, 2012).

44. See Juan Perón, "En la proclamación de su candidatura al Pueblo. 12 de Febrero de 1946," in Juan Domingo Perón, *Obras Completas* (Buenos Aires: Docencia, 1998), T. VIII, 28.

45. *Archivo Cedinci*. Folleto "Unión Democrática. 22 millones de muertes costó al mundo el nazismo."

46. See Folletos "Proclama de la Agrupación Femenina Democrática de Avellaneda" and "El Hitler Argentino" in *Archivo Cedinci*.

47. See, for example, "Grupos de personas provocaron incidentes en el radio céntrico," *La Prensa*, January 3, 1946. This identification was shared by Argentine antifascist groups which constantly made reference to "Nazi Peronismo" and Perón's supposed intention to "kill the Jews" see for example, "Aire acondicionado," *La Vanguardia*, January 26, 1946; "No hay derecho," *La Vanguardia*, February 19, 1946.

48. See US Department of State, *Consultation among the American Republics with Respect to the Argentine Situation* (Washington, DC, 1946). See also "Prueba documental de la propaganda nazi," *La Prensa*, January 19, 1946; "Los argentinos reclamamos la publicación del archivo nazi," *La Vanguardia*, January 25, 1946; "U.S. denounces Argentine Fascism," *Life*, February 25, 1946, 27–32; "La Unión mantendrase firme frente al régimen militar argentino, manifestó Braden en un discurso," *La Prensa*, February 14, 1946; "El 'libro azul'" (editorial), *La Prensa*, February 15, 1946. On previous accusations in Latin America and especially in the United States about the military dictatorship's links with Nazism, see *Archivo del Ministerio de Relaciones Exteriores y Culto. Argentina*, Guerra Europea. Mueble 7. Casilla 43. Exp. 549. Año 1943.

49. See Juan Perón, "En la proclamación de su candidatura al Pueblo. 12 de Febrero de 1946," in Juan Domingo Perón, *Obras Completas*, T. VIII, 27. See also " El coronel Perón formuló declaraciones a los perodistas chilenos," *El Federal*, November 27, 1944.

50. See Juan Perón, "En la proclamación de su candidatura al Pueblo. 12 de Febrero de 1946," in Juan Domingo Perón, *Obras Completas*, T. VIII, 28. See also "Dirigió un mensaje al país el candidato por el Partido Laborista," *La Prensa*, February 11, 1946. On Perón's view of himself as a "product" of the military regime of 1943, see "El coronel Perón expuso a dos periodistas peruanos sus

propósitos de gobierno," *La Prensa*, March 21, 1946, 8. On Perón and his denial of Nazism see Coronel Juan Perón, *El pueblo quiere saber de qué se trata*, 91, 132, 140, 153, 157, 169.

51. Juan D. Perón, *El libro azul y blanco* (Buenos Aires, 1946), 5–7.

52. See Juan Perón, "En la proclamación de su candidatura al Pueblo. 12 de Febrero de 1946," in Juan Domingo Perón, *Obras Completas*, T. VIII, 44. On Perón's having no relation to the "two extremes" of foreign ideological "hatred," see also "El coronel Perón hizo declaraciones al diario imparcial de Chile," *La Prensa*, April 26, 1946.

53. *AGN.* Fondo Documental Secretaría Técnica. Legajo 484. Mensajes Presidenciales editados en libreto. *"El Pueblo no se equivoca nunca," dijo Perón a los dirigentes y delegados del movimiento peronista* (Buenos Aires: Presidencia de la Nación, 1954) (April 19, 1954), 18.

54. See "A los obreros de la Federación Argentina de la Alimentación" (July 19, 1945) in Coronel Juan Perón, *El pueblo ya sabe de qué se trata*.

55. See "Habla Eva Perón," *Mundo Peronista*, July 1, 1951; Eva Perón, "Diez consignas para la mujer peronista," *Mundo Peronista*, August 1, 1951, 5; Eva Perón, "Movimiento femenino peronista," *Mundo Peronista*, July 15, 1951, 5. See also Loris Zanatta, *Eva Perón: una biografía política* (Buenos Aires: Sudamericana, 2011); Isabella Cosse, *Estigmas de nacimiento: Peronismo y orden familiar 1946–1955* (Buenos Aires: FCE, 2006); Carolina Barry, *Evita capitana: El Partido Peronista Femenino, 1949–1955* (Buenos Aires: EDUNTREF, 2009).

56. See *AGN.* Fondo Documental Secretaría Técnica. Legajo 484. Mensajes Presidenciales. Clase dictada por el EXCMO Señor Presidente de la Nación, General Juan Perón en la Escuela Superior Peronista. Julio 2, de 1953. 62/70.

57. *AGN.* Fondo Documental Secretaría Técnica. Legajo 484. Mensajes Presidenciales editados en libreto. Folleto *"No queremos hacer el proletariado campesino: Queremos hacer agricultores felices," Dijo Perón a los hombres del campo* (Buenos Aires: Presidencia de la Nación, 1953) (June 11, 1953), 11.

58. "La navidad de Perón," *La Vanguardia*, December 24, 1946.

59. See *AGN.* Fondo Documental Secretaría Técnica. Mensajes presidenciales Clase dictada por el EXCMO Señor Presidente de la Nación, General Juan Perón en la Escuela Superior Peronista. Julio 2, de 1953. 61, 91; "La familia en el pensamiento vivo de Perón," *Mundo Peronista*, January, 1952, 5. See also Silvia Sigal, "Intelectuales y peronismo," in Juan Carlos Torre (ed.), *Los años peronistas, 1943–1955*, 518.

60. See Mariano Plotkin, "Rituales políticos, imágenes y carisma: la celebración del 17 de octubre y el imaginario político peronista 1945–1951," in Juan Carlos Torre (ed.), *El 17 de octubre de 1945* (Buenos Aires: Ariel, 1995), 206–10.

61. See Sandra McGee Deutsch, *Las Derechas*, 330; Tulio Halperín Donghi, "El populismo de Manuel Fresco a la luz de su impacto electoral," in Darío Cantón and Raúl Jorrat (eds.), *La investigación social hoy* (Buenos Aires: Inst. Gino Germani, 1997).

62. *Choque*, January 3, 1941, 2.

63. See *AGN*. Fondo Documental Secretaría Técnica. Legajo 483. Conferencias Doctrinarias. Informe Confidencial, Buenos Aires, 22 de octubre de 1951. See also SG 658. Diciembre 7, 1953.

64. See Eva Perón, "Palabras pronunciadas el 29 de Mayo de 1951, en el acto organizado por la colectividad japonesa residente en el país, en el Salón Blanco de la Casa de Gobierno," in Eva Perón, *Mensajes y discursos* (Buenos Aires: Fundación pro Universidad de la Producción y del Trabajo: Fundación de Investigaciones Históricas Evita Perón, 1999) T. III, 244. See Virgilio Filippo, *El plan quinquenal de Perón y los comunistas* (Buenos Aires: Lista Blanca, 1948), 10 and 485.

    See also Mariano Plotkin, *Mañana es San Perón: Propaganda, rituales políticos y educación en el régimen peronista (1946–1955)* (Caseros: Eduntref, 2007), 135, 137, 139, and Loris Zanatta, "El populismo, entre religión y política. Sobre las raíces históricas del antiliberalismo en América Latina," *E.I.A.L.* 19(2), 2008, 29–44.

65. Loris Zanatta, *Perón y el mito de la nación católica.*

66. For an analysis of Peronist textbooks for children, see Mariano Plotkin, *Mañana es San Perón*, 176.

67. *AGN*. Fondo Documental Secretaría Técnica. Legajo 483. Conferencias Doctrinarias. See Memorandum 2827, 10 de Julio de 1953. For a list of absentees and topics of the lectures, see for example Memorandums SG # 179, Mayo 5, 1953; SG # 205, Mayo 20, 1953; SG # 219, Mayo 27, 1953; SG # 228, Junio 5, 1953; SG # 333, Julio 22, 1953; SG # 338, Julio 24, 1953; SG # 350, Julio 29, 1953; SG # 368, Agosto 7, 1953; SG # 374, Agosto 12, 1953; SG # 385, Agosto 21, 1953; SG # 394, Agosto 27, 1953; SG # 417, Septiembre 4, 1953; SG # 435, Septiembre 14, 1953; SG # 475, Octubre 5, 1953; SG # 574, Octubre 28, 1953; SG # 672, Diciembre 7, 1953; SG # 312, Mayo 31, 1954; SG # 308, Mayo 31, 1954; SG # 330, Junio 8, 1954; SG # 673, Noviembre 23, 1954; SG # 707, Diciembre 17, 1954; SG # 32, Enero 11, 1955. For movies see also Memorandums 5121, Septiembre 30, 1953; 705, Febrero 14, 1954; SG # 280, Junio 25, 1953. For links between the indoctrination of state personnel and the office of the President, see Memorandum 5605, Noviembre 2, 1953.

68. *AGN*. Fondo Documental Secretaría Técnica. Legajo 483. Conferencias doctrinarias. See Letter from Enrique Olmedo, Subsecretario de Asuntos Técnicos to Doctor Jorge Sosa: Secreto. 2 de Julio. S-N 86. 2 de Julio. See also Confidencial. 22 de Octubre, 1951.

69. *AGN*. Fondo Documental Secretaría Técnica. Legajo 484. Mensajes Presidenciales. Discurso del General Juan Perón en la Escuela Superior Peronista. 25/8/53. 3, 4.

70. José Luis Romero, *Las ideas políticas en la Argentina*, 246–63.

71. Populist Peronism is ideological in Arendt's sense of the term. To believe in an ideology, first you must accept, through an act of faith, that the word of the principal ideologue represents the truth. See Hannah Arendt, "Ideology and

Terror: A Novel Form of Government," *Review of Politics* 15(3), 1953. See also Hannah Arendt, *The Origins of Totalitarianism* (New York: Meridian, 1959).

72. Daniel James, *Resistencia e integración: el peronismo y la clase trabajadora argentina, 1946–1976* (Buenos Aires: Sudamericana, 1990), 27, 58–59.

73. *AGN*. Fondo Documental Secretaría Técnica. Legajo 483 Conferencias. 15 de Diciembre de 1952. Disertación de Srta. Edelma Arauz. "Para un Peronista no puede haber nada major que otro peronista."

74. Carlos Altamirano, "Ideologías políticas y debate cívico" in Juan Carlos Torre (ed.) *Los años peronistas, 1943–1955*, 210–11, 232. On Peronist political culture, see Altamirano, *Peronismo y cultura de izquierda* (Buenos Aires: Temas, 2001). On Mussolini, see Federico Finchelstein, "On Fascist Ideology," Constellations 15(3) (2008).

75. See Juan Perón, "Al constituirse el Directorio del Instituto Nacional de Previsión Social. 15 de Diciembre de 1944," in Juan Domingo Perón, *Obras Completas*, T. VI, 499, and Juan Perón, *Perón expone su doctrina*, 87 (February 24, 1947).

76. Universidad Nacional de Cuyo, Actas del primer Congreso Nacional de Filosofía, Mendoza, Argentina, Marzo 30–Abril 9, 1949 (Buenos Aires: Platt, 1950), 136.

77. Juan Perón, *Perón expone su doctrina*, 29.

78. Universidad Nacional de Cuyo, Actas del primer Congreso Nacional de Filosofía, 135.

79. Ibid. 137.

80. Ibid. 144.

81. Ibid. 148–49, 150.

82. Ibid 153.

83. Ibid. 157.

84. Ibid. 157, 162, 163.

85. Ibid. 171.

86. "Discurso pronunciado por el vicepresidente y Ministro de Guerra, Coronel Juan Perón en representación de las 'alas de la Patria,'" *Retaguardia*, July 8, 1945, 6.

87. "Florilegio del Sr. Presidente," *La Vanguardia*, July 8, 1947.

88. "El último decálogo," *La Vanguardia*, September 21, 1948, 2.

89. "Matar como a víboras," *La Vanguardia*, July 8, 1947.

90. "El último decálogo," *La Vanguardia*, September 21, 1948, 2.

91. See Descartes (Perón), "Las quintas columnas imperialistas," *Mundo Peronista*, October 10, 1951, 9; Descartes (Perón), "Enfermedad de los imperios," *Mundo Peronista*, March 1, 1952, 30.

92. See Fabián Bosoer, *Braden o Perón. La historia oculta* (Buenos Aires: El Ateneo, 2011) 60–61.

93. Descartes (Perón), "Política y estrategia: Conducción política y de guerra," *Mundo Peronista*, August 15, 1951, 8. On anti-imperialism and Peronist doctrine, see also "Doctrina para todos," *Mundo Peronista*, August 15, 1951, 4.

94. Juan Domingo Perón, *Memorial de Puerta de Hierro* (Buenos Aires: Honorable Congreso de la Nación, 2001), 173.

95. See Mariano Plotkin, *Mañana es San Perón*, 105.

96. See, for example, "Sobre partidos políticos: Fragmento de un discurso presidencial," *Nuevas Bases*, September, 1953, 2.

97. "Los descamisados en el pensamiento vivo de Perón," *Mundo Peronista*, May 15, 1952, 5.

98. Speech by Perón, August 14, 1946, in "Mi oficio es pelear," *La Vanguardia*, July 8, 1947.

99. *AGN.* Fondo Documental Secretaría Técnica. Legajo 484. Mensajes Presidenciales. Discurso del General Juan Perón en la Escuela Superior Peronista. 25/8/53. 1, 2.

100. Juan Perón, "Desde los balcones de la Casa de Gobierno. 17 de octubre de 1946," Juan Domingo Perón, *Obras Completas*, T. VIII, 171.

101. This was not necessarily the case. Recent works have emphasized the importance of rituals and manipulation but also the clear material benefits behind the success of Peronism among its followers. See, among others, Eduardo Elena, *Dignifying Argentina: Peronism, Citizenship, and Mass Consumption* (Pittsburgh: University of Pittsburgh Press, 2011); Matthew Karush, *Culture of Class.*

102. Juan Domingo Perón, "Aspiramos a una sociedad sin divisiones de clase. En el Cine Park, 12 de agosto de 1944," in Coronel Juan Perón, *El pueblo quiere saber de qué se trata*, 149.

103. Ibid., 149. See also Juan Perón, "Cátedra conducción política," *Mundo Peronista*, August 1, 1951, 37–44. See also *AGN.* Fondo Documental Secretaría Técnica. Legajo 484. Mensajes Presidenciales editados en libreto. *"No queremos hacer el proletariado campesino: Queremos hacer agricultores felices," dijo Perón a los hombres del campo* (Buenos: Presidencia de la Nación, 1953) (June 11, 1953), 25.

104. Sylvia Saitta and Luis Alberto Romero (eds.), *Grandes entrevistas*, 258.

105. See also, "Desde los balcones de la Casa de gobierno despidiéndose de los trabajadores concentrados en la Plaza de Mayo. Octubre 17 de 1945," in Coronel Juan Perón, *El pueblo ya sabe de qué se trata*, 187.

106. *AGN.* Fondo Documental Secretaría Técnica. Legajo 484. Mensajes Presidenciales. Discurso del General Juan Perón en la Escuela Superior Peronista. 25/8/53. 12.

107. See Eva Perón, "Compañeras," *Mundo Peronista*, September 15, 1951, 5.

108. Eva Perón, "Discurso pronunciado el 22 de agosto de 1951, en la asamblea popular, que se constituyó en el Cabildo Abierto del Justicialismo en la Avenida 9 de Julio," Eva Perón, *Mensajes y discursos*, T. III, 254.

109. See Descartes (Perón), "Política y estrategia. La tercera posición. La 'guerra fría,'" *Mundo Peronista*, November 15, 1951, 8. See also "El Premio Nobel al

General Perón," *La Fronda*, August 11, 1947, and "Tercera posición," *La Fronda*, July 8, 1947.

110. "Evita Capitana," *Mundo Peronista*, June 1, 1952.

111. On indoctrination of Peronist cadres and embassy personnel see *AGN*. Fondo Documental Secretaría Técnica. Legajo 484. Campaña de difusión del Plan Quinquenal Argentino.

112. *AGN*. Fondo Documental Secretaría Técnica. Legajo 484. Carpeta Editoriales. Mensaje Cuerpo Diplomático Argentino en el exterior con motivo del 9 de Julio.

113. Silo Gismo, "Supongamos que usted es...Mr. Truman," *Mundo Peronista*, September 1, 1951, 17. For Ernesto Ché Guevara see his *Notas de Viaje* (La Habana: Ediciones Abril, 1994), 65, 70, 72. For Cambodia, I thank Ben Kiernan for this reference. See also his book *Blood and Soil: A World History of Genocide and Extermination from Sparta to Darfur* (New Haven: Yale University Press, 2007), 544.

114. Eva Perón, "Historia del Peronismo. Causas del Justicialismo–El Comunismo," *Mundo Peronista*, October 15, 1951, 45.

115. *AGN*. Fondo Documental Secretaría Técnica. Legajo 484. Presidencia de la Nación. Subsecretaría de Informaciones. Dirección General de Prensa. H 737. 29 de Agosto de 1951. Síntesis del discurso pronunciado por el General Perón ante obreros de la industria vitivinícola.

116. *AGN*. Fondo Documental Secretaría Técnica. Legajo 484. Presidencia de la Nación. Subsecretaría de Informaciones. Dirección General de Prensa. H 735. 29 de Agosto de 1951. Síntesis del discurso pronunciado por el Presidente de la Nación ante delegados de 'La Fraternidad.' 29 de Agosto de 1951, 2.

117. *AGN*. Fondo Documental Secretaría Técnica. Legajo 484. Mensajes Presidenciales. Discurso del General Juan Perón en la Escuela Superior Peronista. 25/8/53. 1.

118. Perón cited in Cristián Buchrucker, *Nacionalismo y Peronismo*, 325.

119. See Descartes (Perón), "Política y estrategia. La guerra popular," *Mundo Peronista*, September 1, 1951.

120. On Perón's visit to Italy at the time of fascism, see "La Missione militare argentina esalta l'organizzazione delle Forze Armate Italiana," *Il Giornale d'Italia*, September 12, 1940; *Archivo del Ministerio de Relaciones Exteriores y Culto. Argentina*, División Política. Mueble 7. Casilla 1. Guerra Europea. Exp. 14. Año 1939. Telegrama. Roma, Julio 4 de 1940. See also my book *Transatlantic Fascism*, 165; Juan Domingo Perón, *Memorial de Puerta de Hierro*, 64–65; Juan Domingo Perón, *Correspondencia 1* (Buenos Aires: Corregidor 1983) 19 (Roma, 9 de Mayo de 1939).

121. Juan Domingo Perón, *Memorial de Puerta de Hierro*, 65.

122. Juan Perón, "En la ciudad de Santa Fe. 1 de Enero de 1946," in Juan Domingo Perón, *Obras Completas*, T. VIII, 18.

123. *Archivo Cedinci.* Folleto "Dijo el Coronel Perón."
124. See Descartes (Perón), "Política y estrategia. La preparación como causa de la guerra," *Mundo Peronista*, October 10, 1951, 9. "20 verdades del justicialismo peronista," *Mundo Peronista*, July 15, 1951, 11; Juan Perón, *Perón expone su doctrina*, 95.

CHAPTER 5

1. "Revelación del caudillo," *Política*, October 24, 1945, 1.
2. Carlos Ibarguren, *El sistema económico de la Revolución* (Buenos Aires: Banco de la Nación Argentina, 1946), 5.
3. "Definición!" *Ahijuna*, July 24, 1946, 3. See also "La Revolución cumplió su etapa política," *Política*, March 20, 1946; Emilio Gutiérrez, "Concepción revolucionaria," *Liberación. Movimiento Revolucionario Nacional Sindicalista*, September 15, 1946.
4. From the pages of Father Julio Meinvielle's magazine *Balcón*, many of them formulated "Peros a Perón" (Objections to Perón), but these "objections" were mild and had none of the fascist violence that nacionalismo had presented before 1945. See Marcelo Sánchez Sorondo, *Memorias: conversaciones con Carlos Payá* (Buenos Aires: Editorial Sudamericana, 2001), 97. See also "Odio ideológico," *Balcón*, August 16, 1946, 1.
5. Julio Meinvielle, *Política argentina, 1949–1956* (Buenos Aires: Editorial Trafac, 1956), 323. See Julio Meinvielle, "Hacia un nacionalismo marxista," *Presencia*, December 23, 1949, reproduced in *Cabildo*, August 2, 1973; Marcelo Sánchez Sorondo, *Memorias*, 89.
6. Jordán B. Genta, *La masonería y el comunismo en la revolución del 16 de setiembre* (Buenos Aires: [s.n.], 1955). As late as in 1970, Genta would continue to be reactive towards Peronism and equally paranoid in his anti-Semitism. See *Archivo Dipba.* Legajo 12728. Folio 70/p.7.
7. See "No hay 'frente,'" *Segunda República*, March 27, 1963, 1. See also *Archivo Dipba.* Legajo 10411. 3 de 1960. Folios 193–94.
8. Richard Gillespie, *Soldados de Perón: historia crítica sobre los Montoneros* (Buenos Aires: Editorial Sudamericana, 2008), 98–99; Carlos Altamirano, *Peronismo y cultura de izquierda* (Buenos Aires: Temas, 2001), 121–40.
9. See Hugo Vezzetti, *Sobre la violencia revolucionaria.* See also Pilar Calveiro, *Política y/o violencia: una aproximación a la guerrilla de los años 70* (Buenos Aires: Norma, 2005). For militarism in ERP, which, all in all, did not have an extreme-right pedigree regarding its notions of violence, see Vera Carnovale, *Los combatientes: historia del PRT–ERP* (Buenos Aires: Siglo XXI Editores, 2011). On violence in this period, see also Samuel Amaral, "El avión negro: retórica y práctica de la violencia," in Samuel Amaral and Mariano Ben Plotkin (eds.), *Perón: del exilio al poder* (Buenos Aires: Cántaro, 1993); Marina Franco, *Un*

enemigo para la nación. Orden Interno, violencia y 'subversión', 1973–1976 (Buenos Aires: Fondo de Cultura Económica, 2012); Sebastián Carassai, *Los años setenta de la gente común. La naturalización de la violencia* (Buenos Aires: Siglo XXI, 2013); and Omar Acha, "Dilemas de una violentología argentina" in his *Un revisionismo histórico de izquierda y otros ensayos de política intelectual* (Buenos Aires: Herramienta, 2012).

10. Hugo Vezzetti, *Pasado y presente* (Buenos Aires: Siglo Veintiuno Editores, 2002), 125.

11. On the differences between legality and legitimacy as generally conceived by the extreme right see the influential text by Carl Schmitt, *Legality and Legitimacy* (Durham: Duke University Press, 2004). On "legality" and the dictatorship, see Victoria Crespo, "Legalidad y dictadura" in Clara Lida, Horacio Crespo and Pablo Yankelevich (eds.) *Argentina, 1976: Estudios en torno al golpe de Estado* (Buenos Aires: Fondo de Cultura Económica, 2008)

12. Rogelio García Lupo, "Diálogo con los jóvenes fascistas," in his *La rebelión de los generales* (Buenos Aires: Jamcana, 1963), 70.

13. On transnational fascism after 1945 in Europe, see Andrea Mammone "Revitalizing and De-territorializing fascism in the 1950s: the Extreme Right in France and Italy, and the Pan-national ('European') Imaginary," *Patterns of Prejudice*, 45(4), 2011.

14. Alberto Ezcurra, "Uriburu," *Tacuara* 15(8) (n/d), cited in Daniel Gutman, *Tacuara: Historia de la primera guerrilla urbana argentina* (Buenos Aires: Vergara, 2003), 80–81.

15. *Ofensiva MNT* 11, November, 1962, 1.

16. "Aguilas, svásticas, violencia y un viejo enigma ¿quien mueve a Tacuara?" *Primera Plana*, February 5, 1963, 20–22. See also Collins, *Archivo Dipba*. Legajo 10411. Tacuara Segundo Congreso Nacional.

17. *Archivo Dipba*. Legajo 10411. La Plata, Marzo 3 de 1960.

18. See "Tacuara: Recurrimos a la violencia solo cuando nos obligan," *El Mundo*, February 2, 1963.

19. On the origins and early organizational structure of Tacuara see *Archivo Dipba*. Legajo 15. C. 75. 2/6/1960. Movimiento Nacionalista Unificado "Tacuara." Orígenes. The most accurate report from Argentine intelligence on the origin and ideology of Tacuara is the one written by the Naval Intelligence Service. See also Legajo 14199. Caso Pendiente. Estudio ideológico efectuado por el delegado del Servicio de Inteligencia Naval. Legajo 7374. Folios 413-415-419. Octubre de 1972.

20. See *Archivo Dipba*. Legajo 12218. Policia de la Provincia de Buenos Aires, Central de Inteligencia. Festival Internacional de Cine de Mar del Plata, 1959. On the Sixties, see Jeremy Varon, "Time is an Ocean: The Past and Future of The Sixties," *The Sixties* 1(1), 2008.

21. See *La Prensa*, March 24, 1964, 6; *La Prensa*, March 28,1964, 5; *La Prensa*, March 25, 1964, 12; *New York Times*, March 25, 1964, 1; *New York Times*,

September 30, 1966, 17. See also "Busca la policia a Joe Baxter Jefe de la banda terrorista," *La Prensa*, March 26, 1964, 3; "El esclarecimiento del asalto al policlínico," *La Razón*, March 24, 1964; "Joe Baxter estaría por caer," *Pregón*, March 25, 1964; "Una organización terrorista sorprendente," *El Plata*, March 26, 1964; "Fueron reconocidos en rueda de presos los autores del asalto al policlínico," *El Mundo*, March 29, 1964; "Conexión entre asaltantes comunes e ideológicos," *La Nación*, May 21, 1970; *Archivo Dipba*. Legajo 1715. Carpeta daños. Tandil, 13 de diciembre, 1962; Ibid. Legajo 12721.

22. "Argentine Youths in Nazi Group Salute and Cry: 'Hail Tacuara!'" *New York Times*, September 16, 1962, 30; "Resurrecting the Swastika," *Time*, September 21, 1962; "Los jóvenes fascistas descubren su país," in his *Nosotros decimos no: crónicas, 1963–1988* (México: Siglo Veintiuno, 1989), 137.

23. Rogelio García Lupo, "Diálogo con los jóvenes fascistas," 74. See also *Archivo Dipba*. Legajo 12739. Folio 60.

24. *New York Times*, March 25, 1962, 41; Eduardo Galeano, "Los jóvenes fascistas descubren su país," 146. See also *Archivo Dipba*. Legajo 1352. Carpeta daños. 29/30 de marzo, 1961. See also Legajo 12459. R. 12459. 1963.

25. *Archivo Dipba*. Legajo 12242. DSN 73. 1963.

26. On the realms of memory in nacionalismo see Federico Finchelstein, *Fascismo, Liturgia e Imaginario*, 95–111.

27. *Tacuara*, 1, 2, Quincena, October 1963.

28. *La Prensa*, September 10, 1962, 4; *La Prensa*, September 11, 1962; *New York Times*, September 11, 1962, 11; "CGT a la cola de Tacuaras," *El Popular*, July 29, 1964. See also *Archivo Dipba*. Legajo 14199. Memorándum, San Nicolás, Noviembre 22 de 1966.

29. *Archivo Dipba*. Legajo 1745. Carpeta daños. Campana, 15 de abril de 1963; Ibid. Legajo 2022. Carpeta daños. Azul, 7 de diciembre de 1967; Ibid. Legajo 15456. Mar del Plata, Noviembre 9, 1969. Folios 36, 52.

30. See "Nuestra Guerra Justa," Movimiento Nacionalista Tacuara. *Boletín del Comando 1 de Mayo*, Segunda Quincena, August, 1963. On violence, power, and desire in transatlantic fascist ideology see Federico Finchelstein, "Fascism Becomes Desire: On Freud, Mussolini and Transnational Politics," in Mariano Plotkin and Joy Damousi (eds.), *The Transnational Unconscious* (London: Palgrave Macmillan, 2009).

31. "Documentamos la barbarie," *Nueva Sión*, May 19, 1962; *La Prensa*, July 1, 1962, 3.

32. Federico Finchelstein, *Transatlantic Fascism*, 73–75.

33. See "Una comunicación acerca del caso Sirota dió la Policía," *La Prensa*, July 3, 1962, 4; "El gobierno y las recientes agresiones," *La Prensa*, July 2, 1962, 1; *La Prensa*, July 1, 1962, 3; *New York Times*, July 3, 1962, 4. See also Movimiento Nacionalista Tacuara. Secretaría de Prensa y Propaganda, *El caso Sirota y el problema judío en la Argentina* (Buenos Aires, 1962), 5, 7, 8.

34. Leonardo Senkman, *El antisemitismo en la Argentina* (Buenos Aires: Centro Editor de América Latina, 1989), 52. See also "Otra vez, atentados y crímenes políticos," *Primera Plana*, March 10, 1964, 6; "El Caso Alterman," *El Popular*, March 18, 1964.

35. Leonardo Senkman, *El antisemitismo en la Argentina*, 53, 91.

36. See "Hubo otra atentado racista," *El Mundo*, March 19, 1964; *Archivo Dipba*. Legajo 12721. For this situation in the concentration camps during the Dirty War see the next chapter.

37. The poem was published in *Ofensiva*, August 9, 1962; Alejandra Dandan and Silvina Heguy, *Joe Baxter: del nazismo a la extrema izquierda: la historia secreta de un guerrillero* (Buenos Aires: Editorial Norma, 2006), 65–67; Daniel Gutman, *Tacuara*, 76–78.

38. *New York Times*, January 18, 1962, 3; *Archivo Dipba*. Legajo 10411. Asunto: Informar Novedad sobre actuación grupo Tacuara, Folio 194.

39. *Ofensiva*, August 9, 1962; Alejandra Dandan and Silvina Heguy, *Joe Baxter*, 65–67; Daniel Gutman, *Tacuara*, 76–78.

40. On Sassen and the importance of the interview to understand Eichmann, see Saul Friedlander, *Memory, History, and the Extermination of the Jews of Europe* (Bloomington: Indiana University Press, 1993), 110–11, and also 33. On the De Mahieu, Hitler, Mussolini, and other fascists' influences see *Mazorca* 2(16), 1968, 4–11. See also *Mazorca* 3(3), 1969. On Tacuara's links with Nazi escapees see also *Archivo Dipba*. Legajo 169. Carpeta Material Bélico. Memorandum and especially folio 2.

41. *New York Times*, August 3, 1962, 22; Daniel Gutman, *Tacuara*, 86. See also *Archivo Dipba*. Legajo 1609. Carpeta daños. 10 de Julio de 1962.

42. David Rock, *Authoritarian Argentina*, 206. For similar views in other naciona-lista organizations see also *La Escoba*, January 15, 1962; "Crónica del gueto," *Combate*, October 27, 1960. On the Eichmann kidnapping and its effects on Argentine–Israeli relations and the Argentine Jewish community see Raanan Rein, *Argentina, Israel, and the Jews: Perón, the Eichmann Capture, and After* (College Park, MD: University Press of Maryland, 2003). See also *Archivo Dipba*. Legajo 10411. Memorándum 895. 2 de junio de 1960. See ibid., Memorándum 879.

43. See Hannah Arendt, *Eichmann in Jerusalem*, 252.

44. See Christopher R. Browning, *Collected Memories: Holocaust History and Postwar Testimony* (Madison: University of Wisconsin Press, 2003); Deborah Lipstadt, *The Eichmann Trial* (New York: Schocken, 2011).

45. Session No. 105. 7 Av 5721 (20 July 1961) in *The trial of Adolf Eichmann: Record of proceedings in the District Court of Jerusalem* (Jerusalem: State of Israel, Ministry of Justice, 1992–1995).

46. *Archivo Dipba*. Legajo 10411. Folio 87. See also Folios 77–86.

47. See *Mazorca* 2(15), 1968, 3, 10.

48. See Tabaré Di Paula, "Tacuara juega a la milicia revolucionaria," *Ché,* June 2, 1961, 11; *New York Times,* August 2, 1962, 3; *New York Times,* August 21, 1962, 13; "Conversamos con el P. Meinvielle," *Alianza,* October, 1961; *Archivo Dipba.* Legajo 199. See *Archivo Dipba.* Legajo 12312. Folio 7. Buenos Aires, Marzo de 1963.

49. See Arie Zafran, "Un reportaje a los jefes de Tacuara," *Mundo Israelita,* May 5, 1962; "El verdadero rostro de Tacuara," *Nueva Sión,* May 19, 1962.

50. *New York Times,* December 1, 1962, 8. For the Israeli reaction, see also *New York Times* December 7, 1962, 14. On Tacuara's conflation of Zionism and Judaism see also *Mazorca* 12, 1967, 12–13; H. Panigazzi, "Nuestra Acción," *Tradición: Legión Capital* 2(3), 1968, 2; "¿Qué son, raza o comunidad religiosa?" *Mazorca* 12, 1968, 9–10.

51. See *New York Times,* August 9, 1964; *New York Times,* August 16, 1964; *New York Times,* September 3, 1964; "Triki opina sobre política argentina," *Primera Plana,* March 17, 1964. On Triki see also Leonardo Senkman, *El antisemitismo en la Argentina,* 57–59; Mauricio J. Dulfano, "Antisemitism in Argentina: Patterns of Jewish Adaptation," *Jewish Social Studies* 31(2), 1969, 128. See Hussein Triki, *Voici la Palestine* (Tunis: Société L'Action d'édition et de presse, 1972); see especially Chapter 13, "Activité sioniste en Argentine," 287.

52. Leonardo Senkman, *El antisemitismo en la Argentina,* 56; Hussein Triki, *Voici la Palestine,* 316–17. See also Juan Carlos Cornejo Linares, *El nuevo orden sionista en la Argentina* (Buenos Aires: Tacuarí, 1964).

53. See "Triki, la juventud árabe y las 'tacuaras de Perón,'" *Pregón,* April 30, 1964. On Triki see also the peculiar description by Guillermo Patricio Kelly on his interaction with him, in "El imperialismo dirige a Tacuara," *Así,* March 31, 1964, 6; "Confidencial y secreto" *El Aliancista* 1(1), July 28, 1964. See *Archivo Dipba.* Legajo 14199. Caso Pendiente. Legajo 7374. Folio 419. 1972.

54. Julio Rios, "Tacuara," *Tacuara: Órgano del movimiento revolucionario Tacuara* 1(1), October, 1963. "Move to Left Splits Argentine Nazis," *New York Times,* January 19, 1964, 24.

55. MNRT eventually split into two groups, one more "Marxist" than the other. See Daniel Gutman, *Tacuara,* 108; Daniel Lvovich, *El nacionalismo de derecha: Desde sus orígenes a Tacuara* (Buenos Aires: Capital Intelectual, 2006), 80–85.

56. Joe Baxter, "Nacionalismo," *Tacuara: Órgano del movimiento revolucionario Tacuara* 1(1), October, 1963.

57. "MNRT. Violencia revolucionaria," *4161: Órgano de la Juventud Universitaria Peronista,* June 2, 1964.

58. Other group of tacuaras also helped MNRT members on the run after the assault on the policlinic. However, GRN officially denied any links with MNRT: *La Prensa,* March 26, 1964, 3. See also *Archivo Dipba.* Legajo 18744. Agrupación Tacuara, Febrero 1992. P. 3.

59. J. Rios, "Tacuara y el movimiento nacional," *Tacuara: Órgano del movimiento revolucionario Tacuara* 1(3), November, 1963, 4.

60. See "Lealtad al 17," *Tacuara: Órgano del movimiento revolucionario Tacuara* 1(2), October, 1963, 1, 2. See also Roberto Bardini, *Tacuara: la pólvora y la sangre* (México: Océano, 2002), 99; Eduardo Galeano, "Los jóvenes fascistas descubren su país," 144.

61. See "'Los Tacuaristas no somos asesinos' afirma su jefe," *Crónica*, April 4, 1964. In 1989, Ezcurra spoke in support of Carlos Menem's repatriation of the remains of Juan Manuel de Rosas. He died in 1993. Juan Mario Collins succeeded Ezcurra as leader of Tacuara. Collins died in 2000. He was mysteriously strangled. Roberto Bardini, *Tacuara*, 129; Alejandra Dandan and Silvina Heguy, *Joe Baxter*, 162, 197.

62. Eduardo Galeano, "Los jóvenes fascistas descubren su país," 144.

63. Daniel Lvovich, *El nacionalismo de derecha*, 84.

64. "El nacionalismo y el ser o no ser peronista. Un momento, escucha compañero," *Mazorca* 1(3), May, 1966.

65. As an example of this form of memorialization see the book by Roberto Bardini, *Tacuara*. On the different memories of Tacuara, see María Valeria Galván, "Memories of Argentina's Past over Time: the Memories of Tacuara" in Selma Leydesdorff and Nanci Adler (eds.) *The Tapestry of Memory: Evidence and Testimony in Life-Story Narratives*. (New Brunswick: Rutgers-Transaction Publishers, 2013) 111–132.

66. See Jorge Verasi, "Violencia," *Mazorca: Órgano de Difusión de la Guardia Restauradora Nacionalista* 1, 1970, 8.

67. See "Nota del M.N.R. 'Tacuara,'" *Compañero*, March 31, 1964.

68. See "Aforismos," *G.R.N.*, October, 1963, 1. More research is needed on this topic. I have found some exceptions to the all-male prevailing pattern of Tacuara in DIPBA archival materials. For example, a woman participated in a Tacuara squad that shot up a socialist meeting in Miramar in the summer of 1960. One of the bullets injured a socialist man in the testicles, leaving him gravely injured. *Archivo Dipba*. Legajo 10411. Memorándum. Delegación Central de Inteligencia, Mar del Plata, Febrero 21 de 1960.

69. Eduardo Galeano, "Los jóvenes fascistas descubren su país," 141.

70. *Archivo Dipba*. Legajo 10411. Folio 83. See also "Haga patria. Mate un bolche." ("Forge the homeland. Kill a red."), *Mazorca* 2(14), 1968.

71. See "Nuestra Doctrina y el nacionalismo Argentino," *Combate*, October–November, 1963, 1, 4. GRN continued the clerico-fascist tradition. As the GRN members told his comrades: "Camarada: Erguid el cuerpo y sanead (*sic*) tu alma, así llegaras a la RECONQUISTA DE LA PATRIA EN CRISTO." See N. L. Silgueira, "En pie de lucha," *GRN Tradición. Legión Capital* 2(3), 1968?; *Mazorca: Órgano de Difusión de la Guardia Restauradora Nacionalista* 1, ca. 1970, 5. For nacionalismo in the 1960s and 1970s see the descriptive report: "El nacionalismo Argentino," *Carta Política* 2(16), 1975, 14–21. For previous examples of Tacuara and other nacionalista interactions see *Archivo Dipba*. Legajo 10411. La Plata, Marzo 3 de 1960.

72. Some former GRN members would see this ritual as a sign of homoerotic connections between GRN members and Meinvielle. See José Amorín, *Montoneros: la buena historia* (Buenos Aires: Catálogos, 2006), 94. On Meinvielle "advisory" role in GRN see *Archivo Dipba*. Legajo 127. C. 8. Guardia Restauradora Nacionalista.

73. "18 de Marzo de 1964," *Restauración: Órgano de difusión de la GRN*, March–April, 1964. See "Editorial," *Mazorca* 5(21), 1971. See also "Evita, ayer, hoy y siempre jefe espiritual de la causa nacional," *Mazorca* 2(13), July, 1968.

74. "Reportaje al PBRO. Julio Meinvielle," *Azul y Blanco*, July 17, 1967, 16; "Tacuara frente a los lacayos del régimen," *Estudio y Lucha: Órgano oficial de la Unión Nacionalista de Estudiantes Secundarios*, 1968.

75. On bureaucratic authoritarianism see Guillermo O'Donnell, *El estado burocrático autoritario* (Buenos Aires: Editorial de Belgrano, 1982).

76. "Reportaje al Reverendo Padre Julio Meinvielle," *Mazorca* 5, 1970.

77. "Reportaje al PBRO. Julio Meinvielle," *Azul y Blanco*, July 17, 1967, 17; "Testimonio de actualidad," *Segunda República*, March 27, 1963, 3.

78. See "Terrorismo: claro desafio al gobierno," *Primera Plana*, March 31, 1964, 4. See also "Lamentable: el gobierno y justicia aseguran impunidad a Tacuara," *Mundo Israelita*, March 2, 1963. In the mid-1960s the security reports became more detached or even critical of Tacuara's more left-wing elements. See *Archivo Dipba*. Memorándum, 23 de Agosto, 1960. Estudiantil Registro n. 13; Legajo 1829. Carpeta daños. City Bell 17 de junio de 1964; Ibid. Legajo 10411.

79. See *Archivo Dipba*. Legajo 122. C. 3. 14-5-1963.

80. Alejandra Dandan and Silvina Heguy, *Joe Baxter*, 29–36, 239–40, 261–323. On Baxter in Vietnam see "Baxter en Vietnam y un real peligro," *Atlantida*, April, 1965. See also the picturesque intelligence report on Baxter in *Archivo Dipba*. Legajo 14199. Caso Pendiente. Estudio ideológico efectuado por el delegado del Servicio de Inteligencia Naval. Legajo 7374. Folios 418, 419. Octubre de 1972.

81. On the Tacuara links with the security forces who usually provided them with weapons and protection see *New York Times*, September 12, 1962; *New York Times*, May 17, 1963, 11, 15; *New York Times*, March 2, 1964, 10; *New York Times*, February 19, 1965, 18; *La Prensa*, March 28, 1964, 6. See also the denunciation of Tacuara's links by the Liga Argentina por los Derechos del Hombre in *Archivo Dipba*. Legajo 10411. Tacuara-Side-DIPA. The same pattern of links with the Argentine security forces can be attributed to the neo-Nazi organizations of the 1980s and 1990s. See David Rock, *Authoritarian Argentina* 234–35, and Raúl Kollmann, *Sombras de Hitler: la vida secreta de las bandas neonazis argentinas* (Buenos Aires: Editorial Sudamericana, 2001).

82. Ignacio González Janzen's journalistic account remains a significant source for the Triple A. See Ignacio González Janzen, *La Triple-A* (Buenos Aires: Contrapunto, 1986). Many new documents are to be expected from ongoing trials of former members of the Triple A.

83. Alejandra Dandan and Silvina Heguy, *Joe Baxter*, 178–79; Daniel Gutman, *Tacuara*, 191. On Perón and Vandor see James W. McGuire, *Peronism without Perón*, 112–50, and Santiago Senén González and Fabián Bosoer, *Saludos a Vandor* (Buenos Aires: Vergara, 2009). On Baxter's trip to Madrid, which also took him to Prague, Algeria and Vietnam among other places, see *Archivo Dipba*. Legajo 14199. Caso Pendiente Legajo 7374. Folio 418. Octubre de 1972.

84. Before leaving Madrid, Baxter made a visit to Otto Skorzeny, the Nazi commando who had "liberated" Mussolini in 1943. Skorzeny was "exiled" in Madrid at the time. Daniel Gutman, *Tacuara*, 192.

85. Ignacio González Janzen, *La Triple-A*, 14; Marcos Novaro and Vicente Palermo, *La dictadura militar*, 81. On American training and indoctrination of Latin American military officers, see Lesley Gill, *The School of the Americas: Military Training and Political Violence in the Americas* (Durham: Duke University Press, 2004).

86. CONADEP, *Nunca Más* (Buenos Aires: Eudeba, 1984), 69.

87. See "Segunda parte de la entrevista exclusiva al ex dictador argentino Jorge Rafael Videla (1976–1981). 'No salimos a cazar pajaritos, sino al terrorismo y a los subversivos,'" *Cambio* 16 (Spain), March 4, 2012.

88. For an insightful, and yet hyperbolic, fictional account of López Rega see Tomás Eloy Martínez, *La novela de Perón* (Buenos Aires: Legasa, 1987). See also the fine biography of Lopez Rega by Marcelo Larraquy, *López Rega: el peronismo y la Triple A* (Buenos Aires: Aguilar, 2011).

89. See Ignacio González Janzen, *La Triple-A*, 89. See *Archivo Dipba*. Legajo 16135. Disertación sobre Marxismo en Tacuara Peronista. Noviembre 2 de 1973. Folio 1. See also "Curas guerrilleros: el antiperonismo resucita," *El Caudillo*, April 26, 1974.

90. See "La formación de la llamada Triple A," *La Nación*, February 6, 1976.

91. Ignacio González Janzen, *La Triple-A*, 90–91.

92. "El sermón de Vicente López," *Así*, December 12, 1972. Quoted in Ignacio González Janzen, *La Triple-A*, 92. See also Sergio Bufano, "Perón y la Triple A," *Revista Lucha Armada en la Argentina*, 3 (2005). For the Triple A as for Meinvielle the paranoid concept of *sinarquía* was clearly rooted in anti-Semitism. See "Un estudio sobre la sinarquía. Para conocer al enemigo," *El Caudillo*, June 14, 1974, and also *El Caudillo*, June 21, 1974.

93. *Archivo Memoria Abierta*. Fondo Fiscalía Luis Moreno Ocampo. Caja 48. Causa 13. Doc. Anexa Declaraciones. Folio 23. 4E. Testimonio de Deheza.

94. "Religión o muerte," *El Caudillo*, March 19, 1975. See Domingo Rafael Ianantuoni, "La sinarquía contra el Justicialismo," *Las Bases*, April 19, 1973, 9.

95. See Felipe Romeo, "Editorial: Entre enemigos y adversarios," *El Caudillo*, October 23, 1975.

96. *El Caudillo*, March 12, 1975; *El Caudillo*, March 14, 1974. On anti-Semitism, see also *Archivo Dipba*. Doc. 17518. Side 56.714/76. Legajo n. 2708 L. Folio 162.

97. *El Caudillo*, February 12, 1975; "La muerte de un maricón," *El Caudillo*, November 6, 1975.

98. "La maldad del psicoanálisis," *El Caudillo*, January 21, 1975.

99. Tomás Eloy Martínez, *La novela de Perón*.

100. See Roberto Bardini, *Tacuara*, 119. Romeo also liked to sing the anthem of the Spanish Legion with its famous lyrics: "I am the boyfriend of death." "Muere de sida uno de los ideólogos de la Triple A argentina," *El País* (Madrid), May 6, 2009.

101. During the military dictatorship of 1976–1983, Romeo became a close collaborator of General Ramón Camps. In 1988 Romeo was arrested for possession of narcotics in rather unclear circumstances. After being a fugitive from Argentine justice for three years, Romeo returned to Argentina in critical condition and died of HIV/AIDS in April of 2009. Nobody claimed his corpse. Luis Bruchstein, "Criminales y derechistas en las Tres A," *Página 12*, December 27, 2006; Sergio Kiernan, "El órgano oficial de la Triple A del Brujo," *Página 12*, January 7, 2007; "Murió Felipe Romeo, vocero de la banda de ultraderecha 'Triple A'," *Clarín*, May 5, 2009. See also "Perón siempre tiene razón," *El Caudillo*, May 24, 1974. Ruiz de los Llanos stated about Hitler: "Y un día nuestras calles llevaran tu nombre...Fuhrer inolvidable/Fuherer implacable/ Nuestro Fuhrer." See Gabriel Ruiz de los Llanos, *El mejor enemigo es el enemigo muerto* (Buenos Aires: La Camisa, 1976), 43–44, 81–83. On Ruiz de los Llanos see also *Archivo Dipba*. Doc. 17518. Side 56.714/76. Legajo n. 2708 L. Folios 162–67. See also "Soy nacionalista (firmado Isabel Perón)," *El Caudillo*, October 18, 1974.

102. See, for example, "Rosas Perón," *El Caudillo*, March 14, 1974. See also "La patria peronista es la patria federal," *El Caudillo*, November 16, 1973; "Vuelve a la Patria," *El Caudillo*, November 8, 1974; "Habla el caudillo," *El Caudillo*, May 3, 1974; "El Restaurador y sus enemigos," *El Caudillo*, February 1, 1974; Felipe Romeo, "La batalla de Obligado se libra todos los días," *El Caudillo*, November 19, 1974.

103. Irina Hauser, "Los crímenes de la Triple A son de 'lesa humanidad,'" *Página 12*, March 18, 2008; "Confirman que los crímenes de la Triple A son de lesa humanidad" *Clarín*, March 17, 2008.

104. Ignacio González Janzen, *La Triple-A*, 93–106; *El Caudillo*, December 18, 1975; *El Caudillo*, November 19, 1974.

105. *El Caudillo*, March 19, 1975.

106. See "La violencia" and "60.000 personas se retiraron," *Noticias*, May 2, 1974, 6, 12, 13. See, for example, Mario Firmenich, "La provocación de derecha no puede dividirnos," *Noticias*, May 16, 1974, 12. On nacionalismo and Father Mugica see, "Carlos Mugica," *Cabildo*, June 13, 1974, 24.

107. *New York Times*, December 15, 1974.

108. See "La seguridad social," *Noticias*, July 30, 1974, 12; *Las Bases*, June 7, 1973. See also José López Rega, "Anatomía del Tercer Mundo," *Las Bases*, September 21, 1972, 68–69.

109. See "Ivanissevich habló de las huelgas docentes," *La Nación*, June 18, 1975. See also "Ivanissevich: La crudeza necesaria," *El Caudillo*, January 14, 1974; "Ministro Oscar Ivanissevich," *El Caudillo*, December 17, 1974. An editorial in *La Nación* praised the minister's action at the universities and denounced the "subversive ideological penetration" of the educational system. See the editorial, "Guerrilla que no se combate," *La Nación*, April 6, 1975.

110. Interview with Alberto Ottalagano in Darío Macor and Eduardo Iglesias, *El peronismo antes del peronismo* (Santa Fe: Universidad Nacional del Litoral, 1997), 160, 163, 172.

111. See "La semana política," *La Nación*, January 5, 1975; "La Intervención en las universidades extenderían," *La Nación*, March 13, 1975. Ottalagano became later known as the author of the book *I'm a Fascist, So What?* See Alberto Ottalagano, *Soy fascista, ¿y qué? Alberto Ottalagano, una vida al servicio de la Patria* (Buenos Aires: Ro.Ca Producciones, 1983). See also Alberto Ottalagano, *Nacionalismo, peronismo, justicialismo: Tres momentos de una idea* (Buenos Aires: Club Literario, 1986).

112. "Se ofreció una demostración al Dr. A. Ottalagano," *La Prensa*, December 15, 1974, 6; *The New York Times*, December 5, 1974, 12. See also Ignacio González Janzen, *La Triple-A*, 36–37.

113. Felipe Romeo, "Quien le teme a las Tres A?" *El Caudillo*, November 1, 1974. On the Triple A and the university see Felipe Romeo, "El País de diciembre," *El Caudillo*, December 3, 1974. Romeo stated, "La Universidad está al servicio del país, por primera vez en su historia."

114. See "La universidad: su acción disolvente," *El Caudillo*, January 29, 1975.

115. Ciga Correa was later on incorporated into the military's Dirty War as a member of Battalion 601 and also deployed in Honduras as an "adviser" to anticommunist paramilitary formations. See Francisco Martorell, *Operación Cóndor, el vuelo de la muerte: La coordinación represiva en el Cono Sur* (Santiago: Lom Ediciones, 1999), 50; Daniel Gutman, *Tacuara*, 257; María Seoane, "Los secretos de la guerra sucia continental de la dictadura", *Clarín*, March 24, 2006; Miguel Bonasso, "El Cóndor y el Aguila," *Página 12*, October 8, 2000.

116. "Reportaje al PBRO. Julio Meinvielle," *Azul y Blanco*, July 17, 1967, 18. See also "Curas guerrilleros: el antiperonismo resucita," *El Caudillo*, April 26, 1974. "Zardini: A dios rogando y a los zurdos pegando," *El Caudillo*, February 26, 1975.

117. "Sicopolítica," *El Caudillo*, May 17, 1974; "Los 'doctores' del engaño. Quieren destruir al pueblo argentino por medio del psicoanálisis marxista," *El Caudillo*, February 22, 1974; "Los hechos son machos," and "Las palabras son hembras," in *El Caudillo*, February 1, 1974.

118. On Ottalagano, see Adriana Puiggrós, *El lugar del saber: conflictos y alternativas entre educación, conocimiento y política* (Buenos Aires: Galerna, 2003), 337; Oscar Terán, *Historia de las ideas en la Argentina* (Buenos Aires: Siglo XXI, 2008), 294; Pablo Buchbinder, *Historia de las universidades argentinas* (Buenos Aires: Sudamericana, 2005), 206. See also David Rock, *Authoritarian Argentina*, 231. Rock mistakenly presents Ottalagano as having being nominated to his position by the later military dictatorship. Ottalagano's arguments about the role of Freud were rooted in the nacionalista critique of psychoanalysis in the years before 1945. Castellani and Filippo continued this criticism in the 1960s. See Leonardo Castellani, *Freud en cifra* (Buenos Aires: Cruz y Fierro, 1966), and Virgilio Filippo, *Imperialismo y masonería* (Buenos Aires: Organización San José, 1967).

119. *La Prensa*, December 15, 1974, 6.

120. By the end of 1974, Ottalagano had created a university Institute of Defense and National Security and put an army general in charge of it. *La Prensa*, December 21, 1974, 6. See also "Universidad: la ofensiva gorila marxista," *El Caudillo*, November 8, 1974.

121. Ignacio González Janzen, *La Triple-A*, 19.

122. Luis Alberto Romero, *Breve historia contemporánea de la Argentina* (Buenos Aires: Fondo de Cultura Económica, 1994), 204.

123. Paul Lewis, "La derecha y los gobiernos militares 1955–1983," in Sandra McGee Deutsch and Ronald Dolkart (eds.), *La derecha argentina*, 358.

124. Ignacio González Janzen, *La Triple-A*, 127; *New York Times*, December 15, 1974; Marcos Novaro and Vicente Palermo, *La dictadura militar* 53, 80–82.

125. Rodolfo Walsh, "Carta abierta de Rodolfo Walsh a la Junta Militar" (March 24, 1977). Appendix in Rodolfo Walsh, *Operación masacre* (Buenos Aires: Ediciones de la Flor, 1994), 205–13.

CHAPTER 6

1. John Dinges, *The Condor Years: How Pinochet and His Allies Brought Terrorism to Three Continents* (New York: The New Press, 2004).

2. See, for example, Marie-Monique Robin, *Escadrons de la mort*; Mario Ranalletti, "Aux origines du terrorisme d'État en Argentine. Les influences françaises dans la formation des militaires argentins (1955-1976)" *Vingtième Siècle*. 2010/1 (n° 105) and Lesley Gill, *The School of the Americas*.

3. See General Luciano Benjamín Menéndez, "Las intervenciones militares en la vida política nacional," *Revista Militar* 707, January–March (1982) 13. Generals Jorge Rafael Videla and Roberto Viola graduated as officers in 1944 and Admiral Eduardo Emilio Massera in 1946.

4. "Sanciones por la acción política," *La Nación*, June 5, 1976; "Habrá fusilamientos para algunos delitos," *La Nación*, June 26, 1976.

5. In Spanish, Kafka's novel "The Trial" is translated as "El Proceso." The term is popularized and often works in generic terms such as with the novel "Catch-22" in English.

6. On this model see the Guillermo O'Donnell classic, *El estado burocrático autoritario*. See also his *Catacumbas* (Buenos Aires: Prometeo, 2008).

7. Cited in "Conversaciones con José Luis D'Andrea Mohr," *Página 12*, July 20, 1998. See also Horacio Verbitsky and Juan Pablo Bohoslavsky, *Cuentas pendientes: Los cómplices económicos de la dictadura* (Buenos Aires: Siglo XXI, 2013).

8. Marcos Novaro, *La dittatura argentina (1976–1983)* (Roma: Carocci, 2005), 65; Marcos Novaro and Vicente Palermo, *La dictadura militar*, 110; María Seoane and Vicente Muleiro, *El dictador* (Buenos Aires: Sudamericana Debolsillo, 2006), 262; "Kissinger Approved Argentinian 'Dirty War'" *The Guardian*, December 6, 2003; Christopher Hitchens, *The Trial of Henry Kissinger* (New York: Verso, 2001), xiii–xiv. As a private citizen Kissinger later visited Argentina in 1978 for the soccer world cup and often praised the dictatorship. See "Llega hoy al país Henry Kissinger," *La Nación*, June 21, 1978.

9. This classic antifascist reading of fascism was first articulated by Daniel Guérin in the 1930s.

10. See Federico Finchelstein, "On Fascist Ideology."

11. "El Gral: Videla habló al país," *La Nación*, May 25, 1976.

12. Liliana Caraballo, Noemí Charlier, and Liliana Garulli (eds.), *La Dictadura*, 76.

13. See Viola in *La Opinión*, April 20, 1977, cited in Fernando Almirón, *Campo Santo*. On the projective use of the concept of totalitarianism to depict the enemy see also the speech by General Videla in "El discurso de Videla," *La Nación*, July 1, 1976.

14. "El enemigo subversivo," *La Nación*, July 8, 1976. See also "Viola: Solución definitiva y no una mera salida," *La Prensa*, March 31, 1981.

15. See for example, the converging testimonies of the former Sergeant Ibáñez and the former Navy officer Adolfo Scilingo in Fernando Almirón, *Campo Santo* and Horacio Verbitsky, *El vuelo* (Buenos Aires: Planeta, 1995).

16. Nicolaides in *La Razón*, Junio 12, 1976, cited in Marcos Novaro and Vicente Palermo, *La dictadura militar*, 92. "Habrá vencedores y vencidos," *La Nación*, June 23, 1976.

17. "Conceptos del general Bussi," *La Nación*, June 21, 1976.

18. See Enrique Vázquez, *PRN. La última origen, apogeo y caída de la dictadura militar* (Buenos Aires: Eudeba, 1985), 73; Marcos Novaro and Vicente Palermo, *La dictadura militar*, 88–89.

19. "Lambruschini: defenderemos hasta la última consecuencia la soberanía," *Clarín*, November 25, 1977.

20. "El arzobispo de San Juan," *La Nación*, January 2, 1977.

21. "Agosti dio la orden de partida a los cadetes," *Clarín*, November 12, 1977; "Videla habló del proceso económico," *Clarín*, November 17, 1977. See also "Declaración de Videla," *Clarín*, March 12, 1977.

22. "El acto," *Clarín*, November 19, 1977, and "Los mandos del ejército analizaron la propuesta política de 'unión nacional' " *Clarín*, November 29, 1977.

23. "Crear un sistema propio," *La Nación*, July 8, 1978.

24. "Objetivos del Tercer Ejército," *La Nación*, August 26, 1976. See also the speech by General Antonio Domingo Bussi, "La lucha del ejército por un estilo de vida," *La Nación*, August 2, 1976.

25. "Continuar la lucha hasta la Victoria," *La Nación*, September 25, 1976; "Videla habló a gobernadores," *La Nación*, July 1, 1976; "Eliminación total del enemigo subversivo," *La Nación*, July 8, 1976.

26. "La alocución," *La Nación*, June 13, 1976.

27. Pascarelli was one of the main military leaders overseeing *El Vesubio* concentration camp. "Detienen a ex jefes militares por su actuación en 'El Vesubio' " *Clarín*, March 31, 2006; "Mataban con golpes y patadas," *Página 12*, March 31, 2006; "Para los dueños del campo El Vesubio," *Página 12*, May 30, 2006.

28. "Habla el Gral. Riveros," *La Nación*, June 21, 1978.

29. "La alocución," *La Nación*, June 13, 1976

30. "Massera descartó todo compromiso con fechas electorales," *Clarín*, March 4, 1977. It is interesting to compare Massera's expression (*"el futuro por asalto"*) with the famous Karl Marx expression about the Parisian revolutionaries of 1870 and their storming heaven which in Spanish translation is *"tomar el cielo por asalto"* and it is quite used in Argentine and Latin American Marxist discourse.

31. "Videla anunció una amplia consulta a todos los sectores de la comunidad," *Clarín*, March 7, 1977. On the military notion of peace after war, see, for example, "Condenó toda violación de derechos humanos el ejército," *Clarín*, March 7, 1977; "Los conceptos de Viola," *La Prensa*, April 20, 1981.

32. "El terrorismo," *La Prensa*, May 30, 1981.

33. For some examples see especially the speech by General Videla in "Continuar la marcha sin reparar en el sacrificio," *La Nación*, May 30, 1976. See also "Mensaje al país del Gral. Videla," *La Nación*, December 26, 1976. See also Ramón Genaro Diaz Bessone, *Guerra Revolucionaria en la Argentina (1959–1978)* (Buenos Aires: Editorial Fraterna, 1986), 9–15.

34. Emilio Mignone, *Iglesia y Dictadura* (Buenos Aires: Ediciones del Pensamiento Nacional, 1986), 22; Hugo Vezzetti, *Pasado y presente*, 14. See also Paul Lewis, "La derecha y los gobiernos militares 1955–1983," in Sandra McGee Deutsch (ed.), *La derecha argentina*, 358.

35. Liliana Caraballo, Noemí Charlier, and Liliana Garulli (eds.), *La Dictadura*, 92.

36. See the text of Juan Manuel Bayón, "Lo Nacional. El nacionalismo," reproduced in Enrique Vázquez, *PRN*, 83–90. For a similar argument see Alfredo Mason,

"Apuntes de una teoría de la nación," *Revista Militar* 711, July–December (1983), 38. See also "Bayón y Páez se quedan," *Página 12*, February 1, 2009; "La hora del debut en Bahía," *Página 12*, April 9, 2009.7

37. *Carta Política*, no. 34, agosto, 1976. Artícle cited in Marcos Novaro and Vicente Palermo, *La dictadura militar*, 94, and Martín Sivak, *El Doctor: Biografía no autorizada de Mariano Grondona* (Buenos Aires: Aguilar, 2005), 165. Grondona had been a Visiting Professor of International Studies at Harvard in the 1980s and the early 1990s.

38. Emilio Mignone, *Iglesia y Dictadura*, 24.

39. Liliana Caraballo, Noemí Charlier, and Liliana Garulli (eds.), *La Dictadura*, 92. See Ignacio González Janzen, *La Triple A*, 66. See also Chapter 5 of this book.

40. "Un juicio oral para el sacerdote Von Wernich," *Página 12*, March 2, 2007; "Llegó la hora del ex capellán," *Página 12*, October 8, 2007.

41. See Horacio Verbitsky, *El Silencio* (Buenos Aires: Sudamericana, 2005), 71; Martín Obregón, *Entre la cruz y la espada* (Bernal: Universidad Nacional, 2005), 94.

42. Testimony of Ernesto Reynaldo Saman, CONADEP File 4841. See Emilio Mignone, *Iglesia y Dictadura*, 27. On Medina see also Delia Maisel, *Memorias del apagón: La represión en Jujuy: 1974–1983* (Buenos Aires: Nuestra América, 2007), 138.

43. These bishops were Enrique Angelelli (assassinated by the dictatorship in August 1976), Jaime de Nevares, Miguel Hesayne and Jorge Novak. Marcos Novaro and Vicente Palermo, *La dictadura militar*, 99–100.

44. Emilio Mignone, *Iglesia y Dictadura*, 167–69.

45. Ibid. 124.

46. Ibid. 117.

47. Ibid.

48. Horacio Verbitsky, "Con el mazo dando," *Página 12*, April 25, 1999.

49. "Massera 'Reinvidicar los derechos humanos contra la subversión atea,'" *Clarín*, March 13, 1977.

50. General Emilio Bolon Varela, "Grandeza de alma," *Revista Militar* 704, April–June, 1981, 54; Alfredo J. A. Masson, "Teología de la nación," *Revista Militar* 707, January–March, 1982, 79.

51. See CONADEP, *Nunca Más* (Buenos Aires: Eudeba, 1984), 299.

52. Liliana Caraballo, Noemí Charlier, and Liliana Garulli (eds.), *La Dictadura*, 114.

53. CONADEP, *Nunca Más*, 303.

54. Ibid.

55. Liliana Caraballo, Noemí Charlier, and Liliana Garulli (eds.) *La Dictadura* 80.

56. CO.SO.FAM., La violación de los derechos humanos de argentinos judíos bajo el régimen militar 1976–1983 (Buenos Aires: Milá, 2006).

57. Ibid. 48.

58. On absence and loss, see Dominick LaCapra, *Writing History, Writing Trauma* (Baltimore: Johns Hopkins University Press, 2001), Chapter 2.

59. In Israel, Timerman became an antiwar activist and opposed the Israeli war in Lebanon in 1982. See Jacobo Timerman, *The Longest War: Israel in Lebanon* (New York: Knopf, 1982).

60. Jacobo Timerman, *Prisoner without a Name, Cell without a Number* (New York: Vintage, 1982), 77.

61. The CO.SO.FAM. report provides a detailed enumeration of the Jewish victims including 1,117 (disappeared), 12. 47%; 15 (dead), 15.62%; 116 (liberated), 12.96%, 48 (unclear status), 10.10%. The total number of Jewish victims in the CONADEP Truth Commission Report is 1,296 (12.43%). CO.SO.FAM., 79–80, 93–135.

62. Irving Kristol, "The Timerman Affair," *The Wall Street Journal*, May 29, 1981.

63. Patricia Blake, "Now, the Timerman Affair," *Time*, June 22, 1981. On Timerman see Graciela Mochkofsky, *Timerman: El periodista que quiso ser parte del poder 1923–1999* (Buenos Aires: Sudamericana, 2004); David Sheinin, *Consent of the Damned: Ordinary Argentinians in the Dirty War* (Gainesville: University Press of Florida, 2012), 71–92.

64. See, for example, the book by Timerman's torturer, General Ramón Camps, *Caso Timerman: Punto final* (Buenos Aires: Tribuna Abierta, 1982) and *Cabildo*, June, 1981, 11.

65. CONADEP, *Nunca Más*, 72.

66. Jacobo Timerman, *Prisoner without a Name*, 73. Anti-Semitic groups such as a belated configuration of Tacuara in 1978 also considered Timerman as the leader of an imaginary Jewish conspiracy against Argentina. *Archivo Dipba*. Legajo 11526. Sección C. N 610. 26 de abril, 1978.

67. Jacobo Timerman, *Prisoner without a Name*, 66.

68. CONADEP, *Nunca Más*, 75; *Archivo Memoria Abierta*. Archivo Oral. Testimonio de Rebeca "Tita" Sacolsky.

69. Ibid. 74; CO.SO.FAM., 55.

70. CONADEP, *Nunca Más*, 74.

71. Ibid. 71.

72. María Seoane and Vicente Muleiro, *El dictador*, CO.SO.FAM, 53.

73. Jacobo Timerman, *Prisoner without a Name*, 159.

74. Enrique P. Osés, *Medios y fines del nacionalismo* (Buenos Aires: La Mazorca, 1941).

75. See by Dominick LaCapra, *History and Memory after Auschwitz* (Ithaca: Cornell University Press, 1998), 27–30, and *Writing History, Writing Trauma*, 166–69.

76. See Document 161 in Yitzhak Arad, Israel Gutman and Abraham Margaliot (eds.), *Documents on the Holocaust* (Lincoln: University of Nebraska Press, 1999), 344.

77. Ibid. 344.

78. Ibid. 344–45. For an analysis of Nazi "morality" see Claudia Koonz, *The Nazi Conscience* (Cambridge: Harvard University Press, 2003).

79. Nicolaides in *Clarín*, April 26, 1981, cited in Marcos Novaro and Vicente Palermo, *La dictadura militar*, 92.

80. "Este gobierno militar tiene mandato," *La Nación*, May 27, 1978.

81. María Seoane and Vicente Muleiro, *El dictador*, 231.

82. CO.SO.FAM., 53, 164. See also "La mano de obra," *Página 12*, August 5, 2006.

83. Krepplak was born in Poland in 1924. CO.SO.FAM., 53, 154, 155.

84. Archivo Memoria Abierta. Archivo Oral. Testimonio de Nora Strejilevich, Buenos Aires, 2008; CONADEP, *Nunca Más*, 72; Jacobo Timerman, *Prisoner without a Name*, 54.

85. On transgenerational trauma see Dominick LaCapra, *Writing History, Writing Trauma* and Nicholas Abraham and Maria Torok, *The Shell and the Kernel: Renewals of Psychoanalysis* (Chicago: University of Chicago Press, 1994).

86. Jacobo Timerman, *Prisoner without a Name*, 50.

87. CO.SO.FAM., 52–53.

88. See Chapter 5 of this book.

89. Federico Finchelstein, *Transatlantic Fascism*, 163–77.

90. Jacobo Timerman, *Prisoner without a Name*, 103.

91. CONADEP, *Nunca Más*, 71.

92. See the text of Juan Manuel Bayón, "Lo Nacional. El nacionalismo," 86. See the reproduction of Bayón's text in Enrique Vázquez, *PRN*, 83.

93. See *Cabildo*, February 8, 1977.

94. See Federico Finchelstein, *Transatlantic Fascism*, Chapter 5.

95. "Massera habló a la juventud," *Clarín*, November 26, 1977. For converging arguments of the combination of Marx and Freud as seen by the censors of the Secretariat for State Intelligence (SIDE) see *Archivo Dipba*. Doc. 17753/570. Decreto 20216/73. Legajo 2583 L.

96. "Massera habló a la juventud," *Clarín*, November 26, 1977. Similarly, General Viola talked about the subversive use of "Atomization" and "dissociation." "El perfil de una propuesta," *Clarín*, November 20, 1977.

97. "Massera habló a la juventud," *Clarín*, November 26, 1977.

98. "Una enérgica homilía de Mons. Bolatti," *La Nación*, October 8, 1976.

99. "Massera habló a la juventud," *Clarín*, November 26, 1977.

100. Ibid.; "Una enérgica homilía de Mons. Bolatti," *La Nación*, October 8, 1976. See also the symptomatic review of Ariel Dorman's and Armand Mattelarts's *Para leer al Pato Donald* in *Archivo Dipba*. Doc. 17518/220. Decreto 1774/73. Legajo 2719 L.

101. See David Rock, *Authoritarian Argentina*, 230; Jacobo Timerman, *Prisoner without a Name*, 100–101. Mariano Plotkin tends to disagree with Timerman, Rock and myself. See Mariano Plotkin, *Freud in the Pampas* (Stanford: Stanford University Press, 2001), 219–27.

102. On this topic see also Federico Finchelstein, "The Anti-Freudian Politics of Argentine Fascism."

103. For some examples see the speech by Videla in "La condición básica para instaurar la democracia," *La Nación*, September 25, 1976; "El arzobispo de San Juan," *La Nación*, January 2, 1977.

104. "Del almirante Massera," *La Nación*, December 31, 1976. See also "Massera," *Clarín*, November 20, 1977.

105. *Cabildo* opposed the neoclassic economics of the dictatorship while attempting to adopt a vague populist tone to present its economic and social positions.

106. See Liliana Caraballo, Noemí Charlier, and Liliana Garulli (eds.), *La Dictadura*, 96–97. See also *Archivo Dipba*. Doc. 17518/220. Decreto 1774/73. Legajo 2719 L.

107. "El presidente habló de la subversión," *La Nación*, September 8, 1976. See also the curiously mimetic presentation of Colonel Miguel Angel Fernandez Gez, "Panorama de la lucha contra la subversion," *La Nación*, September 18, 1976.

108. "Cuiden el hogar: Preserven su seguridad." See "Una clara advertencia formuló Harguindeguy," *La Nación*, June 19, 1976.

109. Liliana Caraballo, Noemí Charlier, and Liliana Garulli (eds), *La Dictadura*, 132–33. On the dictatorship and the media, see David Sheinin, *Consent of the Damned*.

110. See "El presidente con escritores," *La Nación*, May 19, 1976; "Habló con escritores el presidente de la Nación," *La Nación*, May 20, 1976. See also Margarita Pierini, "Crónica de un almuerzo: El General, los escritores y los desaparecidos," *Extramuros: Movimientos sociales y pensamiento crítico* 2(5), 2006.

111. See Volodia Teitelbaum, *Los dos Borges* (Santiago de Chile: Sudamericana, 2003), 212–13; 226–29. Ironically, many military men from Argentina disliked Borges and his opposition to a war with Chile. For example, Fernando Eduardo Laffont described Borges as posturing to win the Nobel Prize and even as representing "Marxism–Leninism" and the "Antichrist." See Fernando Eduardo Laffont, "Borges, el conflicto austral y los militares," *Revista Militar* 704, April–June, 1981, 89.

112. Oscar Terán, *Historia de las ideas en la Argentina* (Buenos Aires: Siglo XXI, 2008), 296–97 and 299–300. See also Andres Avellaneda, *Censura, autoritarismo y cultura. Argentina 1960–1983* (Buenos Aires: CEAL, 1986); Liliana Caraballo, Noemí Charlier, and Liliana Garulli (eds.), *La Dictadura*, 97; Hernán Invernizzi and Judith Gociol, *Un golpe a los libros: Represión a la cultura ante la última dictadura militar* (Buenos Aires: Eudeba, 2002); "El gobierno salió a exhibir documentos de la dictadura recién hallados" *Clarín*, November 5, 2013.

113. "'La cultura es patrimonio de todos y no solo privilegio de algunos.' El presidente exhortó a reconstruir el país en 'unión y libertad'" *Clarín*, November 20, 1977.

114. Emilio Mignone, *Iglesia y Dictadura*, 191.

115. See all in *Archivo Dipba*. Doc. 17753/1771 C.N.I 32/77; Doc. 17518/165. Side 56.714/76. Decreto 1774/73. Legajo 2708 L; Doc. 17753/552. Side 38074/76. Decreto 1774/73. Legajo 2579 L; Doc. 17518/670. C.N.I. 17/79; Doc. 17753/198. Decreto 1774/73. Legajo 2626 L; Doc. 17518/312. Decreto 1774/73. Legajo 2749 L.

116. See all in *Archivo Dipba*. Doc. 17753/120. Decreto 20216/73. Legajo 2331/6 L.; Doc. 17518/220. Decreto 1774/73. Legajo 2719 L.

117. See the example of the Triple A writer Gabriel Ruiz de los Llanos in *Archivo Dipba*. Doc. 17518/165. Side 56.714/76. Decreto 1774/73. Legajo 2708 L. See also CO.SO.FAM., 39.

118. Oscar Terán, *Historia de las ideas en la Argentina*, 297–98.

119. Marcos Novaro and Vicente Palermo, *La dictadura militar*, 162–63.

120. "Expresivo mensaje del general Videla," *La Nación*, June 2, 1978.

121. Santiago García, "Cine durante la Dictadura," *Leer Cine* 1(5), 2006. See also Judith Gociol and Hernán Invernizzi, *Cine y dictadura: La censura al desnudo* (Buenos Aires: Capital Intelectual, 2006).

122. Santiago García, "Cine durante la Dictadura."

123. See Ricardo E. Rodríguez Molas, *Historia de la tortura y el orden represivo en la Argentina*, vol. 1 (Buenos Aires: Eudeba, 1985), 156.

124. "Este gobierno militar tiene mandato," *La Nación*, May 27, 1978: *Archivo Memoria Abierta*. Fondo Fiscalía Luis Moreno Ocampo. Caja 48. Causa 13. Doc. Anexa Declaraciones. Folio 23. 6.C. Testimonio de Deheza.

125. John Dinges, *The Condor Years*; Raúl Cuestas, *La Dictadura Militar Argentina y el genocidio en Centroamérica* (Cordoba: Sima, 2006); Ariel C. Armony, *Argentina, los Estados Unidos y la cruzada anticomunista en América Central 1977–1984* (Bernal: Universidad Nacional de Quilmes, 1999).

126. See Marcos Novaro and Vicente Palermo, *La dictadura militar*, 256.

127. See, for example, *BDIC*. Nanterre, France. Fonds Argentine. F., 7380. Recueil. Guerre de Malouines. Documents 312. Doc. 68456. Angel B. Armelin. Homilía. 5 de Mayo de 1982. Universidad de Buenos Aires.

EPILOGUE

1. See David Rock, *Authoritarian Argentina*, 233.

2. See "Proyecto nacional," *La Nación*, October 26, 1976; "Tono político," *Clarín*, November 20, 1977; "Los mandos del ejército analizaron los lineamientos del 'Proyecto Nacional,'" *Clarín*, November 30, 1977. See also Enrique Vázquez, *P.R.N.*, 299–327; Hugo Vezzetti, *Pasado y Presente*, 71.

3. In his last interview two months before his death, Videla called a new coup "in defense of the republic" and stated that in the present the "republic has disappeared." See "Videla llamó a sus ex compañeros a 'armarse en defensa de la República,'" *Tiempo Argentino*, March 17, 2013; "Videla pidió que los militares 'se armen en defensa de la República,'" *La Nación*, March 17, 2013.

4. See Hugo Vezzetti, *Pasado y presente*; Carlos Nino, *Radical Evil on Trial*; Emilio Crenzel, *La historia política del Nunca Más* (Buenos Aires: Siglo XXI, 2008).

5. On democracy and popular representation, see Pierre Rosanvallon, *Democracy Past and Future* (New York: Columbia University Press, 2006), 91–2. On

Peronism and de-institutionalization, see Luis Alberto Romero, "El Gobierno se comió al Estado," *La Nación*, July 13, 2012, and "La democracia peronista," *La Nación*, May 4, 2012.

6. In a new affront to the victims, the Kirchner Peronist administration in 2013 called for the creation of a so-called "truth commission," inviting the presumed Iranian perpetrators to participate as equals. See Fabián Bosoer and Federico Finchelstein, "Argentina's About-Face on Terror," *The New York Times*, March 2, 2013.

7. Luis Alberto Romero, "Qué significó," *Clarín*, August 28, 2005. On the historical continuity in the conception of the Other in Argentine political culture, see also Luis Alberto Romero, *La crisis argentina*, 80, and his *La Larga Crisis Argentina* (Buenos Aires: Siglo XXI, 2013).

8. See Horacio Verbitsky, "Dimes y diretes," *Página 12*, September 21, 2003. See, for example, "Al cierre de la edición," *El Caudillo*, March 2, 1975; *El Plan Andinia o, El nuevo estado judío* (Buenos Aires: Nuevo Orden, 1965); Federico Rivanera Carlés, *El "reino" patagónico del judío Popper: un antecedente del Plan Andinia* (Buenos Aires: Instituto de Investigaciones sobre la Cuestión Judía, 1987).

9. See "El jefe del Ejército dijo que hay que 'cicatrizar las heridas' del pasado," *Clarín*, June 11, 2007; "Nuevo cruce entre el Gobierno y el cardenal Bergoglio," *Clarín*, June 9, 2007.

10. See "La Confesión," *Revista El Sur* (Cordoba), July, 2012; "En Argentina no hay justicia, sino venganza, que es otra cosa bien distinta," *Cambio 16* (Spain), February 12, 2012.

11. Hugo Vezzetti, *Pasado y Presente*, 90–1.

12. Emilio Mignone, *Iglesia y Dictadura*, 180, 196.

13. *Clarín*, February 19, 2005.

14. *Clarín*, April 4, 2007.

15. Hugo Vezzetti, *Pasado y Presente*, 15.

16. For a criticism of this approach see Hugo Vezzetti, *Sobre la violencia revolucionaria*. On the notion of "just war," see Benjamin Brower, "Just War and Jihad in the French Conquest of Algeria," in Sohail H. Hashmi (ed.), *Just Wars, Holy Wars, and Jihads* (Oxford: Oxford University Press, 2012), 221–45.

Index

CPSIA information can be obtained
at www.ICGtesting.com
Printed in the USA
BVOW06s0516170118
505444BV00002B/98/P